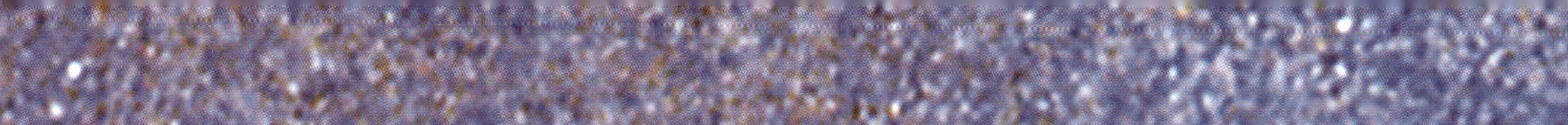

AF544929

KIM POOR

AMAZÔNIA IMAGINED

EDWARD LUCIE-SMITH

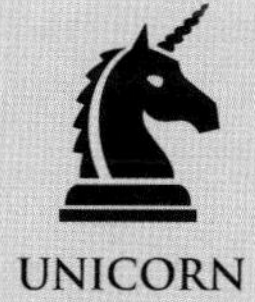

UNICORN

Published in 2017 by
Unicorn, an imprint of Unicorn Publishing Group LLP
101 Wardour Street
London
W1F 0UG
www.unicornpublishing.org

ISBN 978-1-910787-41-0

10 9 8 7 6 5 4 3 2 1

Designed by Jonathan Christie
Printed in Slovenia by Latitude Press Ltd

Dedications

In memory of my wonderful and encouraging mother, Eugenia Weil (Gene), my inspiring father, Robert J Poor and my always supportive stepfather, Roger Weil.

The biggest thanks to my partner, Billy Budis, for always being there to bail me out with his undying love, dedication and, most of all, patience!

Thank you to my brother, Ted Poor, who doesn't realise it but has been an anchor of support and love in my life.

Thanks also to my dear friend Cecilia Bulcão who gave me the intial seed for this project while we were swimming in the waters of Búzios!

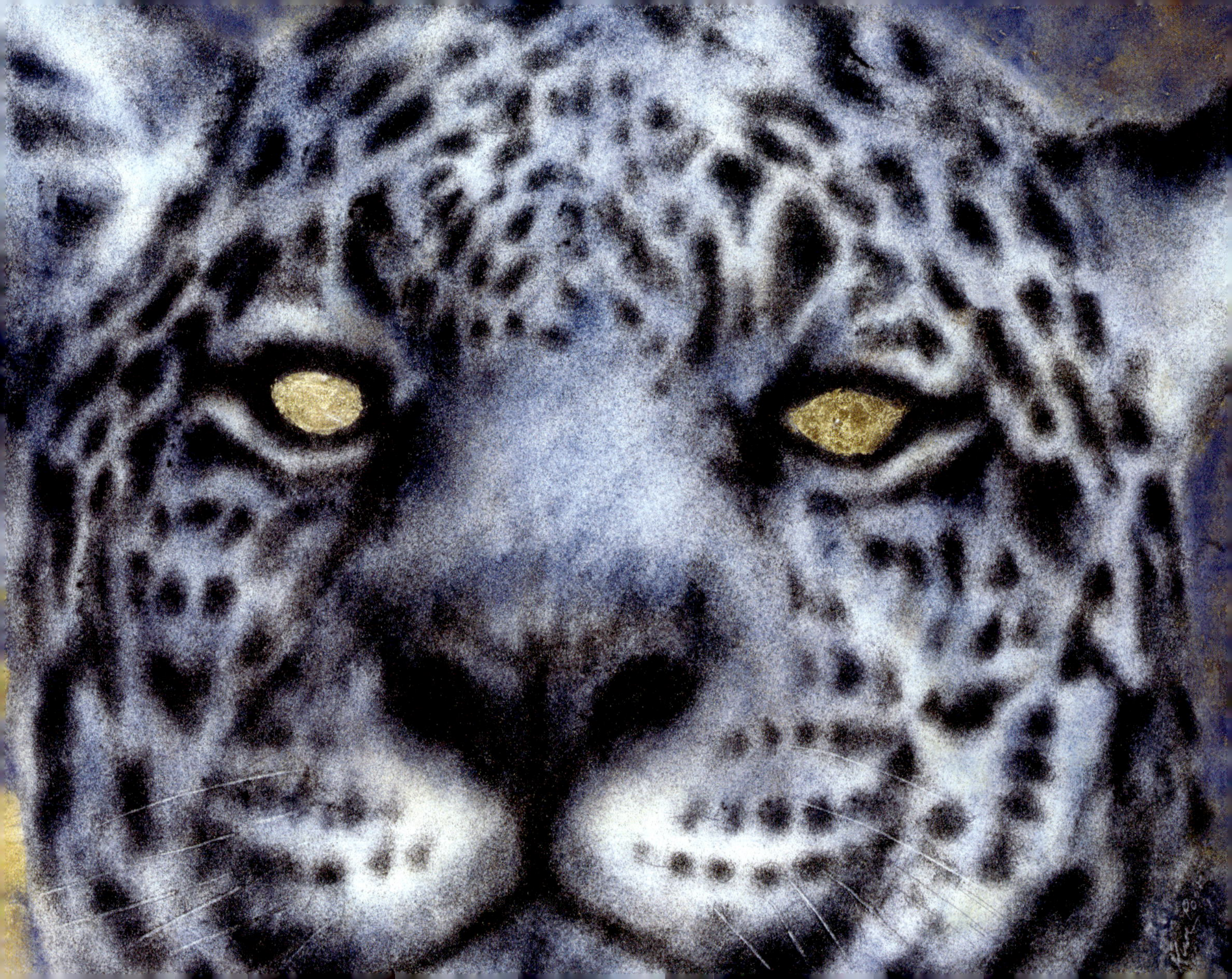

CONTENTS

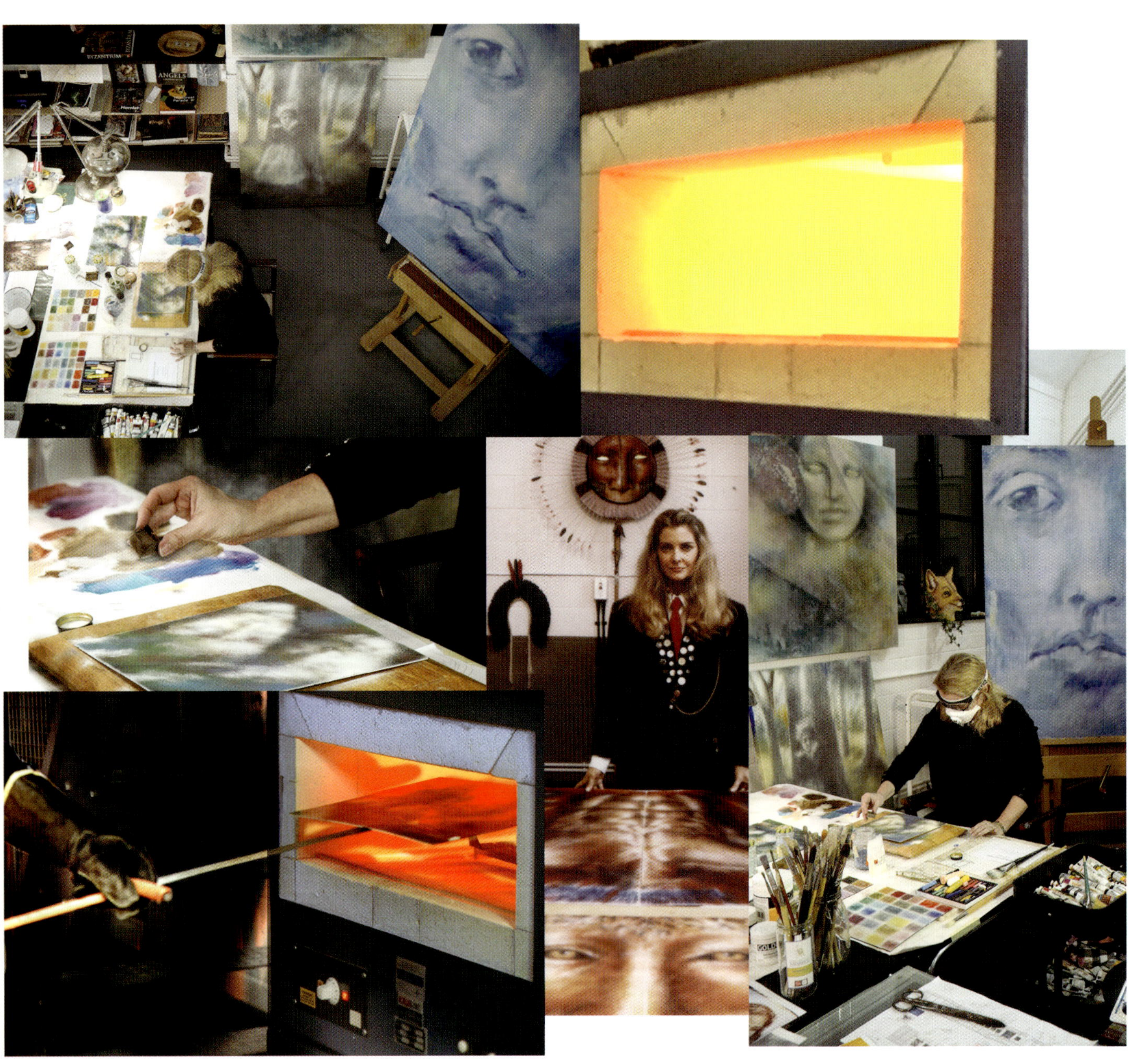
BYZANTIUM
ANGELS

KEEPING FAITH WITH THE LEGENDS

by Edward Lucie-Smith

Brazilian Amazonia is perhaps the least known area of that vast and fascinating country. Least known because of the difficulty of travelling not only to it, but actually within it. Its aboriginal inhabitants often tend to keep themselves to themselves. Poor in material things, they live lives that are rich in stories – stories inherited from their ancestors, handed down from generation to generation by word of mouth, immaterial yet alive.

These stories are suggested by the magical environment that encloses them. Suggested, that is, by forests and water, by friendly creatures and dangerous ones, by the hot sun shining through the heavy canopy of leaves and by the moon sailing clear into the skies, suddenly visible above as a wanderer entering a clearing. They see beasts such as the jaguar, or the planets tracing paths in the sky, as being articulate personalities in their own right, as much part of their extended family as tribal siblings and cousins.

It is this quality of belonging that Kim Poor seizes here, in a magical series of pictures that have already been widely exhibited in her native country. It is not so much that she wants to illustrate Amazonian stories for the edification of others, as that she wants to fuse with the legends of Amazonia in her work – to become fully part of them, an inseparable component of the complex Amazonian matrix.

The paradox is that she chooses highly technological means of doing this. Her paintings are made using an extremely demanding medium: glass and pigment fused, using high heat, onto metal plates. The colours are applied in the form of powder and each hue must be added to the next in an order dictated by its durability and resistance to heat. Some colours can be fired over and over again, but some only once. Before it is fired, the powdered glass (which is applied to the surface using tiny sieves) is extraordinarily vulnerable. The artist says that she has sometimes lost an entire picture in one gust of wind from a window left open at the wrong moment. After firing, however, the glass particles cling firmly to the steel plate and produce colours of astonishing depth and translucency. It s not surprising that some paintings feature images of butterflies, as the effect achieved finds its nearest parallel in the iridescent scales that cover a butterfly's wing.

What Kim Poor is looking for is a way of finding true, durable equivalents for the colours and textures of the Amazonian rainforests and for the shimmering hues of the creatures – birds, beasts and insects – that inhabit them. One of the ways that a painting created with glass powder differs from one made using the more familiar medium of acrylic paint on canvas is that light strikes through the surface and is reflected back from the metal ground. This gives Kim Poor's paintings their characteristic glow and depth. It also means that they change unpredictably as light strikes them from different angles or with varying degrees of intensity.

The bloom of the colour is enhanced by another special characteristic, which is an absence of outlines. Forms are built up from minute speckles of colour; the image has no firm boundaries. This enhances the dreamlike quality of the imagery, which coalesces before the spectator's eye and then seems ready to dissolve again.

There are several paradoxes here. The most obvious is that such an extremely laborious medium is used to produce such delicately evanescent effects. A more profound paradox is that these industrial methods and materials are used to hold a mirror up to a teeming natural world, where everything is in a state of change from one moment to the next. This, the images tell you, is what happens when you look, and hold your breath. The magical moment is yours forever, just as it was for the artist.

None of this would matter if the images didn't have a deeper resonance. We live in a notoriously skeptical and materialistic society. Yet we hunger for something else, something transcendental. How is this to be supplied? The standard forms of religious art, linked to the long established major creeds – Christian, Islamic, Buddhist, Hindu – tend to seem uncomfortably formal and outdated when contemporary artists make images connected to them. It's not that the creeds are themselves out of date. They still command many millions of believers – but their symbolic language is so historically resonant that today's artists often seem to have difficulty in making any very convincing use of it.

An alternative has been what amounts to a retreat into shamanism. The artists – Joseph Beuys and Marina Abramovic are typical figures – now sometimes put themselves forward as a religious figure, without, however, any formal structure of belief or hierarchy of moral values attached. The religious impulse is combined with the solipsism that is now typical of a great deal of contemporary art. In these cases the psychic impact of the responsible personality counts for a great deal more than any actual artwork that an artist of this type may choose to produce. In fact one can even say that the personality becomes the artwork. Any material object linked to it is simply a by-product. This transformation and shift in values is, in a way, the ultimate product -- and surely also the dead end -- of the cult of artistic personality initiated by the European 19th century Romantic Movement.

With these works inspired by Amerindian legends Kim Poor takes a different route. It's clear that her aim is not just to offer pictorial equivalents to the stories themselves. In fact she is very insistent that she is not to be regarded as an illustrator.

What I think she means to do is to offer an equivalent experience, to place the story she is thinking and dreaming about, not in Amazonia, but in the equally magical universe of contemporary art. This book offers not just images of the whole composition associated with each Legend, but numerous details excerpted from the complete paintings. In cinematic terms, you are offered first the wide-screen image, then a tracking shot that finishes with a close up. The paintings are indeed narratives in a way, but much like the fragmented illogical narratives we meet with in our dreams.

The dreamlike quality of Kim Poor's work does, of course, tend to align itself with things that have often aroused comment both in Latin American art and in Latin American literature. In a broad sense we have here yet another example of Magical Realism that can be found in the work of great contemporary Latin American writers such as Gabriel Garcia Marquez, Mario Vargas Llosa and Isabel Allende. Her work shares with theirs not only a dreamlike atmosphere but an undoubted, though often oblique, narrative thrust and, at the same time, a typically Latin American concern with urgent contemporary problems: in this case the ecological problems that threaten the whole Amazon basin, and the tribal peoples who live there.

This magical atmosphere, however, is conjured up with the aid of very specifically modern technology. The materials Kim Poor uses, and the way in which she puts them together to make the effects she wants to create, are very much the product of a sophisticated industrial society. The shifting colours and surfaces do, as I have already suggested, often suggest the effect of the minute scales that one finds of the wings of some gorgeous tropical butterfly. But whereas the butterflies live just for a season – or last a while longer, pinned, dry and dead, in the cabinets of butterfly hunters – these works offer an almost frightening sense of permanence, given the recalcitrant materials from which they are made.

Yet, at the same time, thanks to the properties inherent in these non-organic materials, skillfully deployed as they are here, the images change and shift as one looks at them. They cannot be described as Op or optical art in the strict sense, though this has a well-established tradition in the history of Latin American Modernism, but subtle optical variability is one of their chief properties. The spectator's eye is never quite at rest. As one looks one is always in dialogue with an ever-shifting surface. The compositions come as close as possible to giving permanence to things, both images and the narratives that have inspired those images, that are essentially and tragically impermanent.

If they have one basic function, it is that they open a door into a world that is inexorably fading away. Several generations from now, these works may be thought of as memorials to a world that has completely vanished, never to be recovered. Their impact may be all the greater for that. Time is likely to be their friend. It is not likely, alas, to be the friend of the tribes, the ecology or the stories of Amazonia. Meanwhile the images as we see them now are a moving (in all senses) lament for things that are still with us but that are just about to vanish from the face of the earth.

KIM POOR IN CONVERSATION

with Edward Lucie-Smith

Kim, how did you first become an artist?
I was by all accounts quite a solitary child and, at the same time, very self-sufficient because I loved colouring, I loved colours, I loved crayons, I loved sitting outside as a child and trying to replicate nature as I saw it. In fact my earliest recollection is when I was three years old, sitting outside our house in Petropolis, in Brazil, depicting a very beautiful little colonial church that still exists there. I still think that's probably my best painting to date! It was very, very expressionistic in its colours and in its depiction.

Do you see yourself as a Brazilian artist, or as a European one – or as something between the two?
I identify myself very much today as a Brazilian painting abroad but when I was growing up in Brazil I identified myself as a European or an English painter. I loved the rain, I loved the dark days, which were very few in Brazil, and, at that time, I longed for a mythology of my own which was very connected with Celtic mythology and, I suppose, things I couldn't see - what today we would call the spiritual world. Now, having lived in England for over three decades, I look for colour and light so that's an interesting thing, almost like a negative and positive that's happened in my life. And I still seek mystic and spiritual sources.

What particularly defines your work? Is it something to do with the actual techniques you use?
At university I developed a technique which is probably what I'll be remembered for, which is a process of glass - powdered glass - fused on steel, with amazing natural pigments which I've picked up here, there and everywhere all over the world. It's quite an extraordinary technique as I use the glass in such a way that I go back to it being the consistency of sand, which is what it started out as. I work with sieves so it's an insane process and, I think, probably the only reason that I'm the only one who works like this! It requires a lot of patience and a lot of foresight as sometimes I don't know how the colours are going to react once they've gone in an industrial kiln at over 1000 degrees. Through a lot of mistakes and experimentation I know, for instance, that I'm going to do reds last. And still, today, I'm very happily surprised by effects and textures that can happen spontaneously through this process.

In your earlier years as an artist, were there any personal encounters – with other older artists, for example, that were particularly significant to you?
I was very fortunate to have met Salvador Dali in the Seventies, when I was studying and

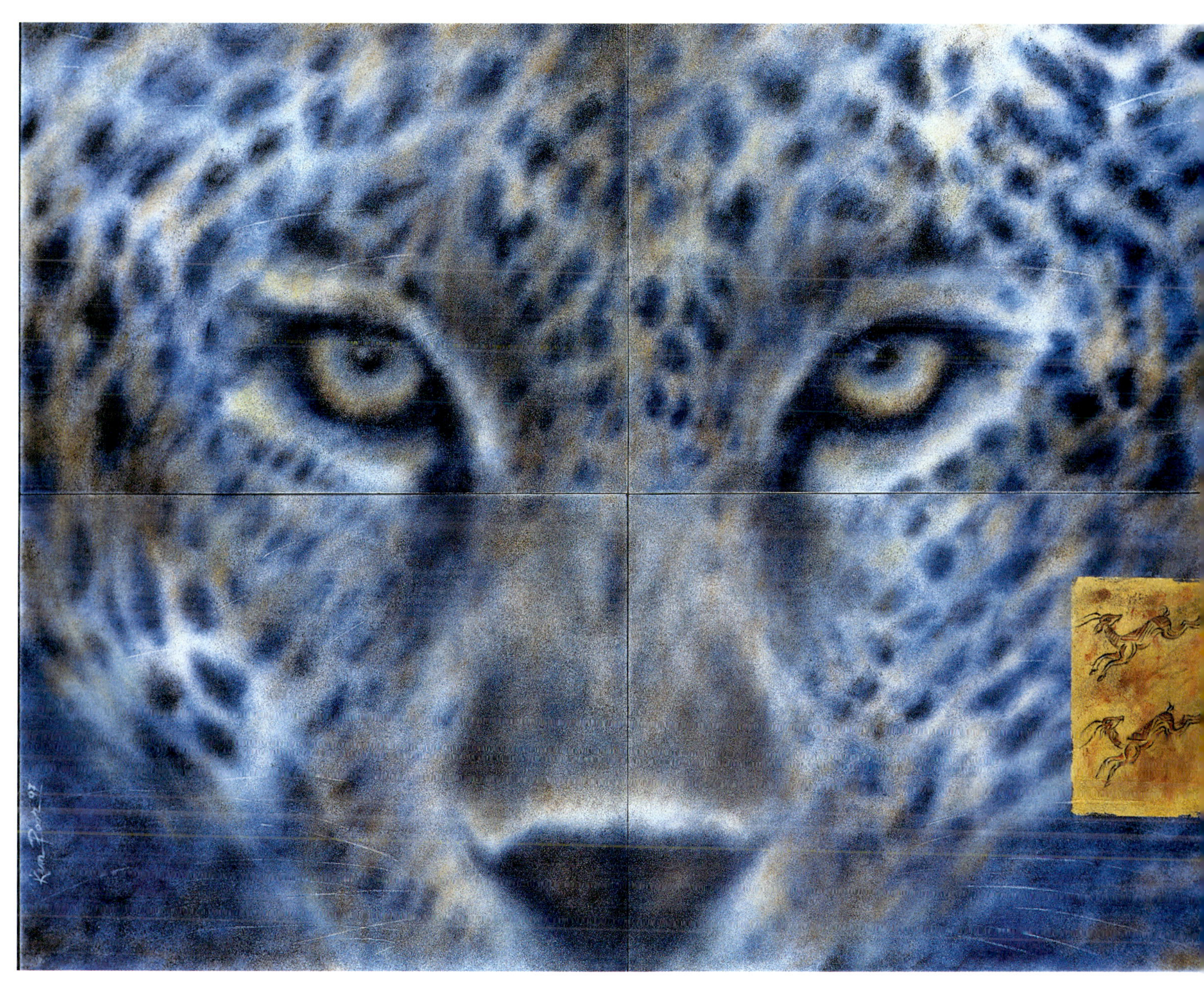

working in New York. He came, with other artists and journalists, to a show that I was a part of. He stopped in front of my paintings and looked, lifted his cane, his wonderful cane, and started banging on my paintings because he couldn't figure out what on earth these pictures were made of. He was fascinated by what he couldn't understand. He started talking to me in Spanish and I stared talking to him in my Portuguese, with a bit of Spanish thrown in. In that particular era of my work it was incredibly spiritual, like looking at the world through different coloured gauzes and very very soft and very unworldly. He started describing this as a 'diáfanismo', 'diáfanismo', and that really coined the term for what my technique was about. It was, really, about breaking up space and the world into tiny little points and tiny little dots, like molecules, and it all somehow coming together in an image. I don't quite know sometimes where the image comes from but it comes together in the painting.

Talking of 'coming together' in a slightly different sense, how do you feel abut having spent so many years as an expatriate? How do you feel when you go back to Brazil, as I know you do quite often now?

Going back to having spent a long time now in England … one day you just wake up and you realise you're still a foreigner in a foreign land. Roots - something I'd never thought about, grab you and I realised that I was in search of something that would take me back to my native Brazil. That would take me back to roots I probably didn't even understand, because even in my own family there are direct connections with the Indians and the Amazon, dating back to my great great great grandfather, Geronimo de Albuquerque, who actually married the daughter of an Indian chief. Almost a Pocahontas type story, where she saved him from the cauldron only to marry him and return to the court in Portugal. She actually learned to speak six languages, which is quite extraordinary! That was a moment, a very critical moment, for me in my work because it all changed. Having probably been much more influenced by European trends I felt that it was time that I did something to … recapture, especially in a cultural sense, things that are disappearing very quickly in my country. Especially in the Amazon region. I've always had this interest in the ecological problems that we are facing and the fact that Brazil still had a chance to preserve so much, whereas other countries had already destroyed so much. It seemed important to do whatever I could, large or small, to get a message across that this is happening. I didn't want a political slant, I really wanted something that was directly connected to the Indians in the Amazon who were losing their culture. It crystallised on a day when I visited The Indian Museum in Rio and saw some pottery there which completely appalled me because it had the face of Mickey Mouse on one of the pieces! I thought "this is just absolutely outrageous". I mean, not only are the lands being taken and they're being massacred, but their whole culture is eroding as well and all of us have to do our part in trying to rescue some of this heritage. So that's when I started to get very interested in trying to do something with the culture that we still have from the Amazonian Indians.

How do you feel about story-telling in art? Many artists now seem to want to separate what they do in art from any suggestion of narrative. What's your attitude to that?

I've always worked with stories and illustrations and believe the written language is a very important part of the visual language. To me they coexist. In the past I'd done quite a lot of work connected to either music or poetry and it was how I felt, or how those pieces moved me, which was then translated onto canvas, onto steel, into clay - whatever medium I'd be interested in at the time. So it was a natural progression for me to be working with what I call legends, except that they're still very alive stories that are still used by the Indians today to educate their children and to show them the phenomena of nature, and how they work and how they've come about, in an almost whimsical way. I think it's done in such a way that children are interested, like our fairy tales or all those stories that we are told or read to as children. It's no different than that and, in researching over the years the different legends and stories from the Amazon basin, the parallels are extraordinary with Celtic, African … the imagery. They all come from the same well. They're just told in different contexts because it's the rainforests versus the Icelandic snows etc. They're all about imagery. In fact, in the Legends of The Amazon exhibitions which I did at The Museum of Modern Art in Rio and then São Paulo, I made sure that several corridors were full of legends. We printed these wonderful stories on the wall and it was very important to send out a message to schools and children to come and be inspired to do work that would reconnect them with their own culture. This is part of a culture that's disappearing. A lot of it has already gone so it's important that we remind the generations that are coming after us that there's such richness in what the Indians have to say and in how they portray nature. It's interesting that things have gone 360 degrees because of the severity of changes, problems like global warming, the reality that we are faced with no longer allows people to doubt that we are reaching a critical point and that a global consciousness has to be reached and acted upon very quickly. Today, rather than being treated with contempt, as they once were, people are looking towards these native people for answers on how to look after our planet, because we've gotten it so wrong.

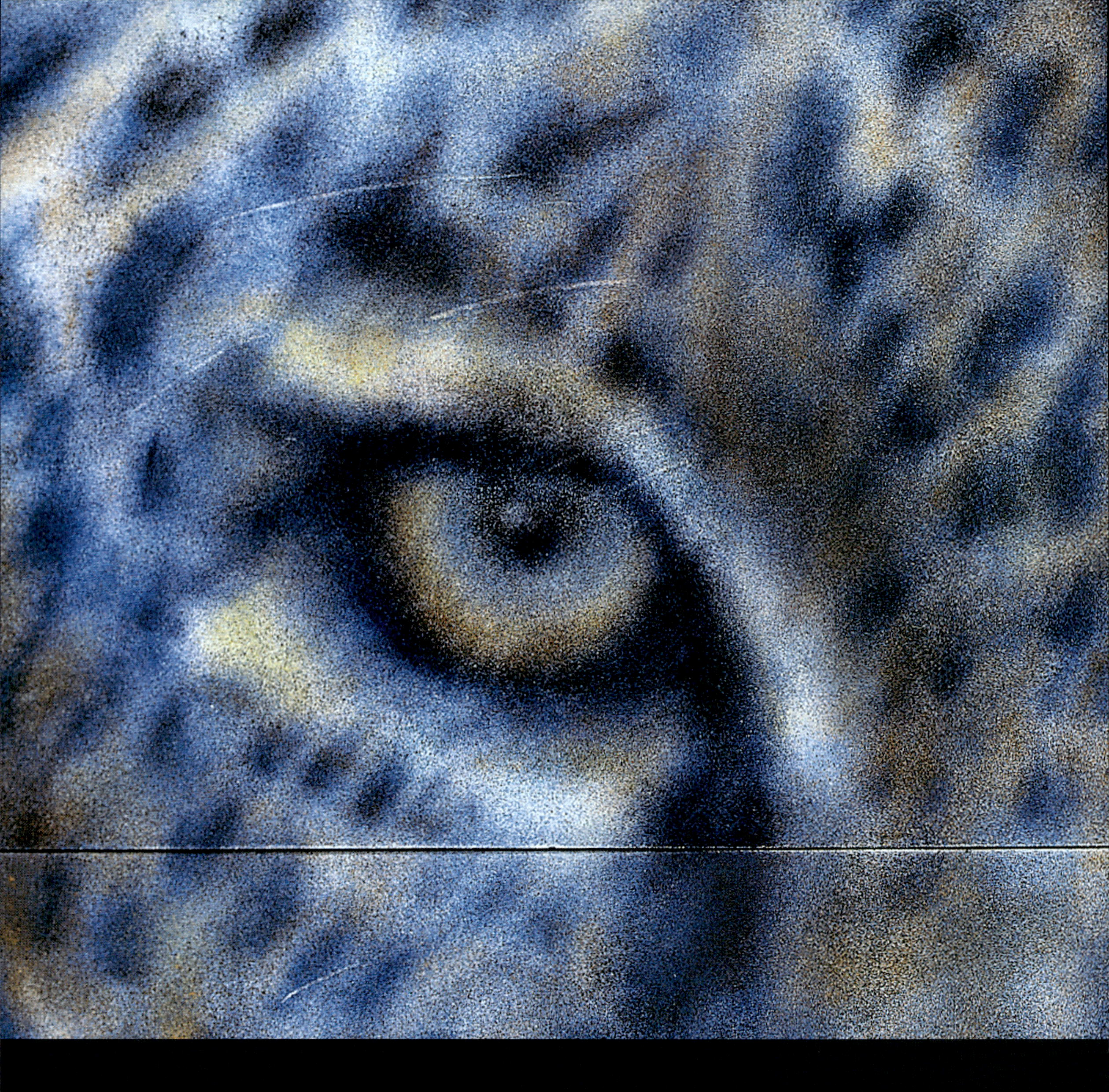

HE LAY IN WAIT FOR TURTLE, BUT TURTLE VERY VERY QUIETLY

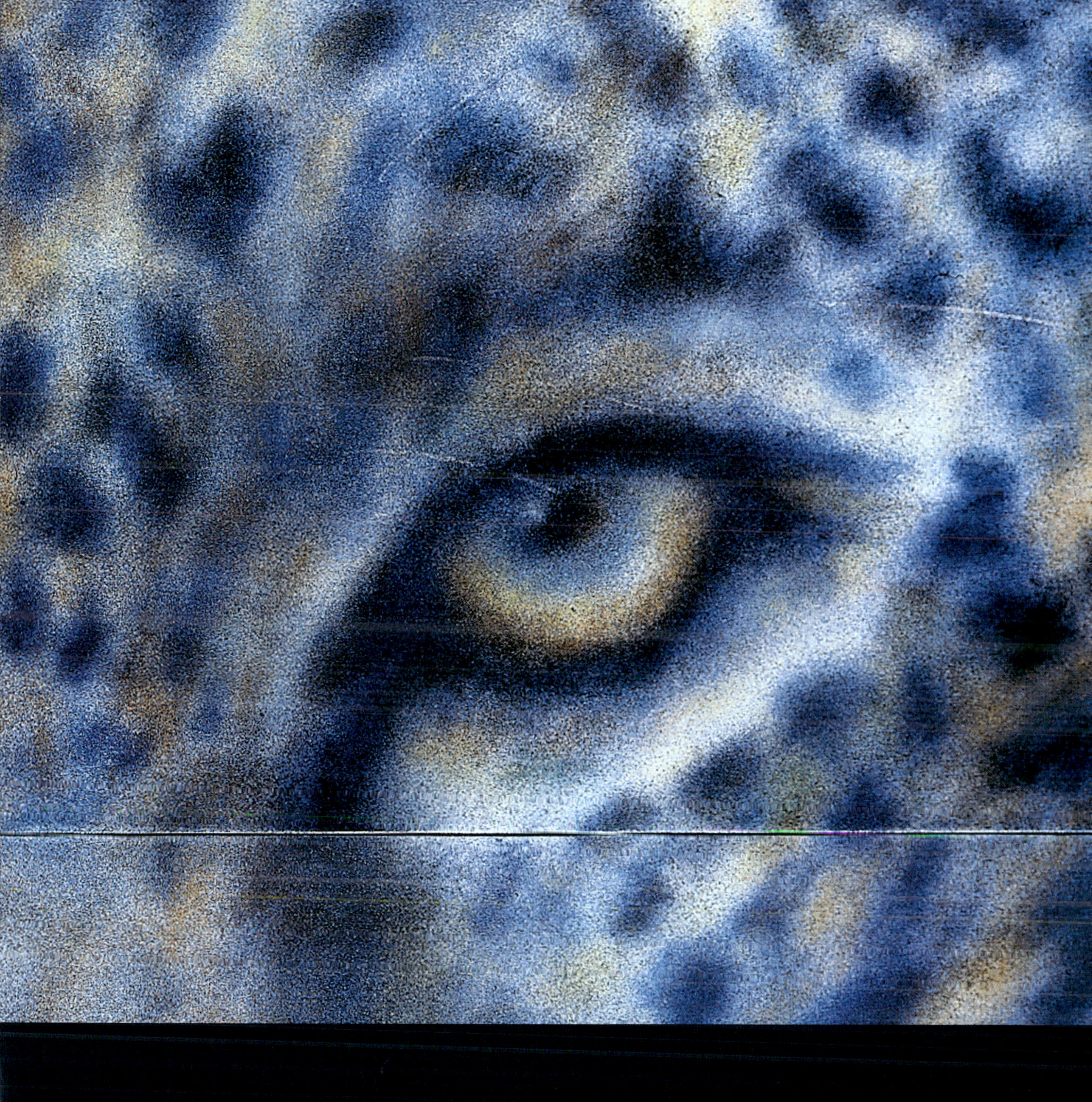

PULLED INTO HIS SHELL AND WENT PEACEFULLY TO SLEEP

EYES

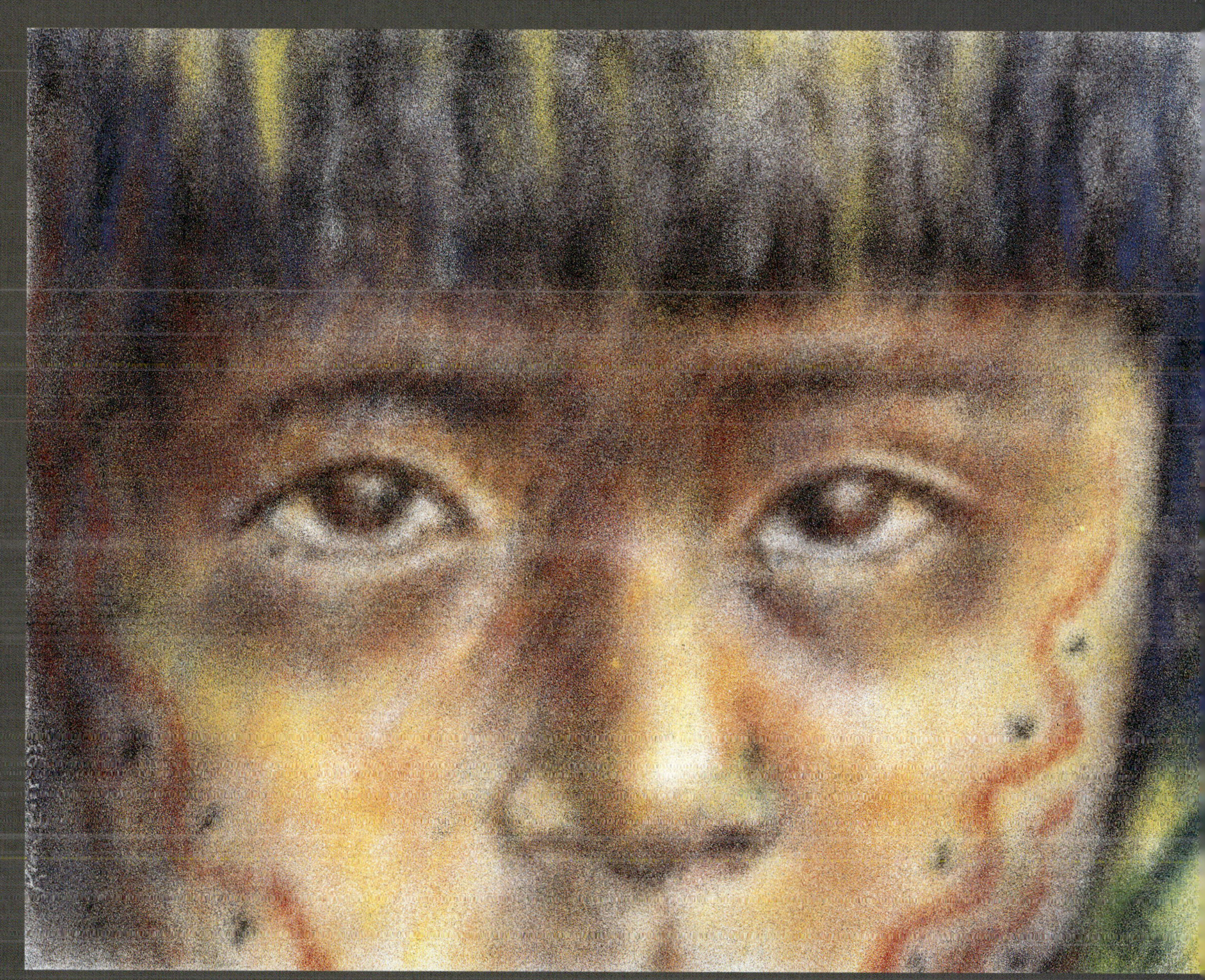

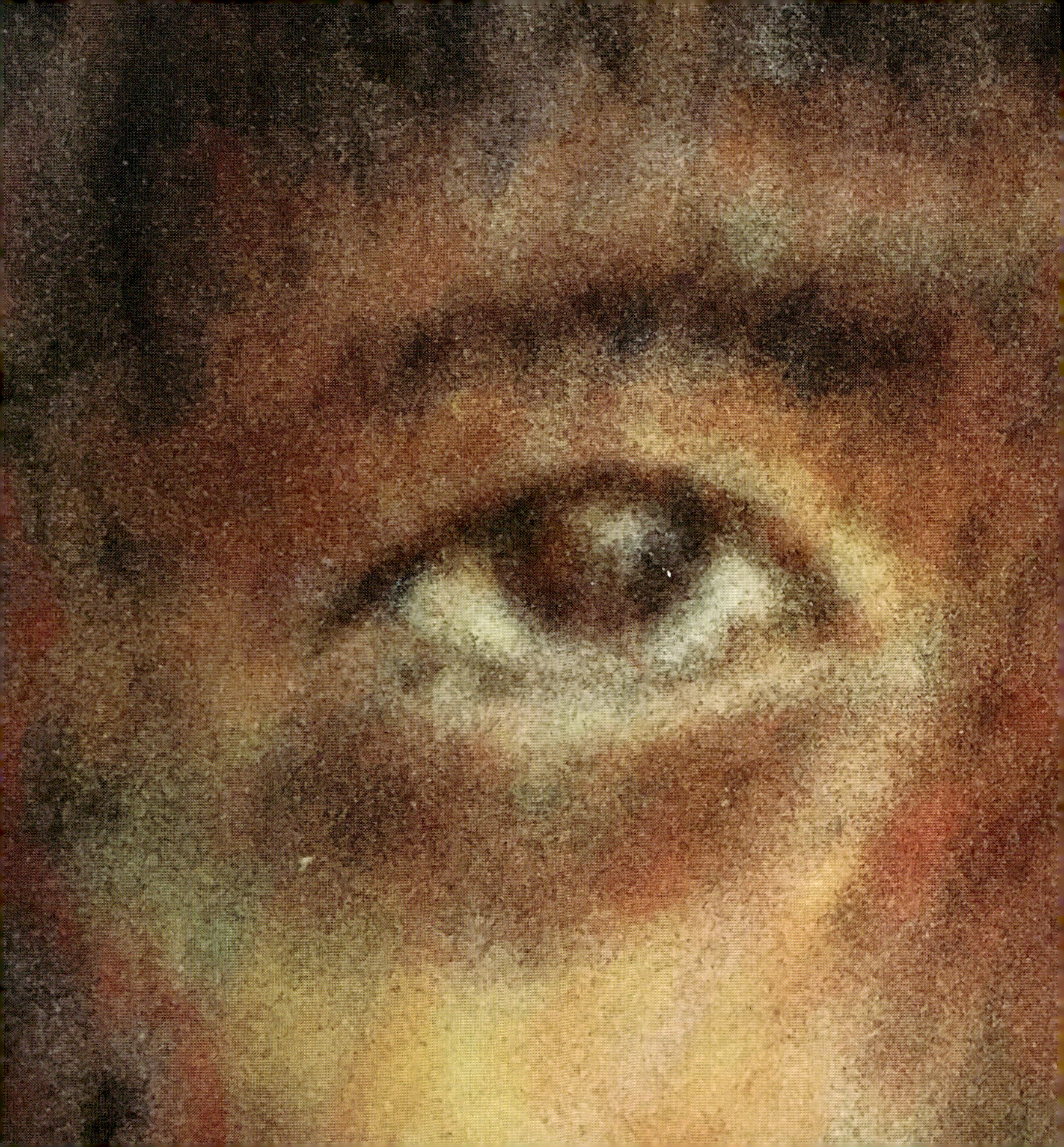

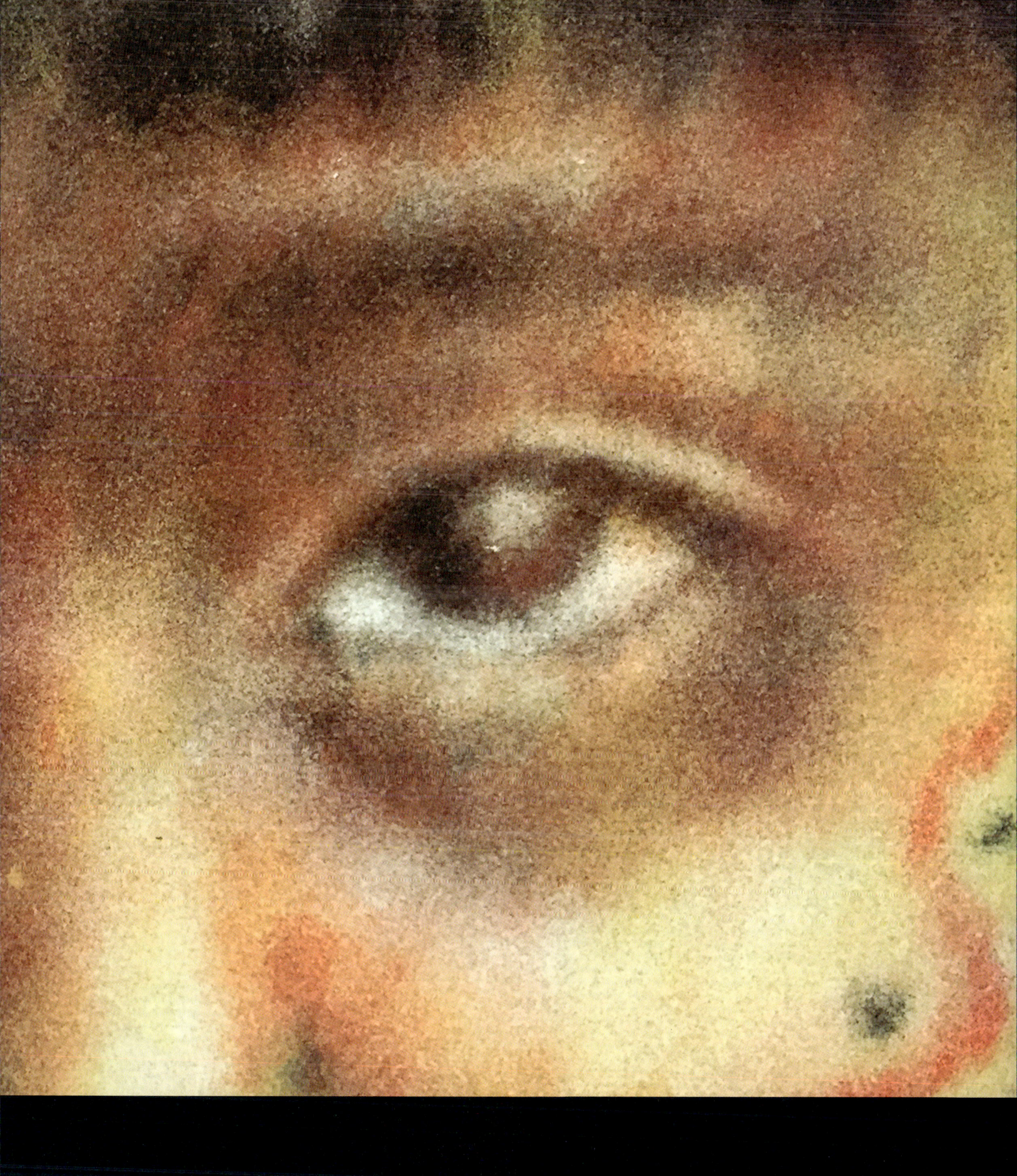

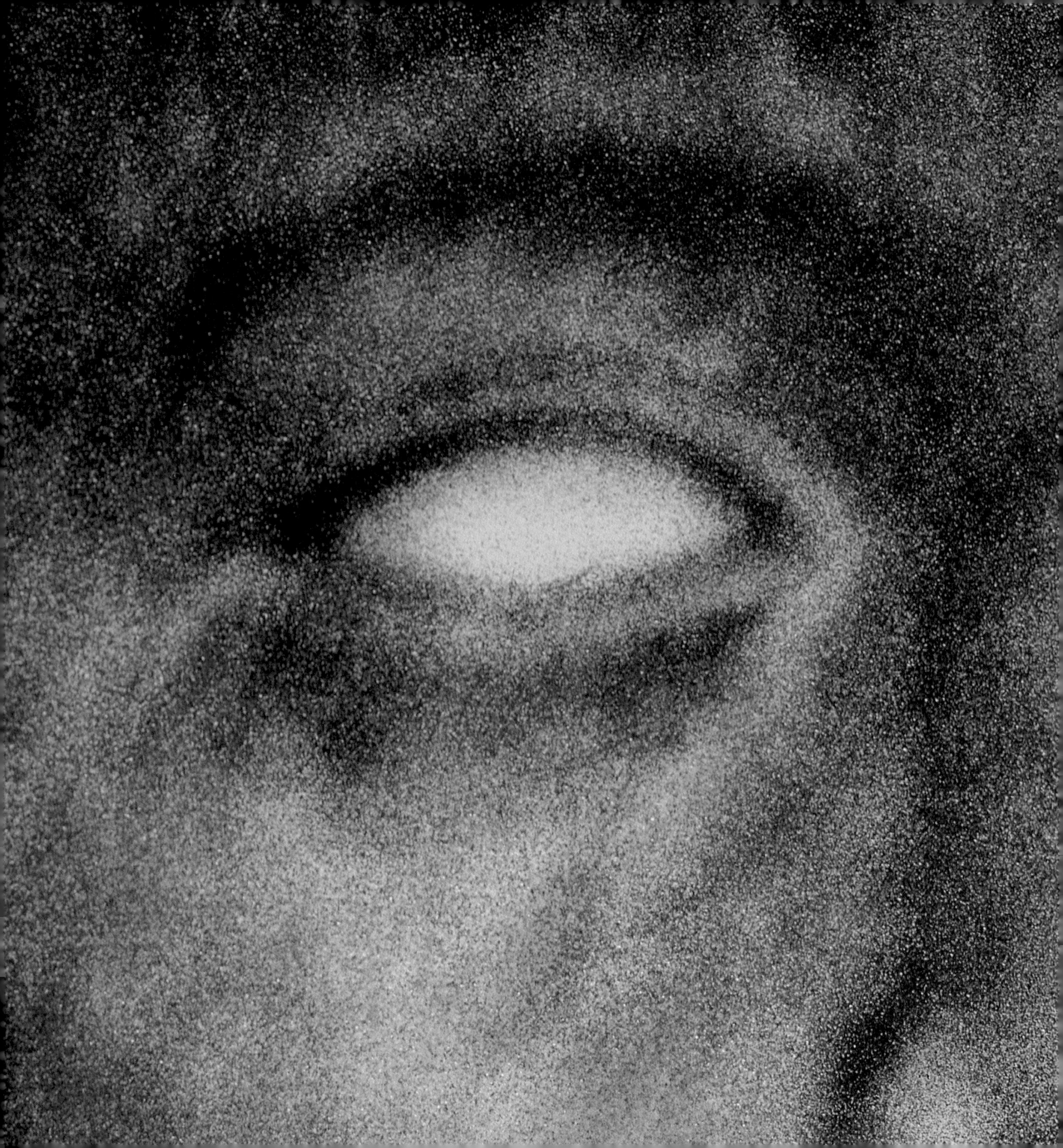

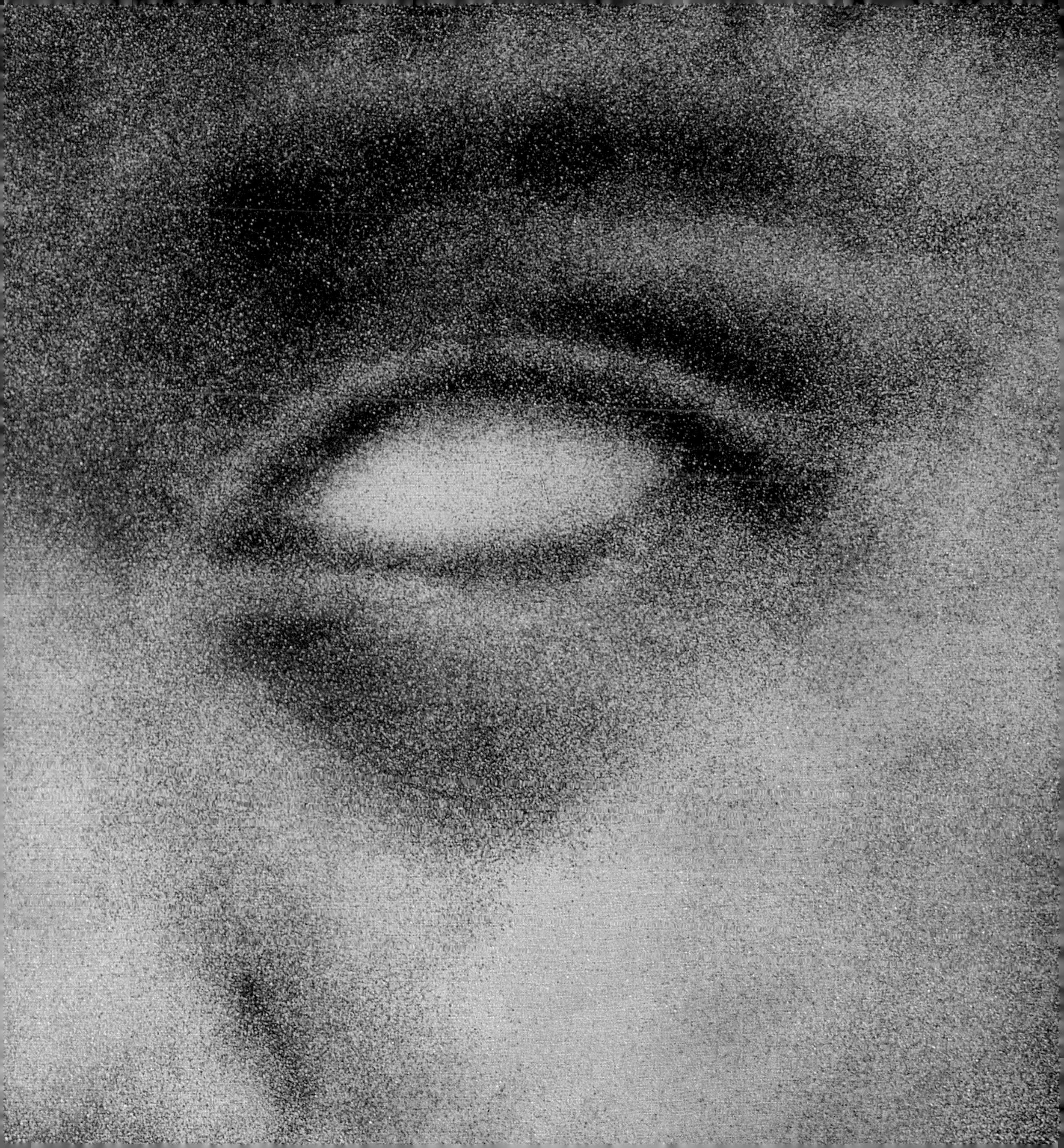

"I WANT TO SEE THAT AGAIN.
SEND YOUR EYES AWAY, COUSIN."

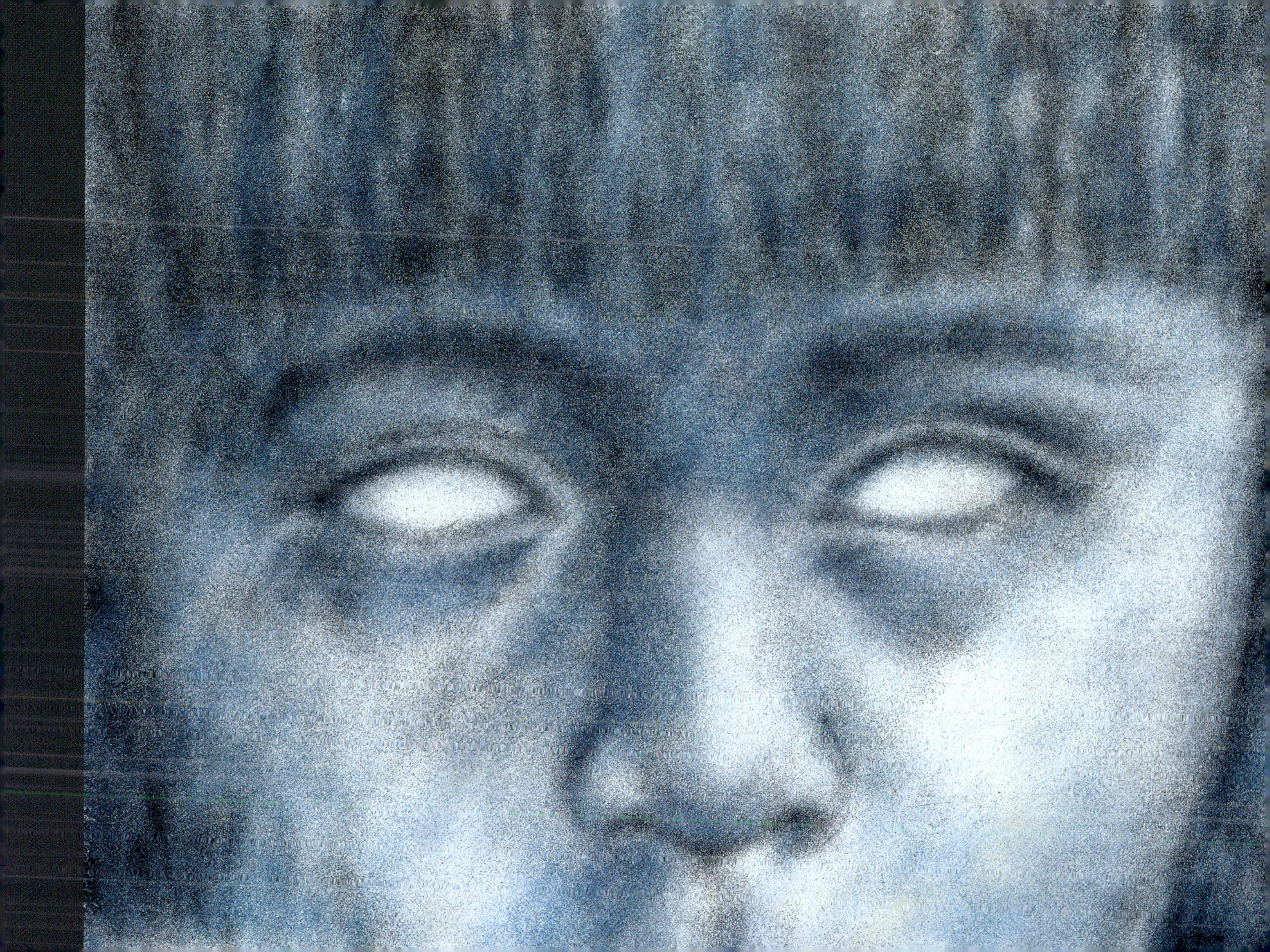

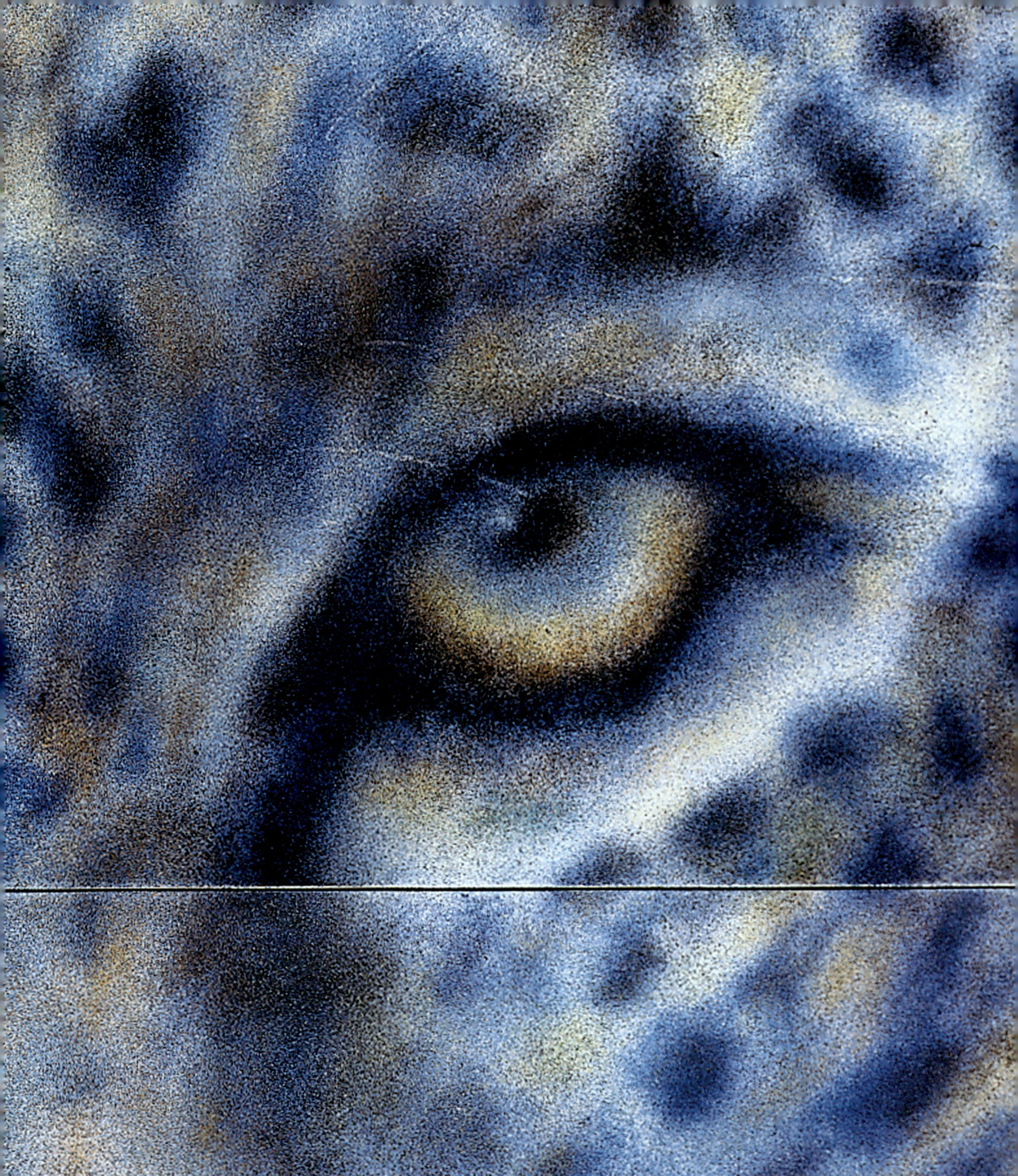

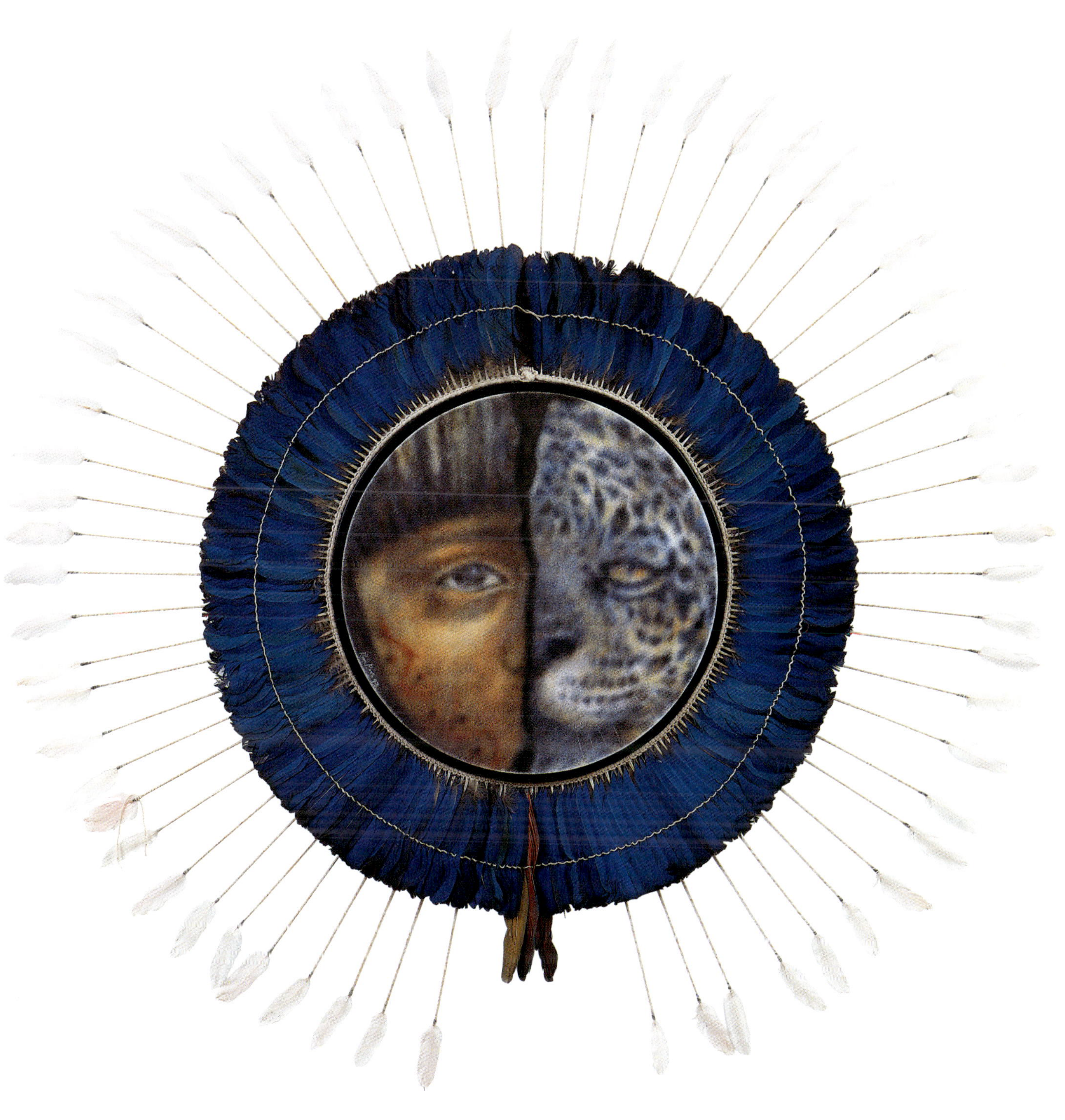

Jaguar's Kiss
The Eye Game

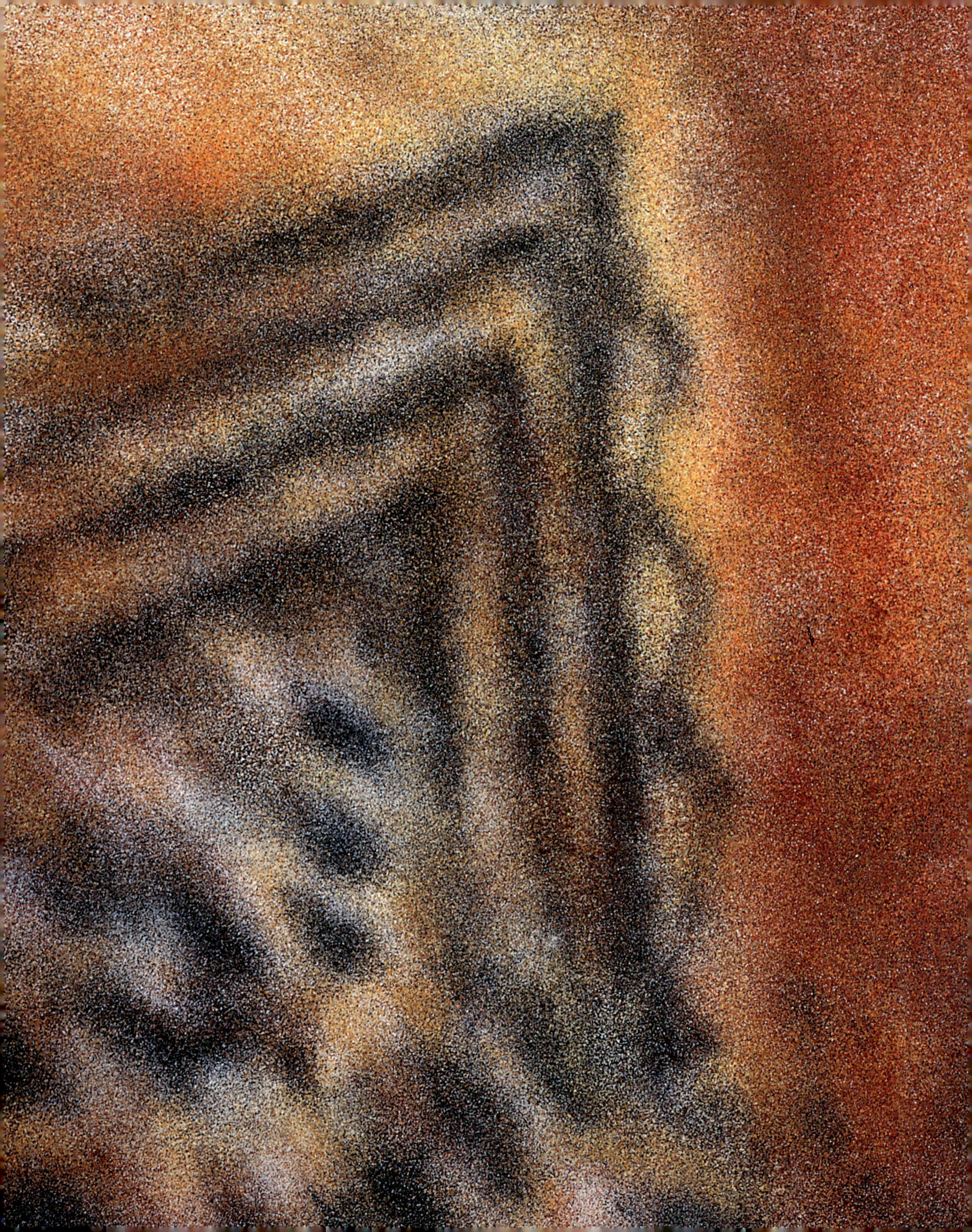

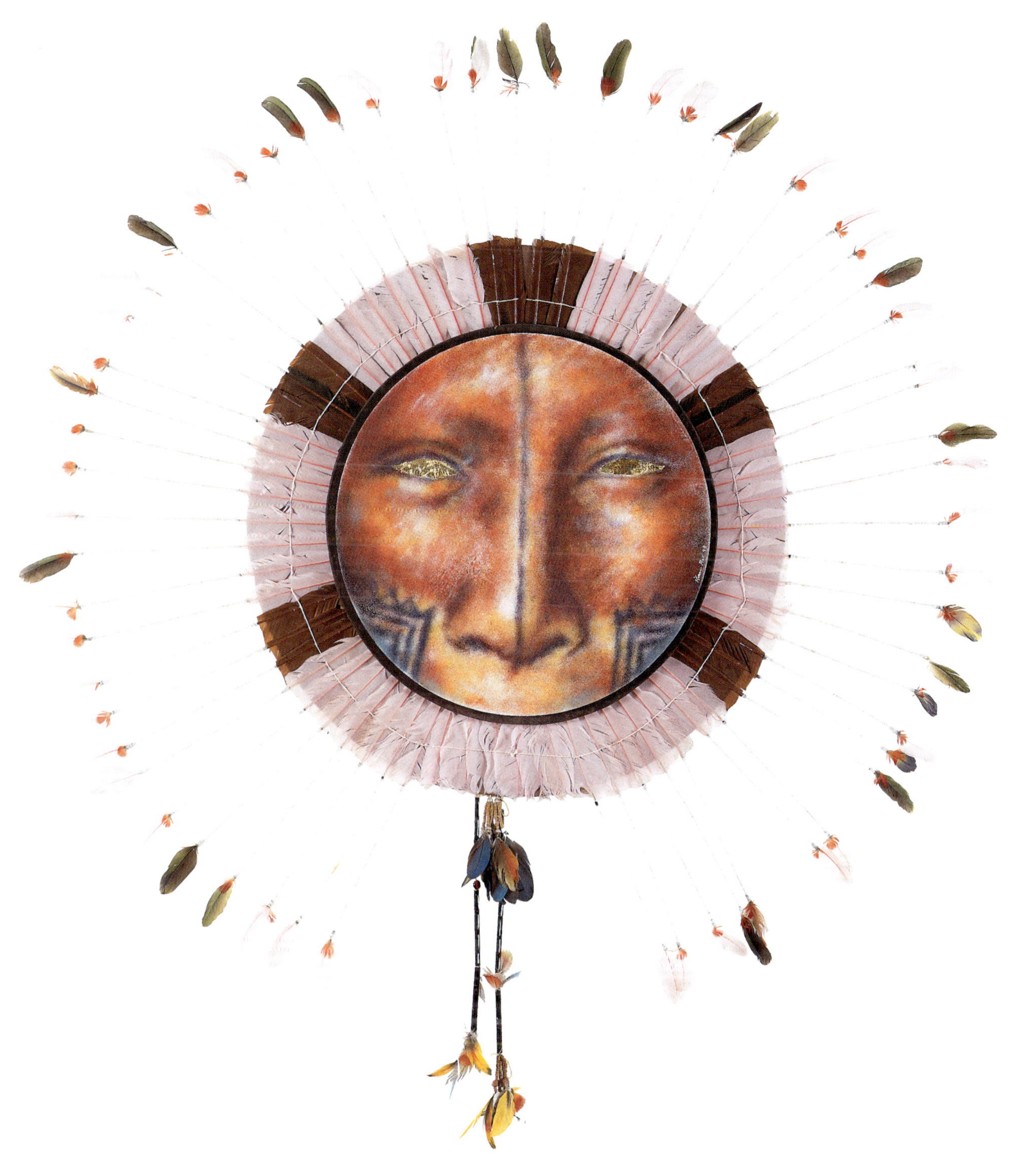

Tupã

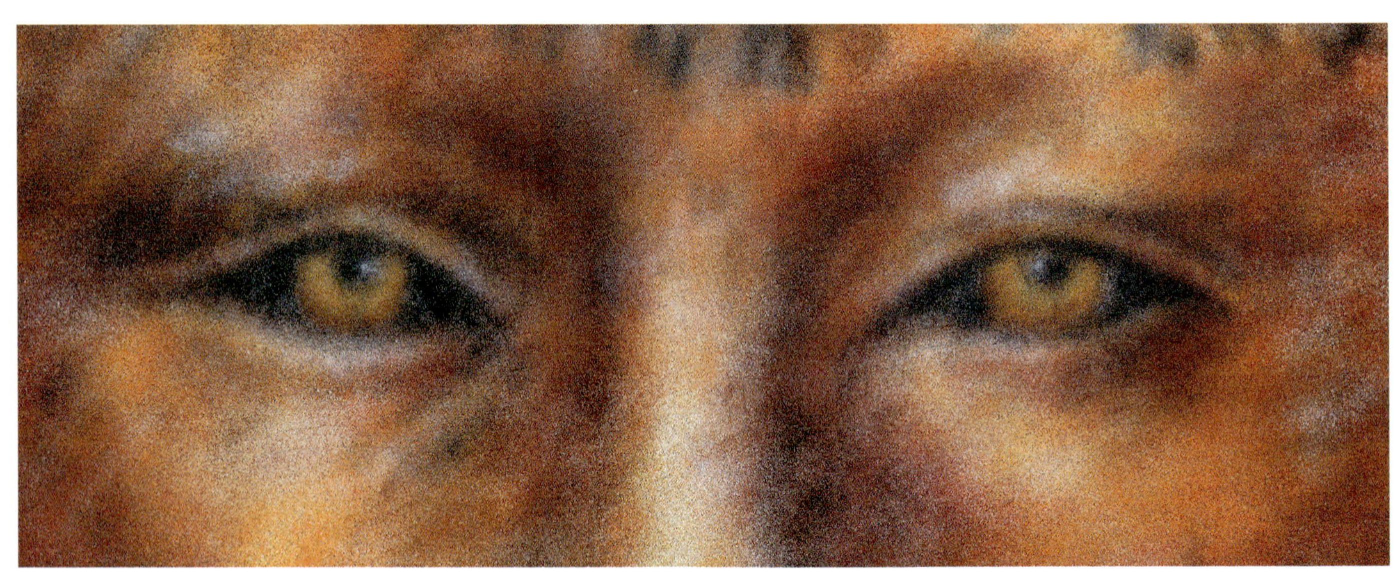

"KANAXIWÉ WARNED THEM THAT THEIR CRAZY IDEA ABOUT LIVING ON THE EARTH WOULD BRING DESTRUCTION TO THAT STEAMY EQUATORIAL PARADISE."

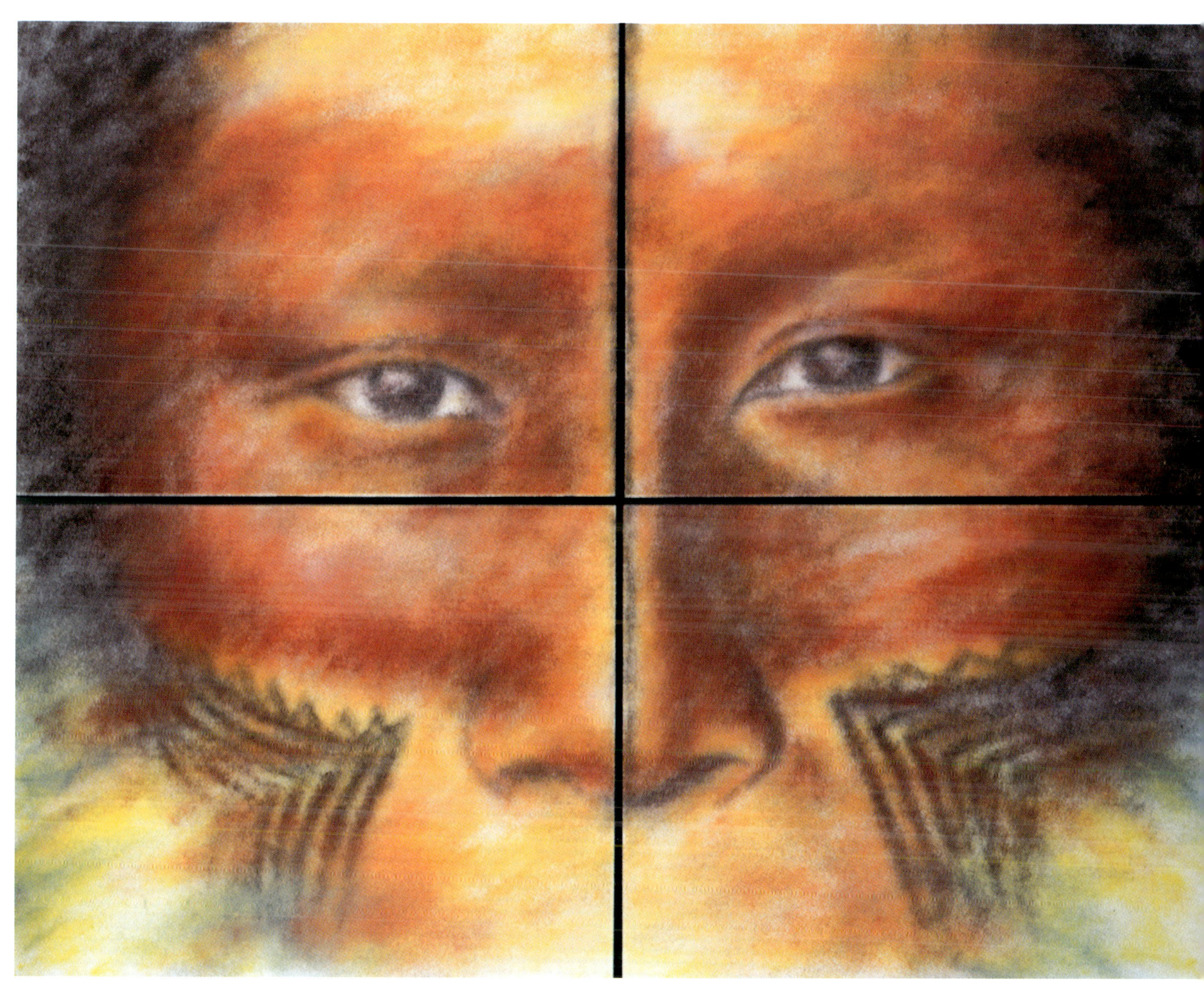

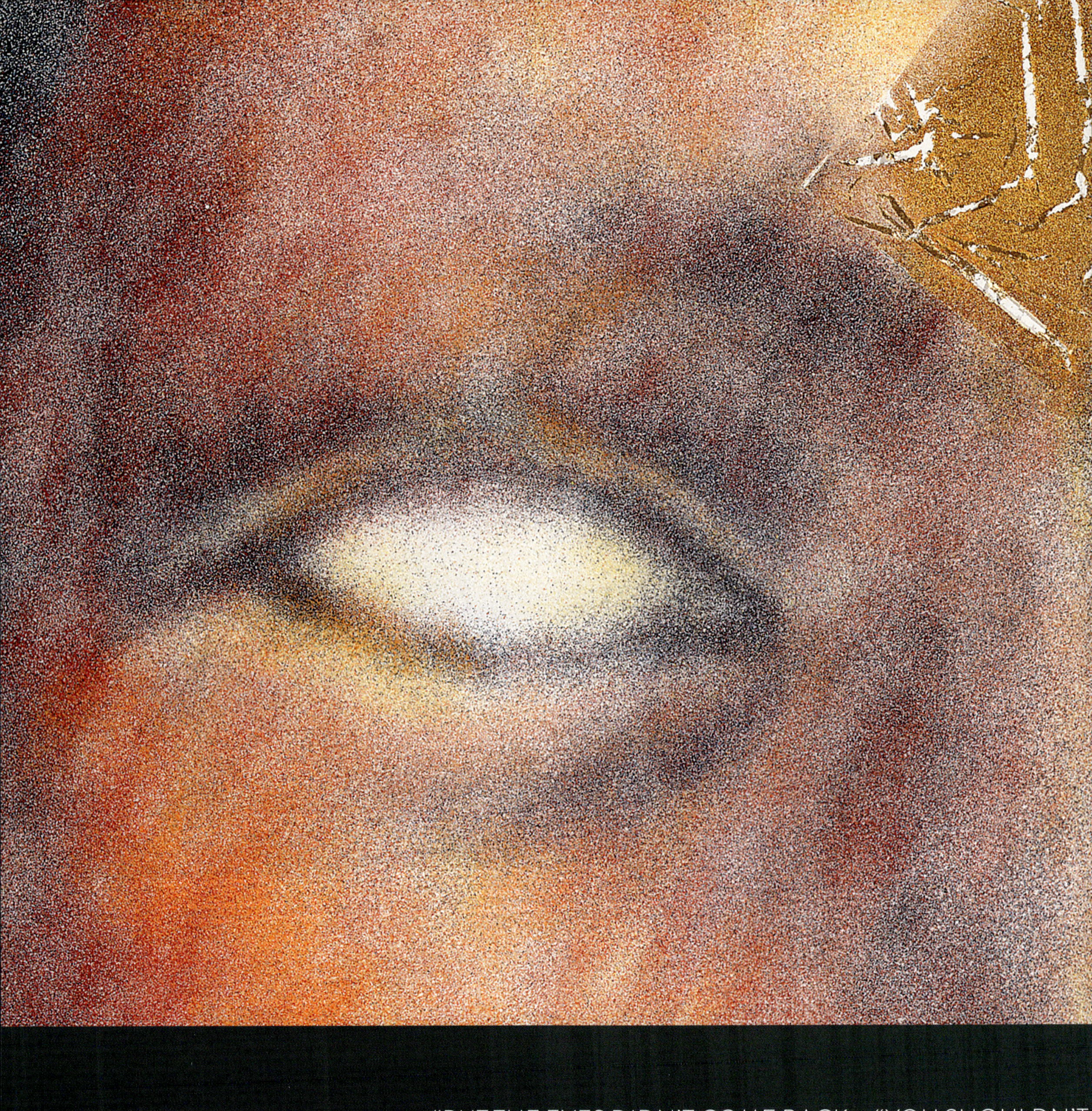

"BUT THE EYES DIDN'T COME BACK ... "YOU SHOULDN'T

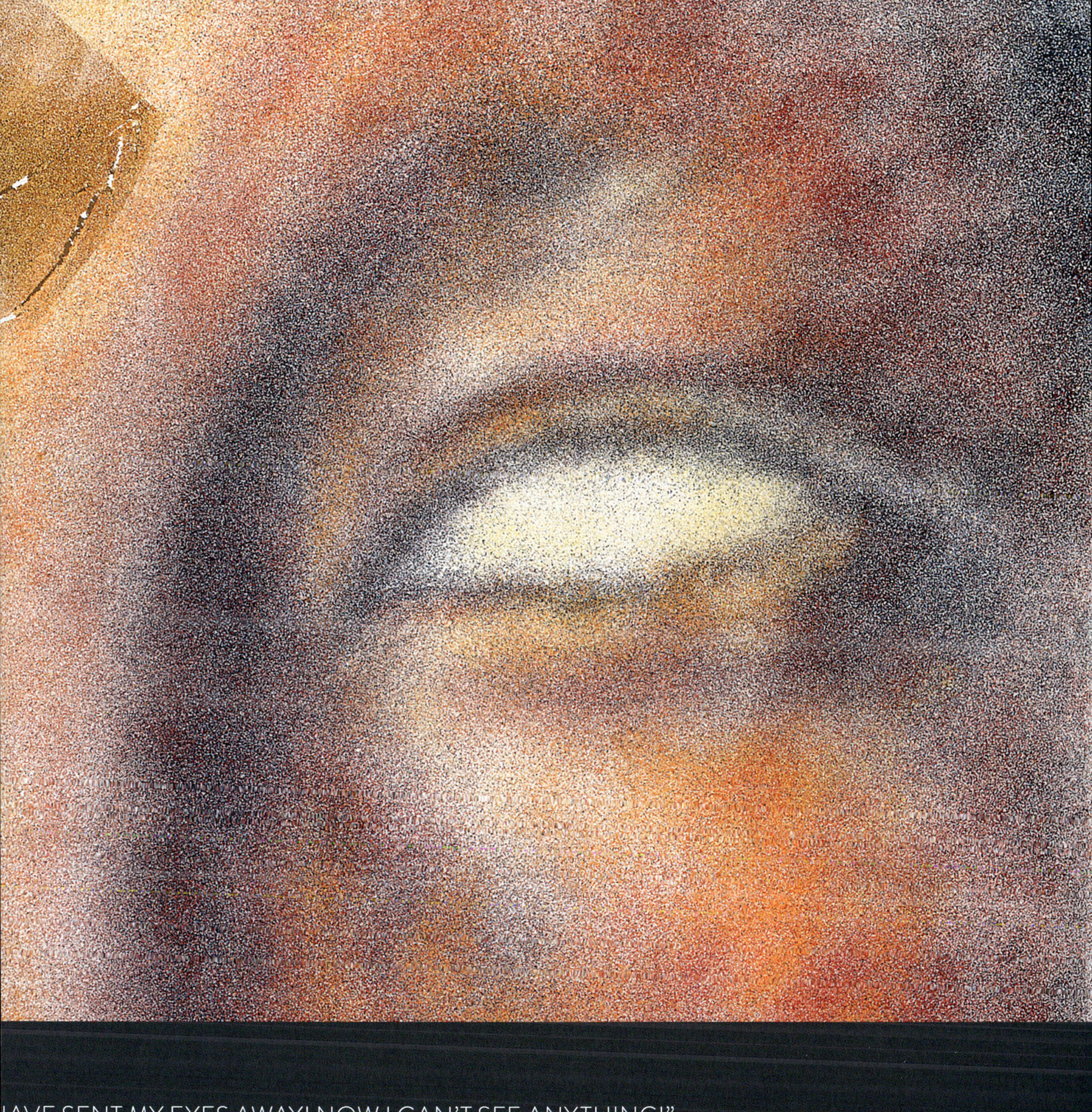

HAVE SENT MY EYES AWAY! NOW I CAN'T SEE ANYTHING!"

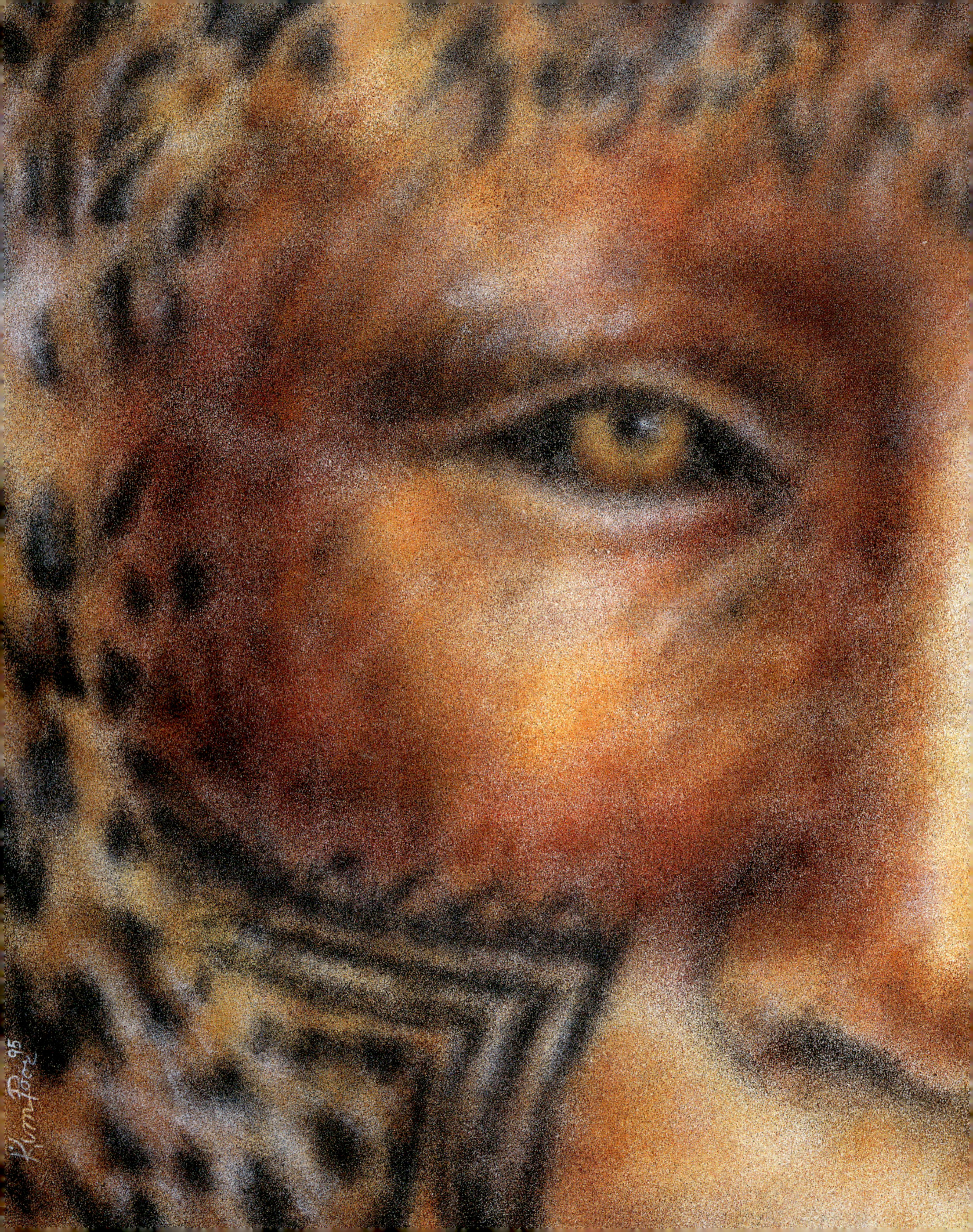

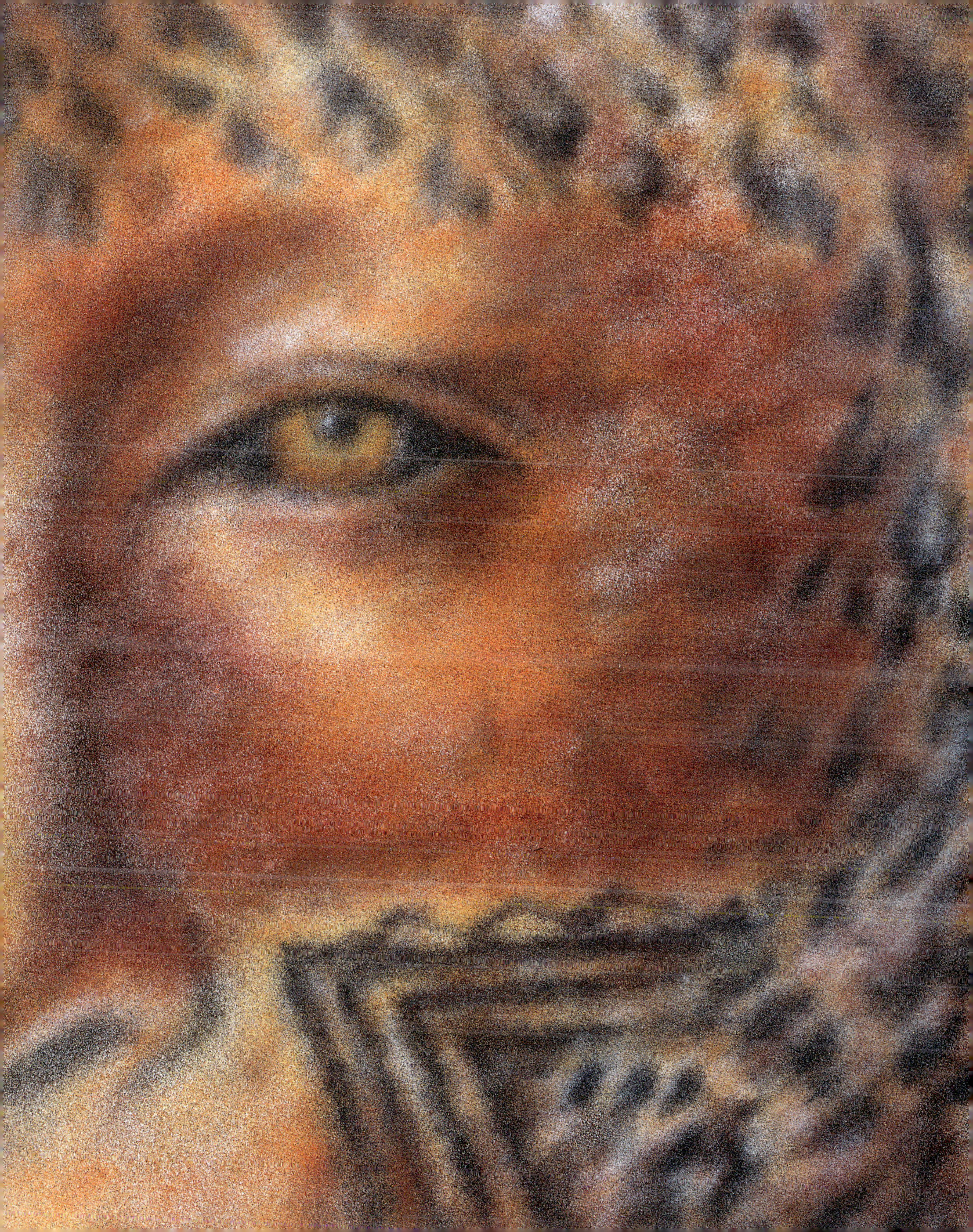

JAGUARS

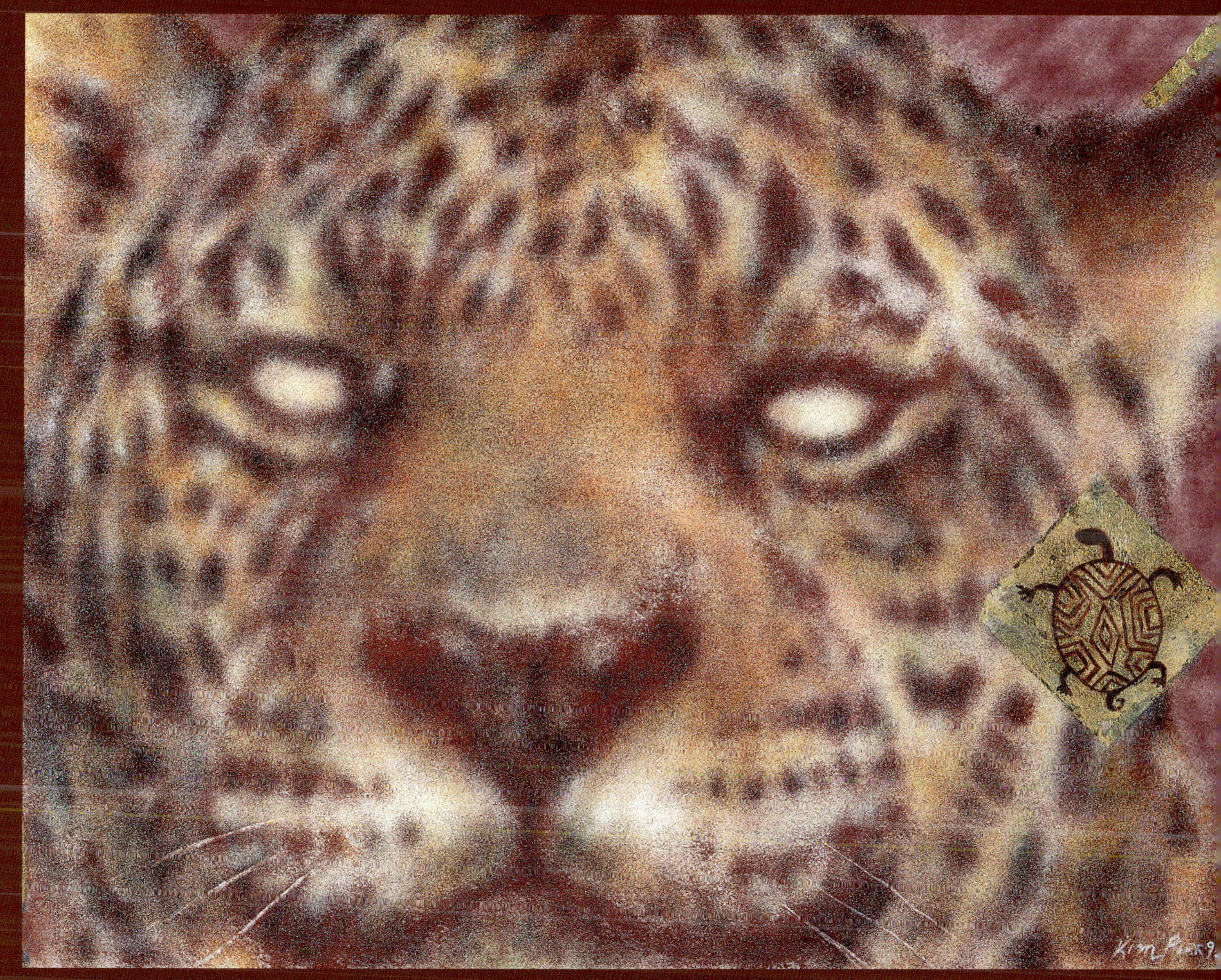

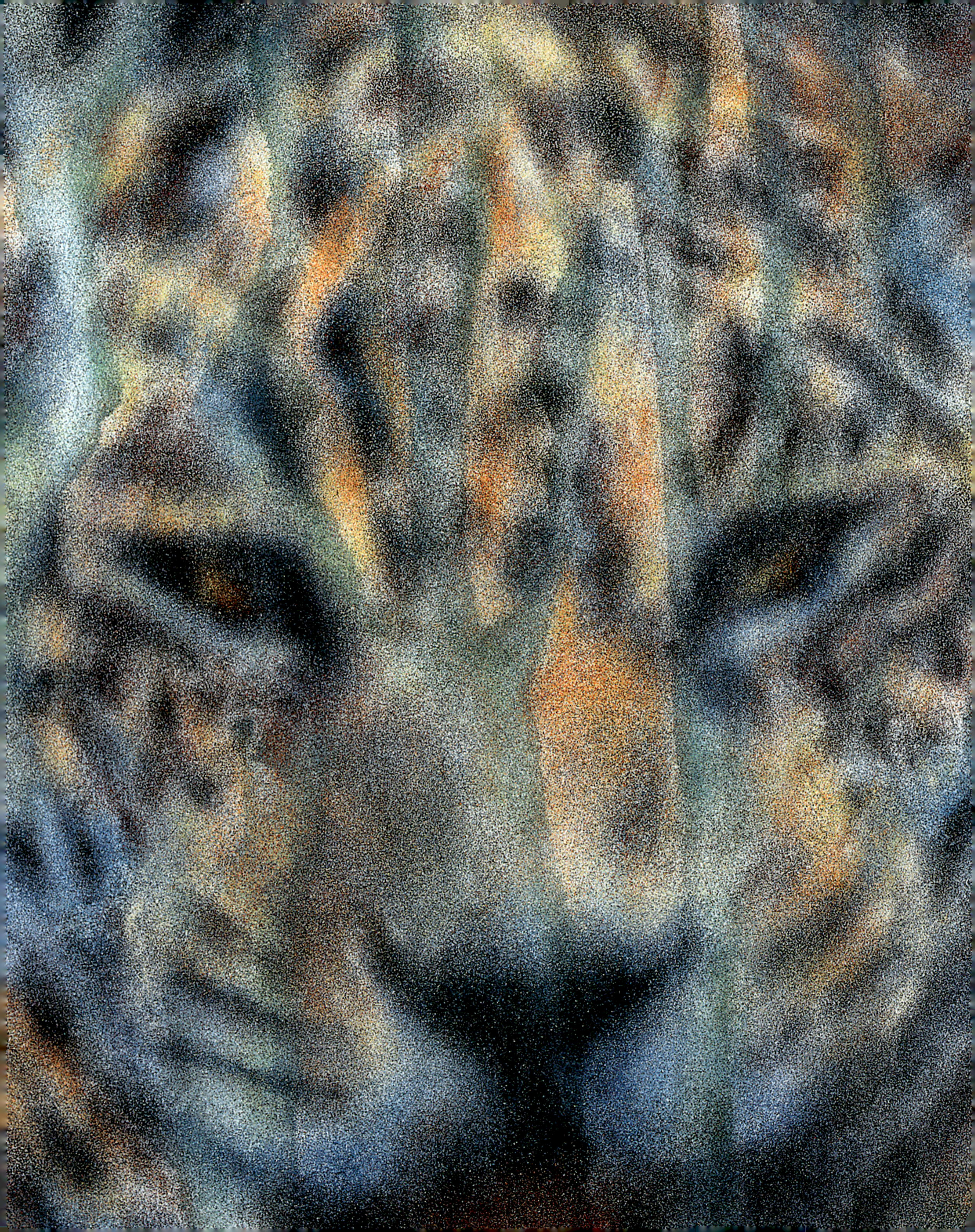

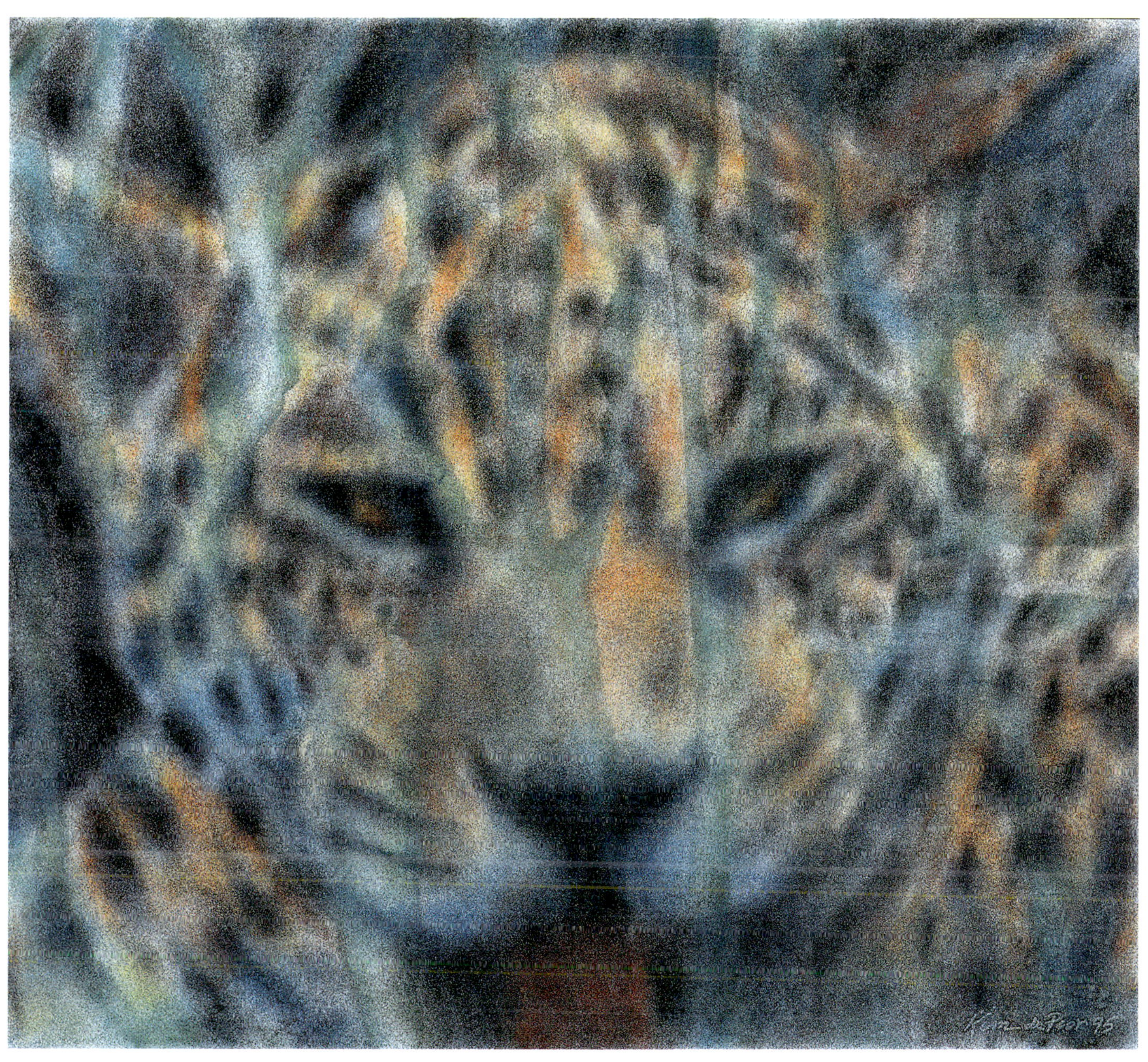

Camouflage

"... BUT ALL OF THEM WERE CHANGED INTO JAGUARS"

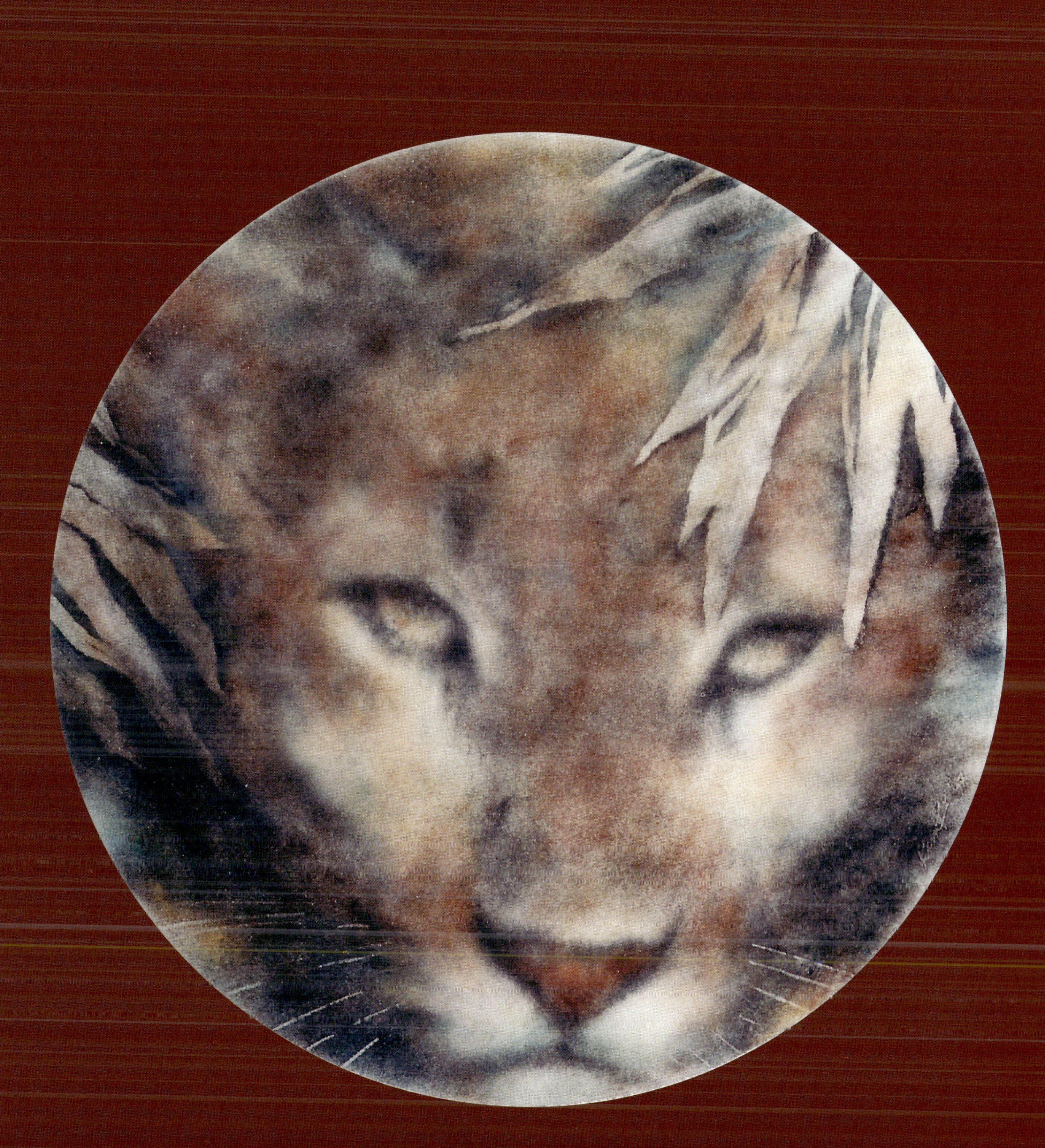

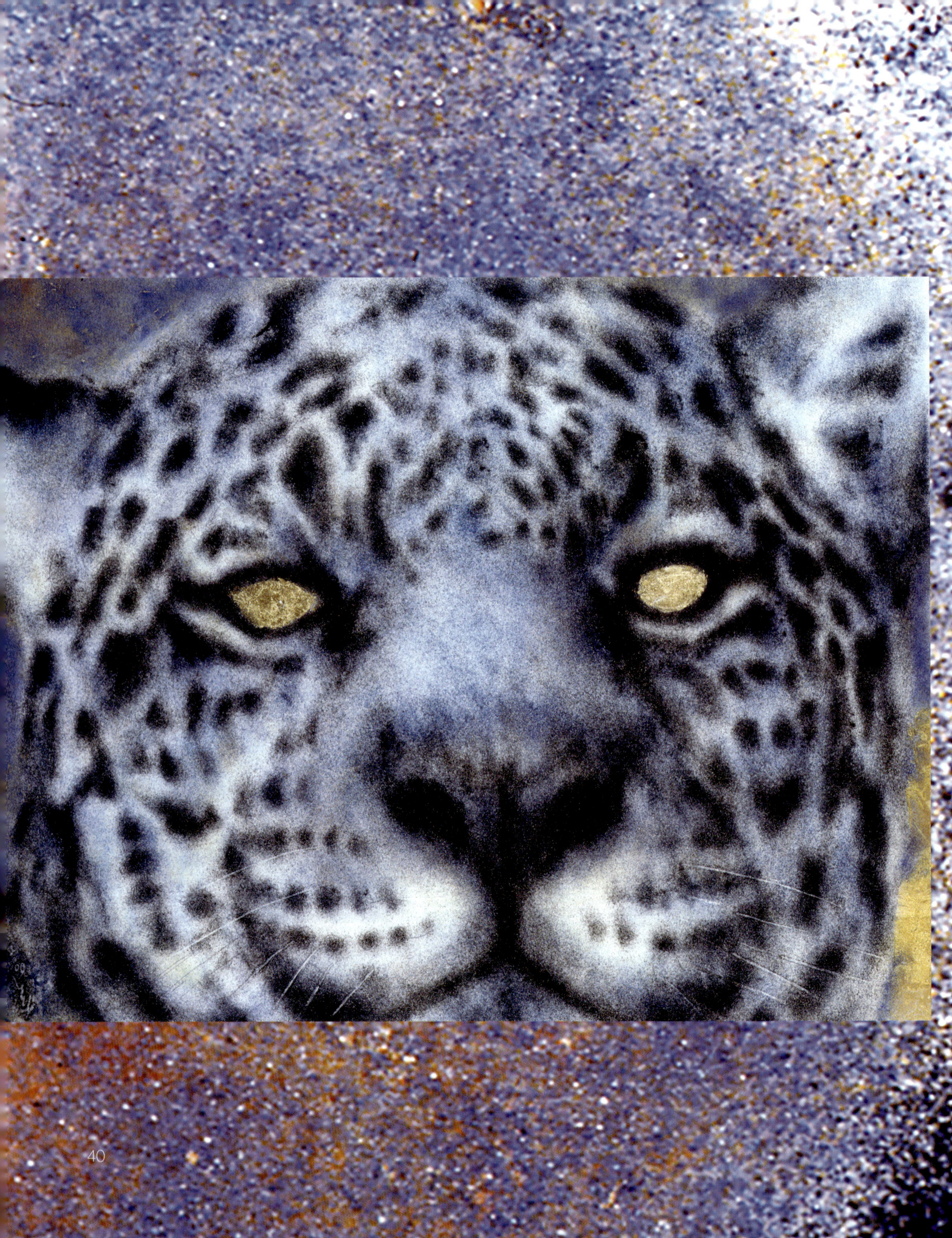

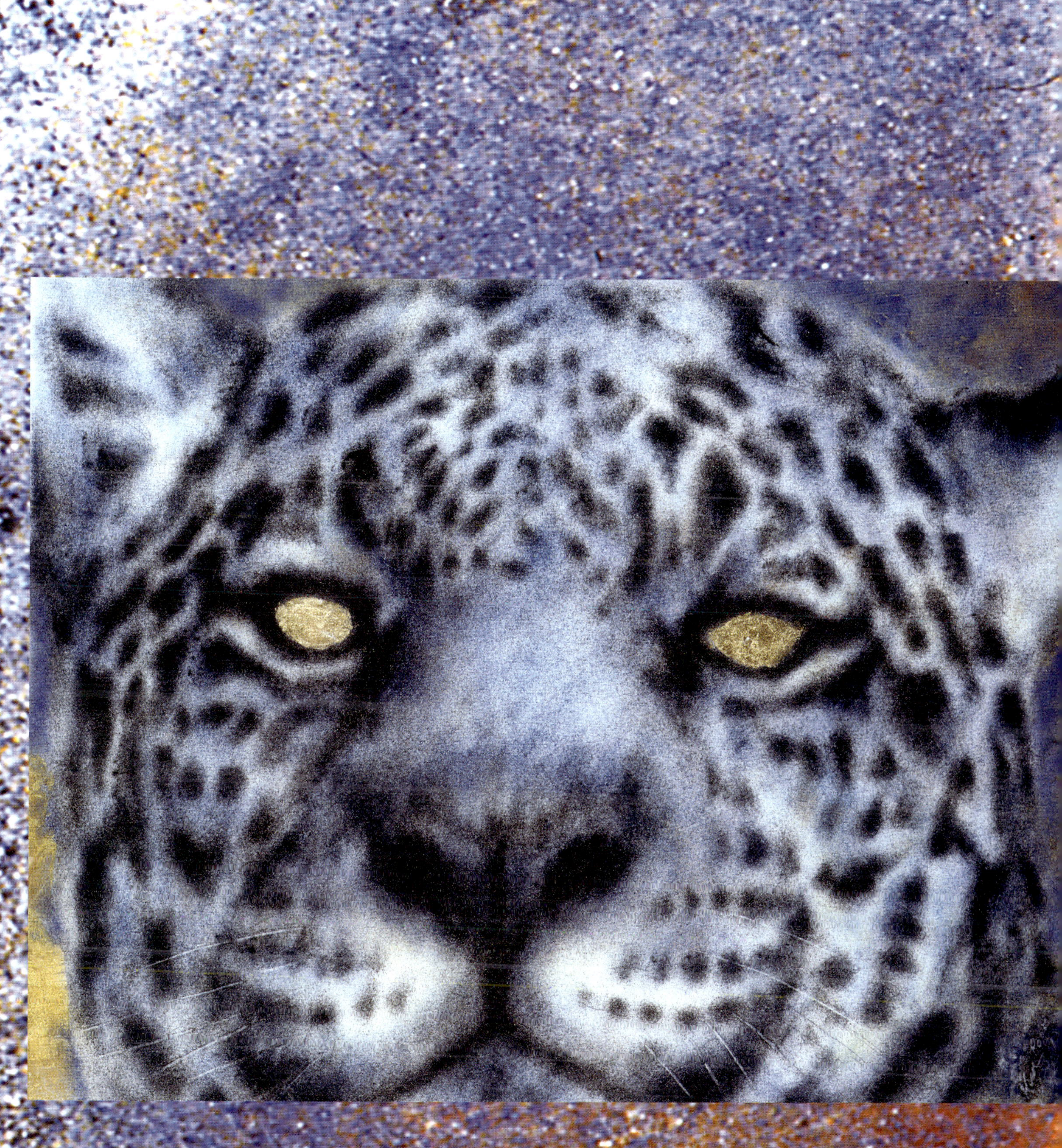

Night Jaguar

MYTHICAL & SPIRITUAL

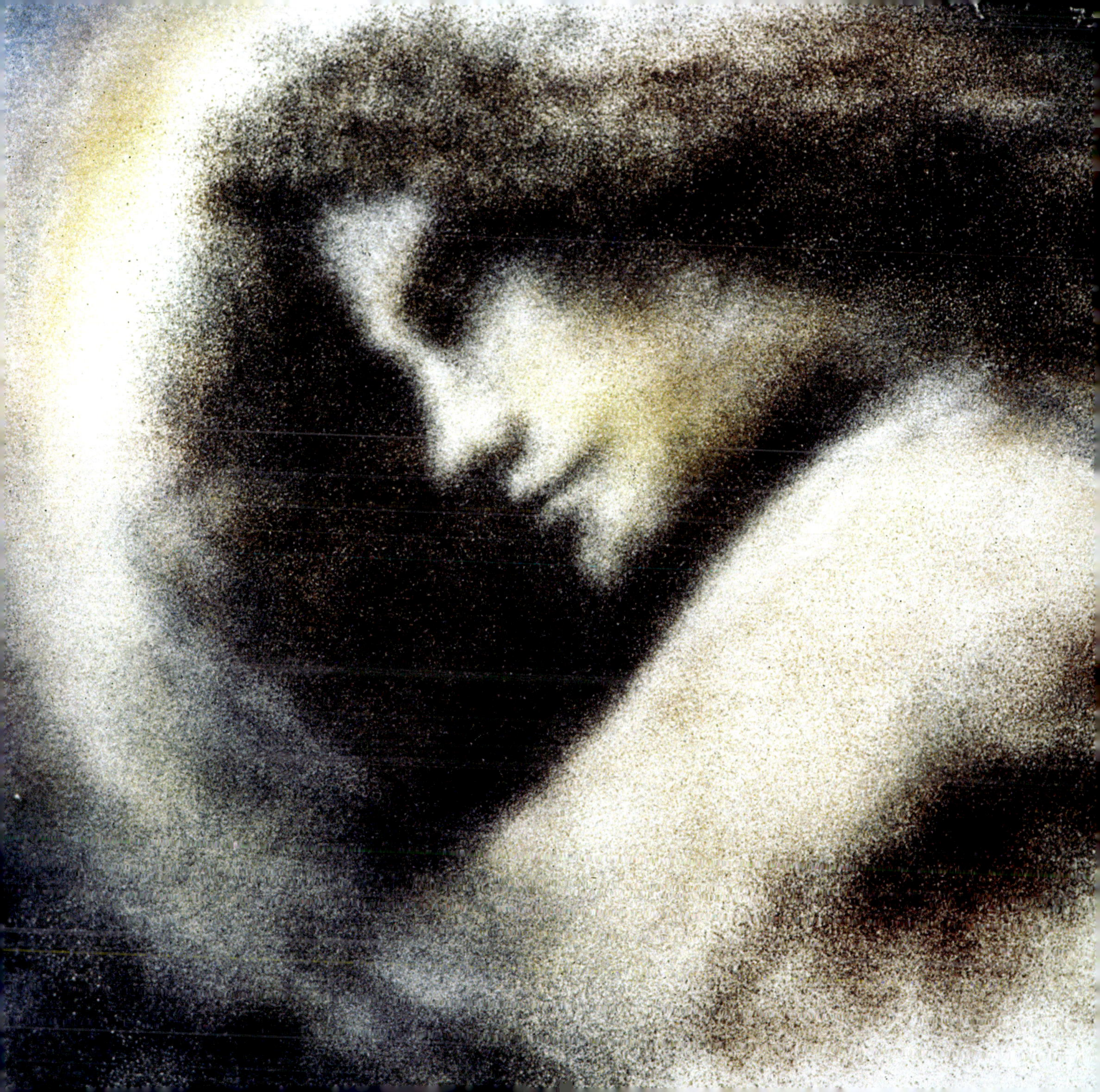

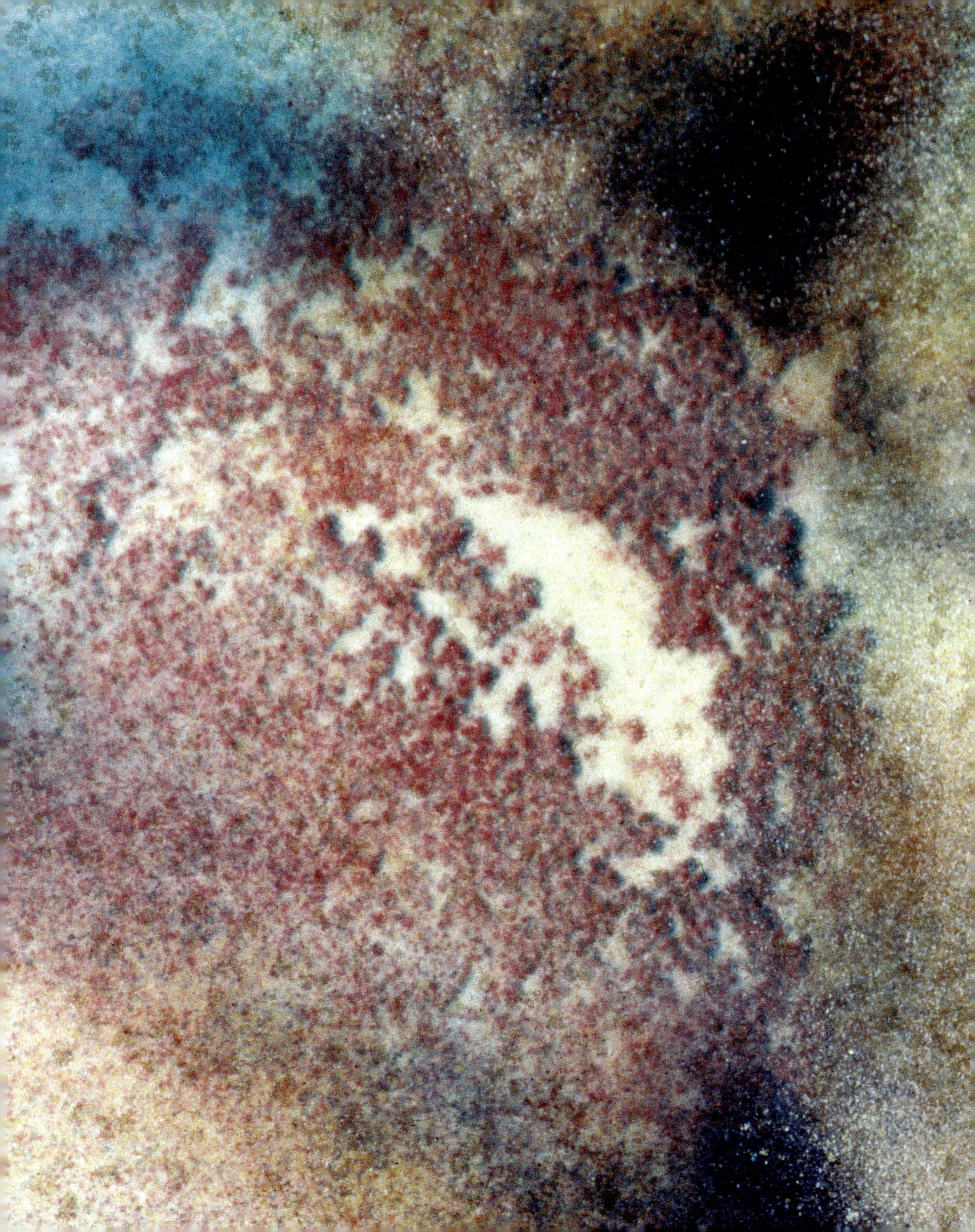

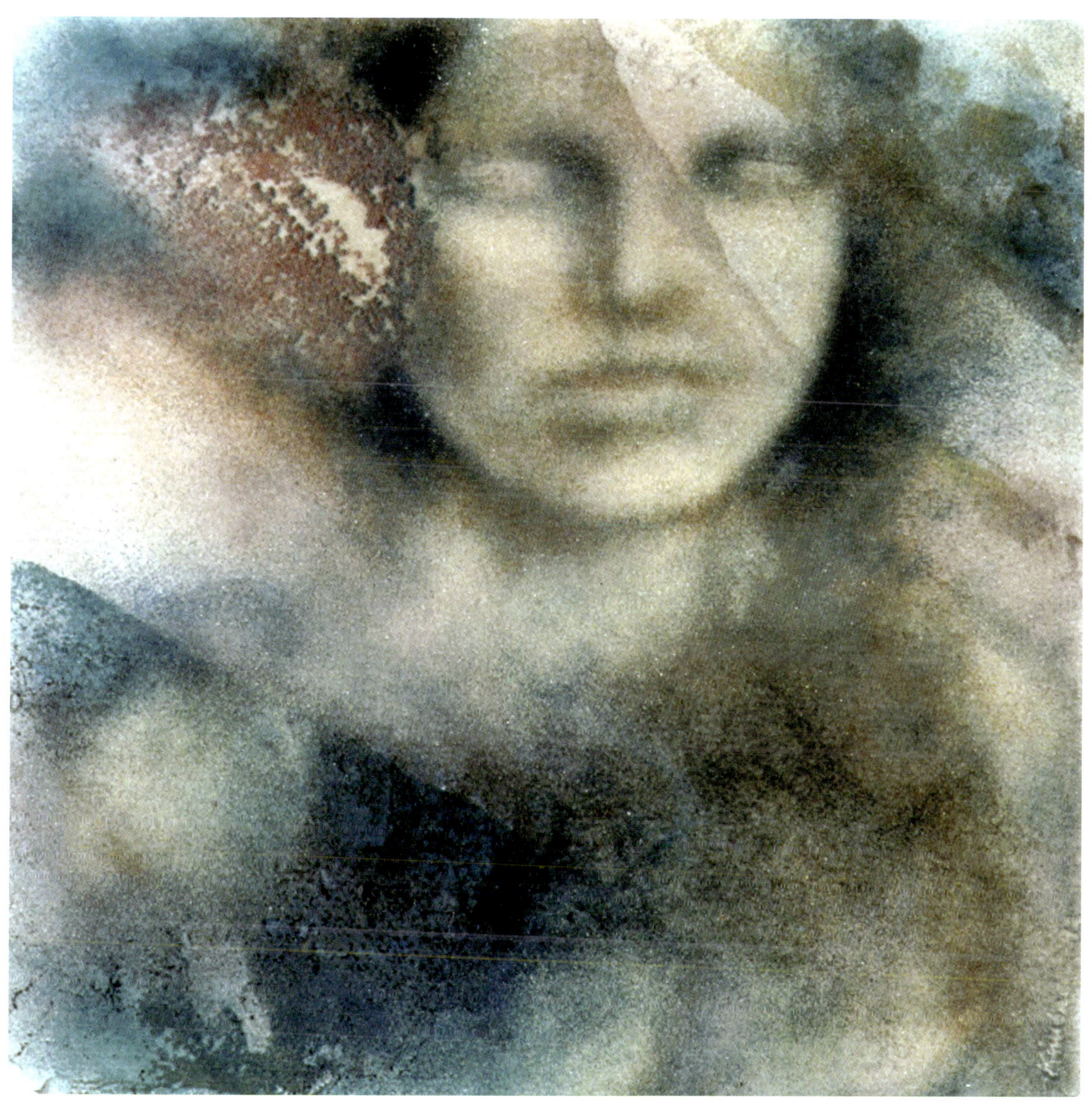

Amazon Angel

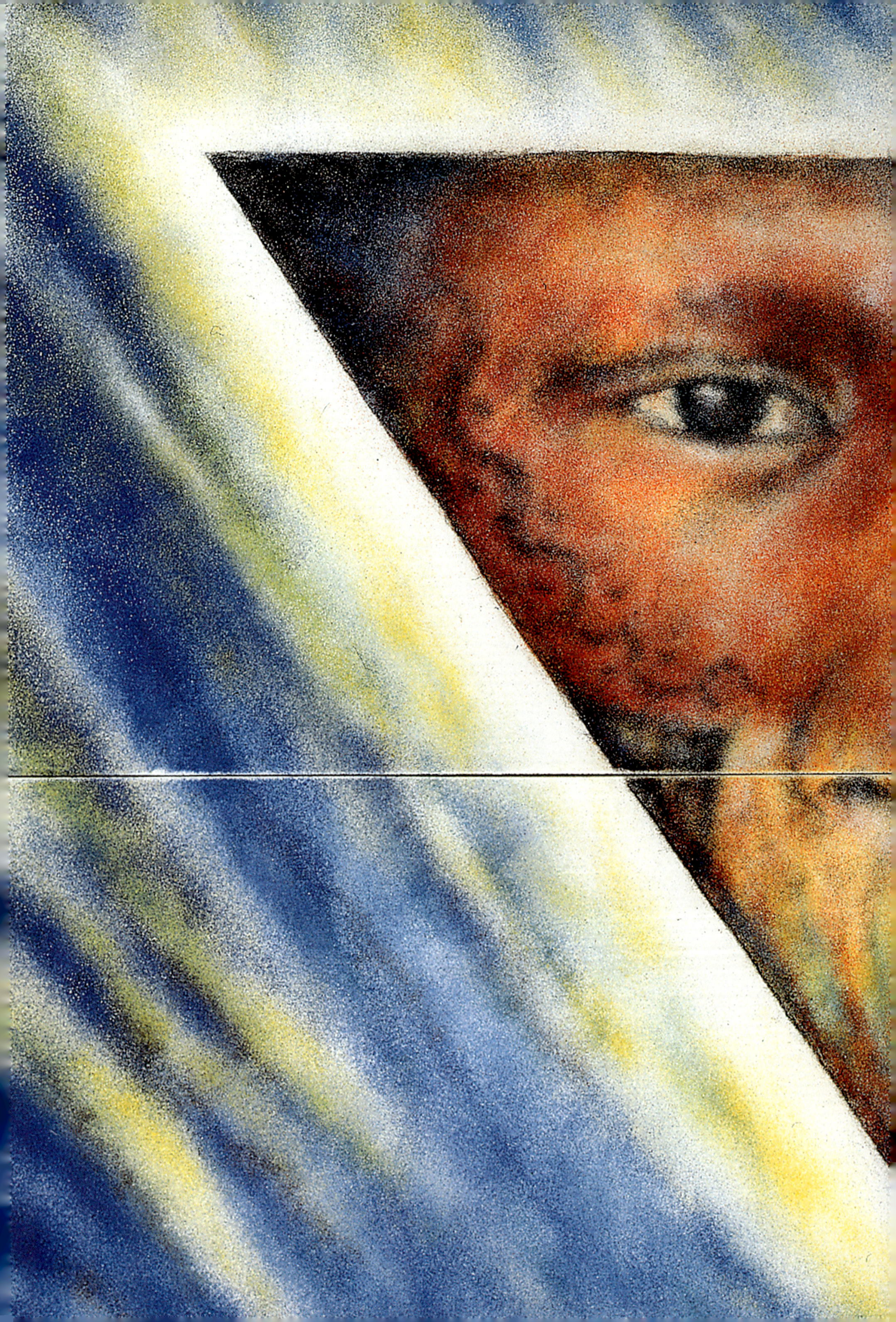

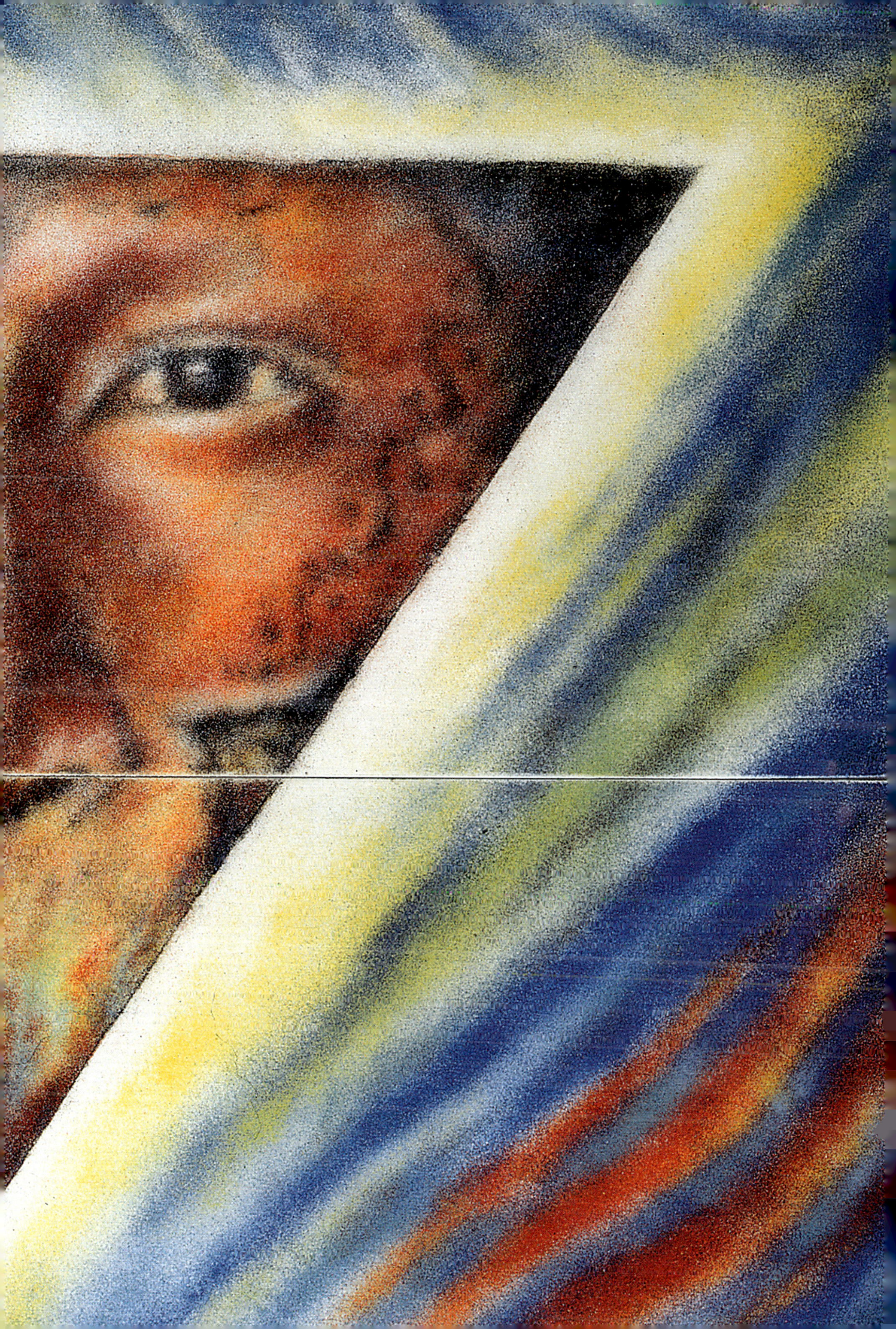

DOES THE WATER HAVE AN OWNER?

NO!

DOES THE SUN HAVE AN OWNER?

NO!

ARE THE EARTH OR THE FLOWERS OWNED BY ANYBODY?

NO!

SO, WHY DOES THE FIRE HAVE AN OWNER?

IT'S NOT RIGHT; FIRE SHOULD BELONG TO EVERYONE!

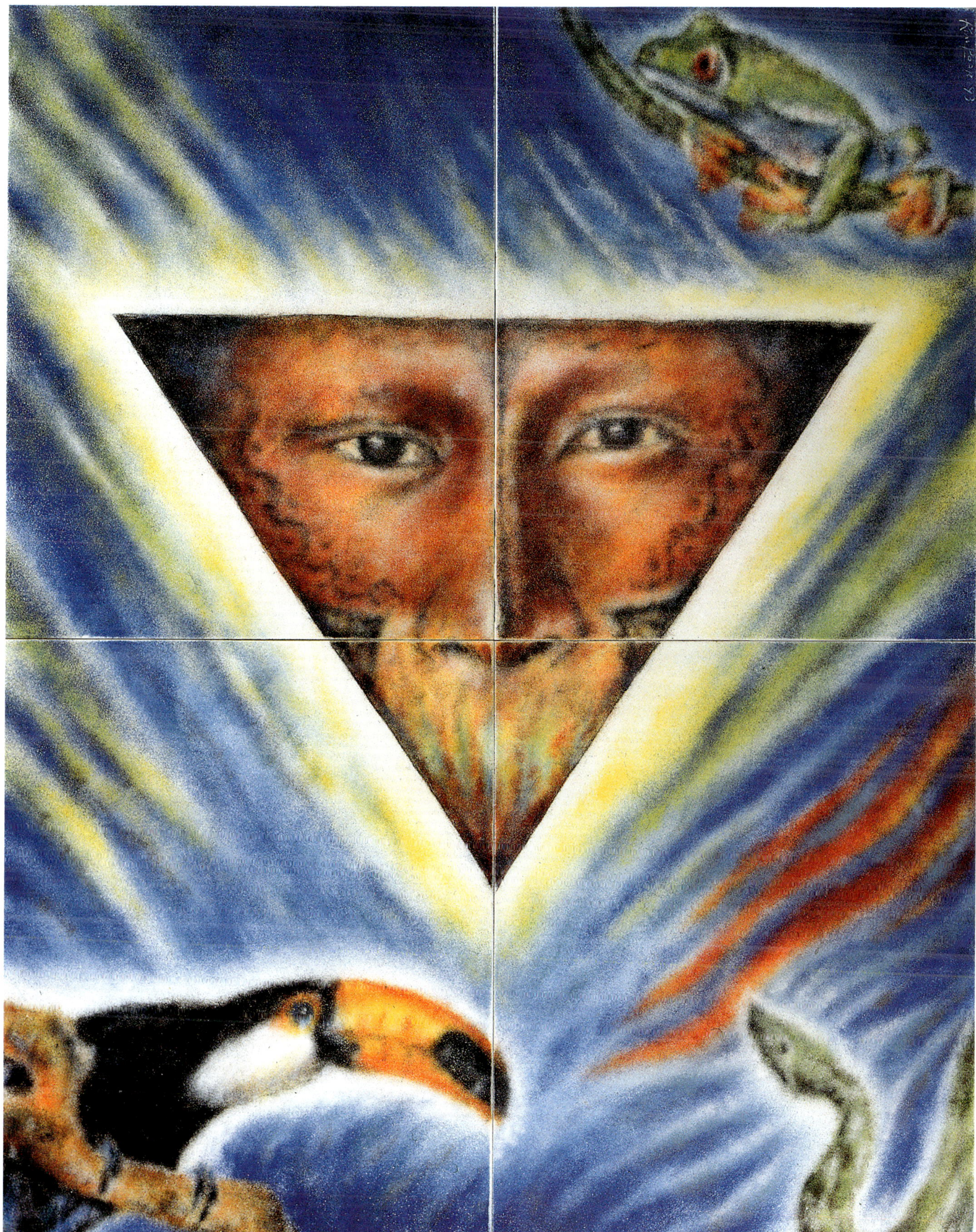

THE TUCANO WASTED NO TIME. HE FLEW TO THE BODY, BRINGING THER FIRE UNDER HIS WINGS.

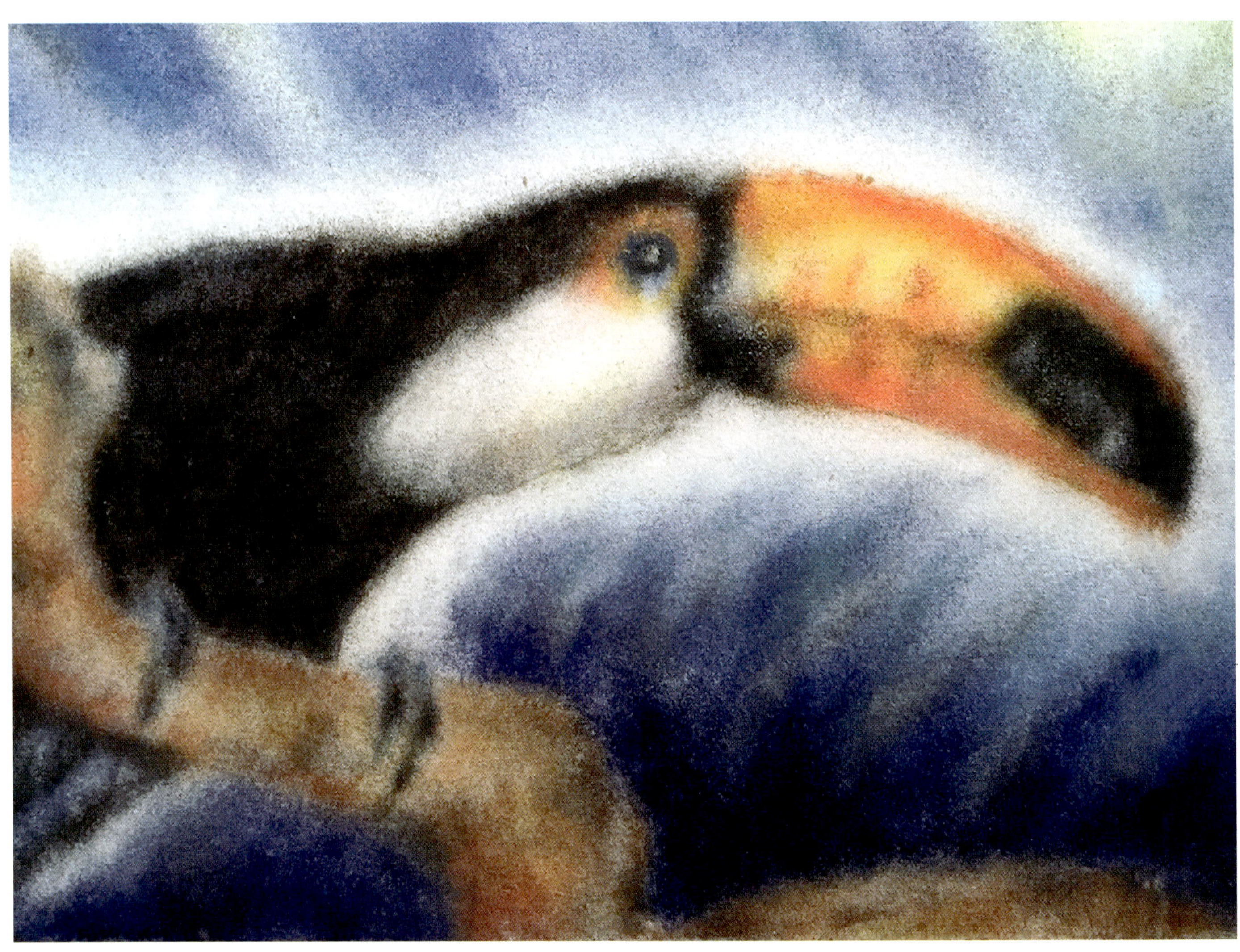

SAPO-CURURU ON THE BANK OF THE RIVER,
WHEN THE SAPO SINGS, THE CURURU IS COLD ...

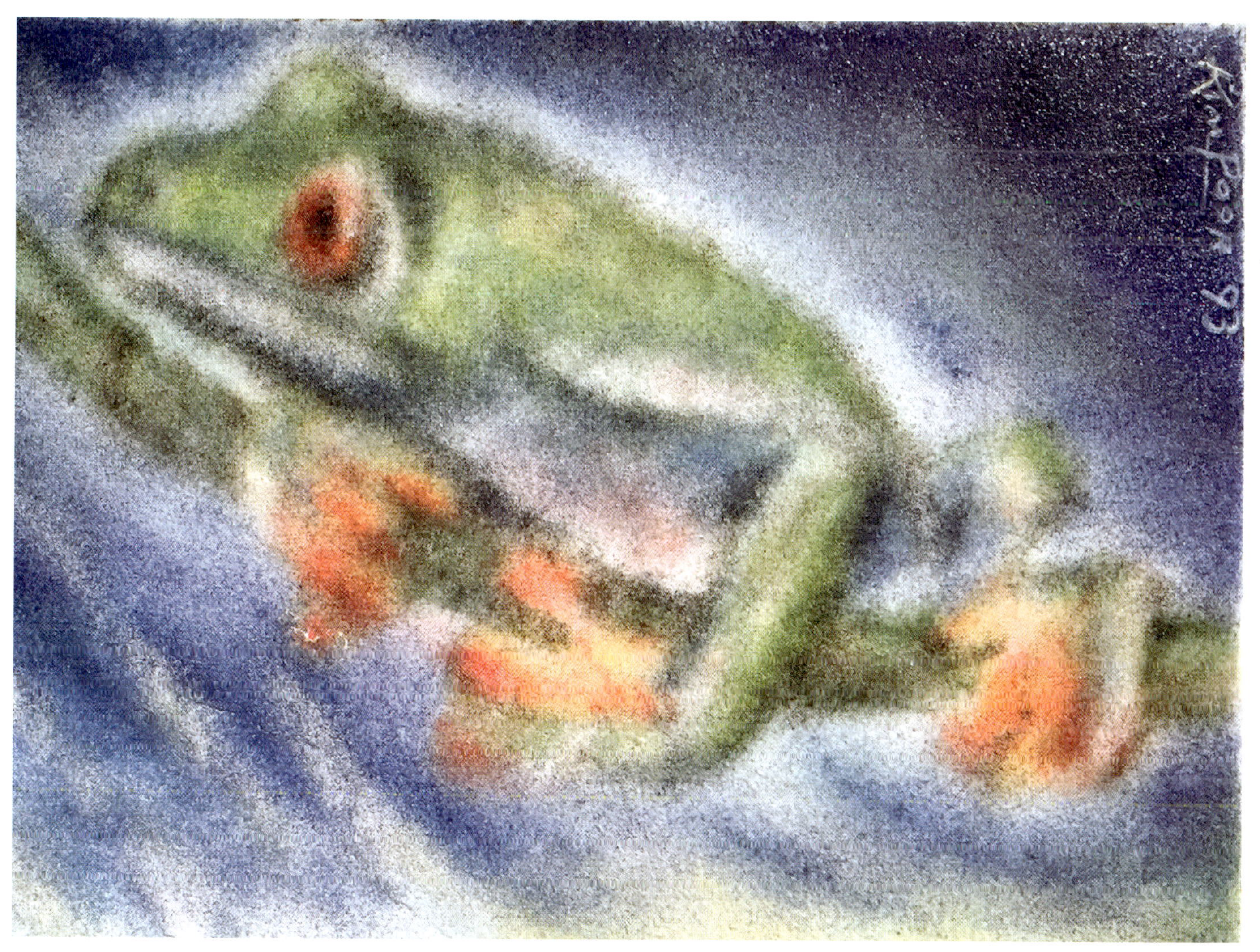

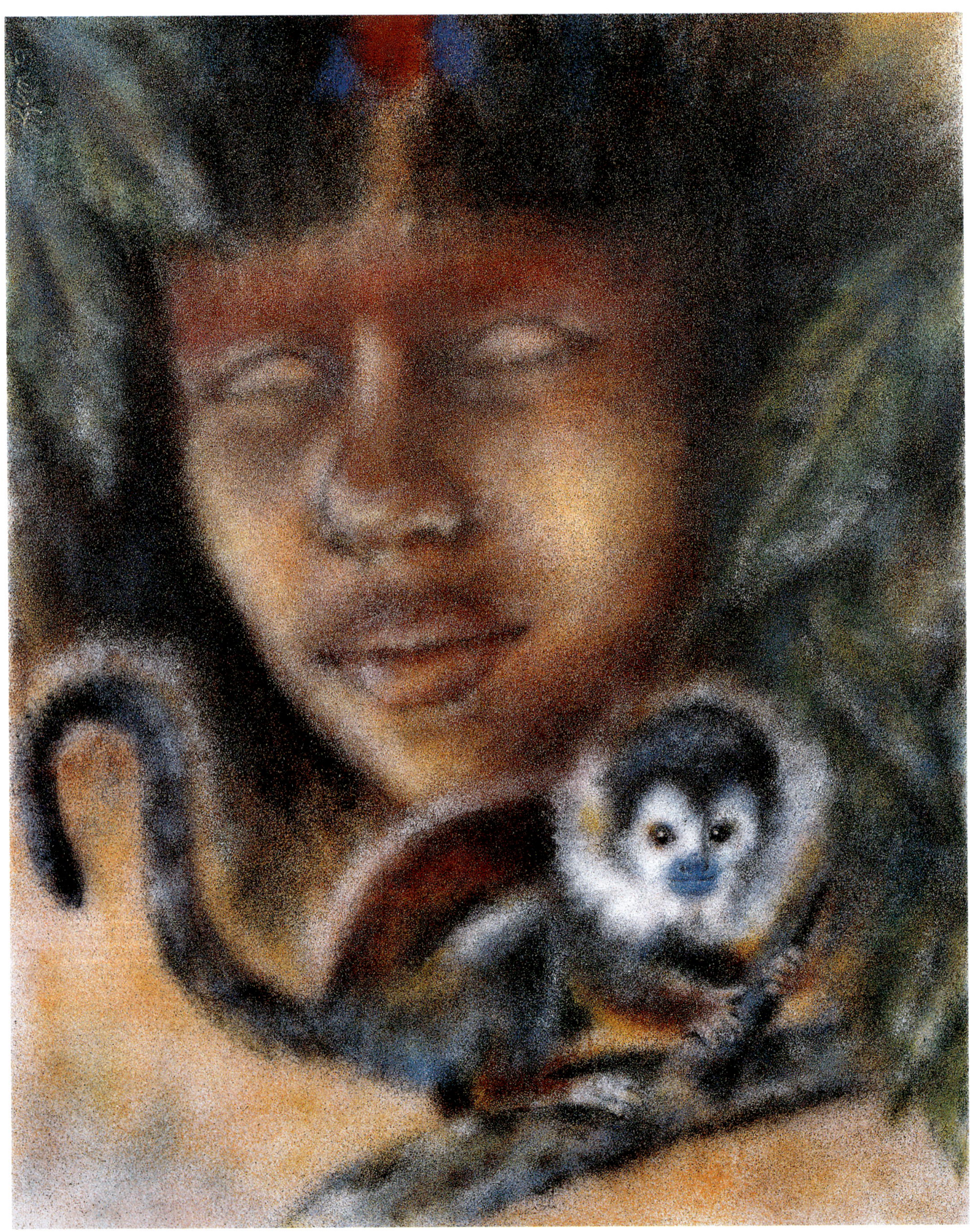

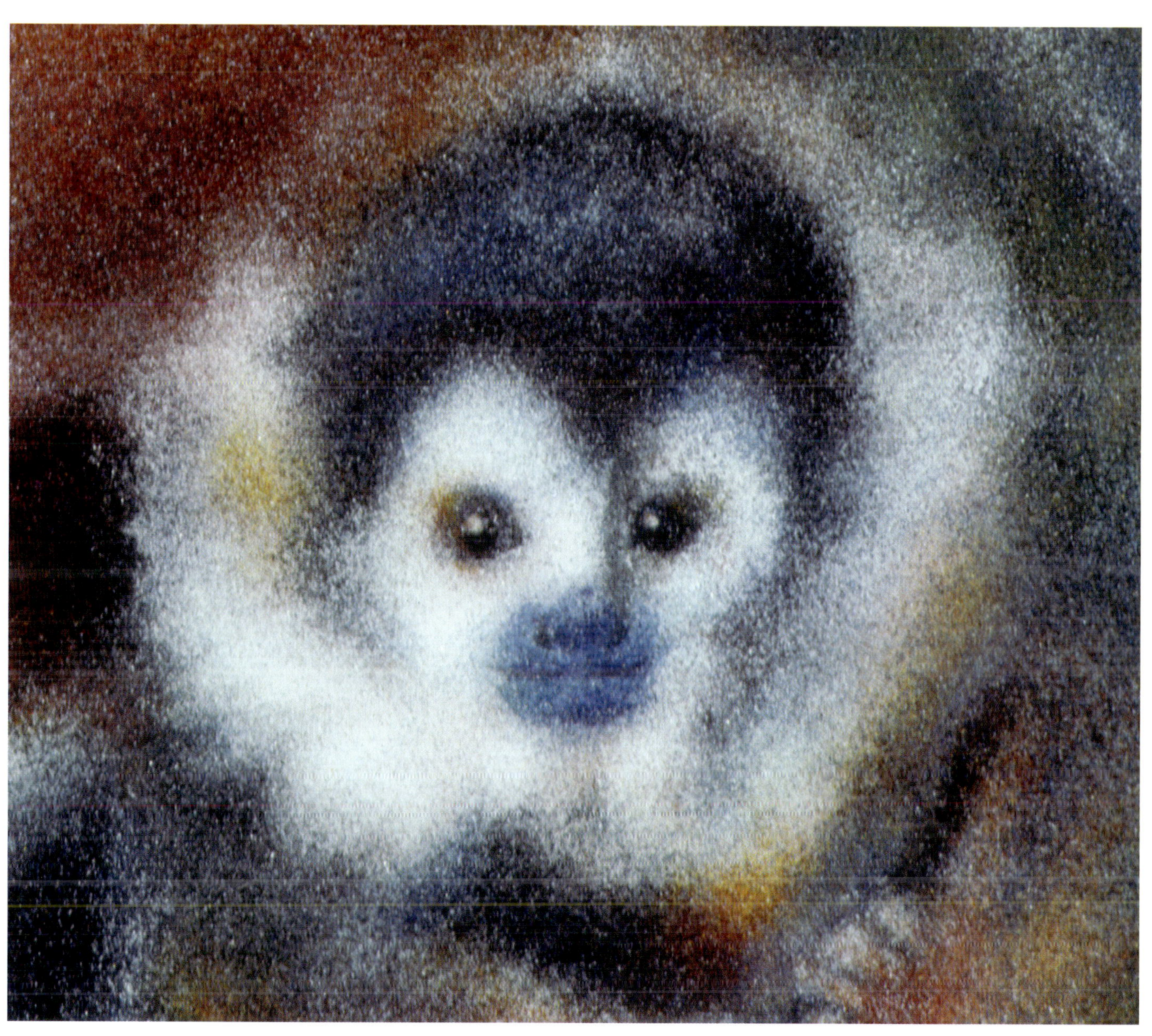

Mico Leão

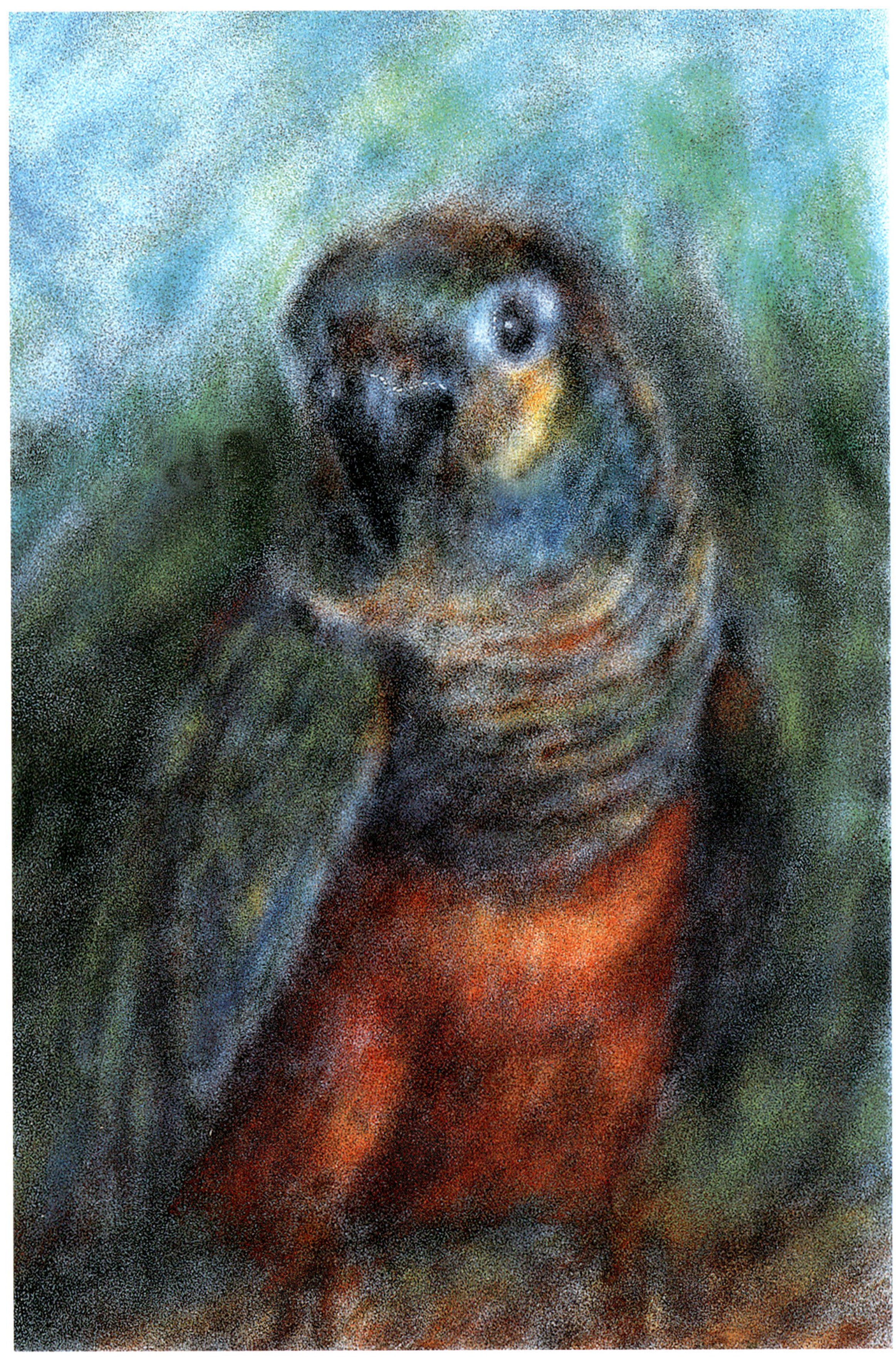

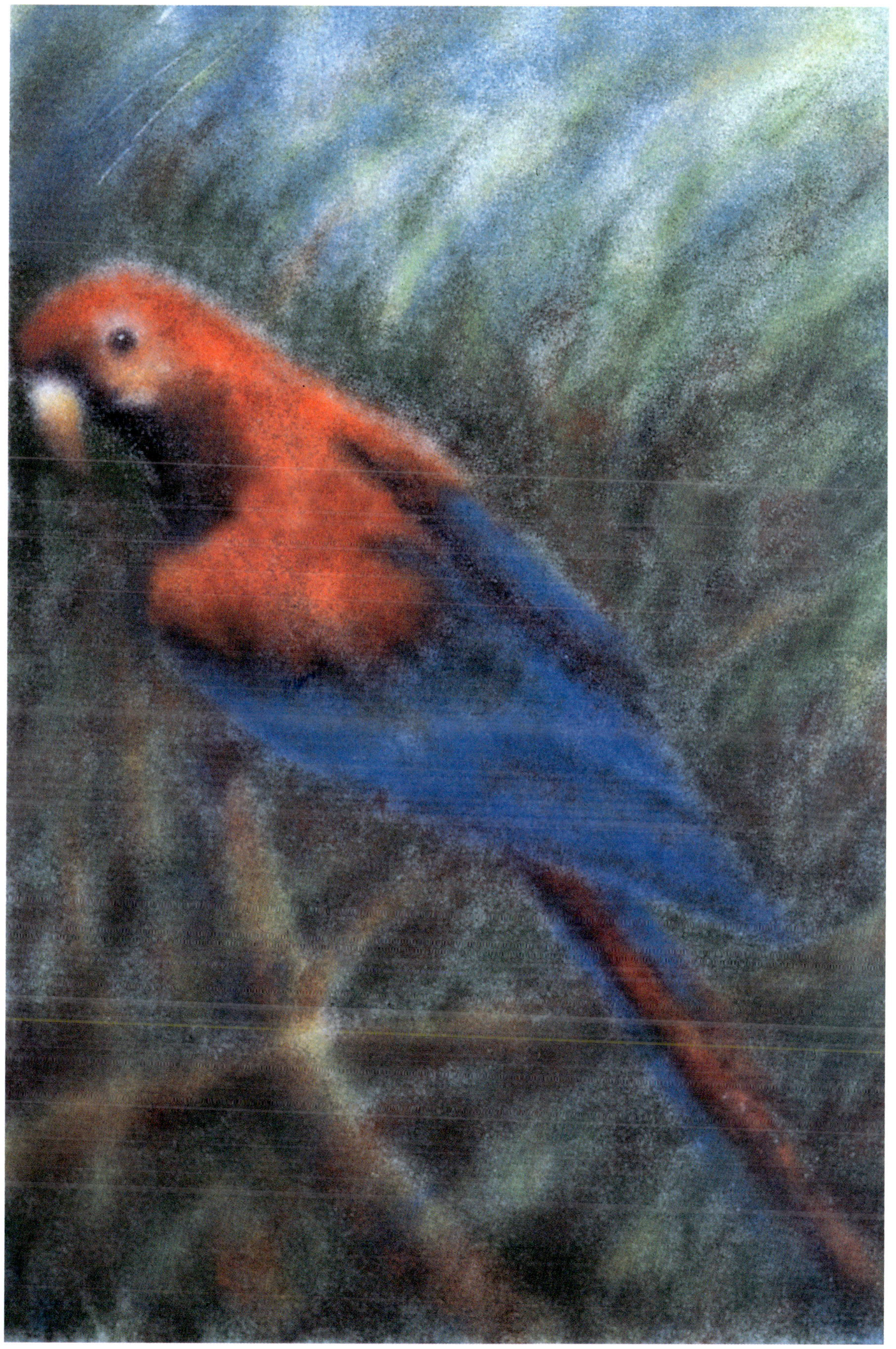

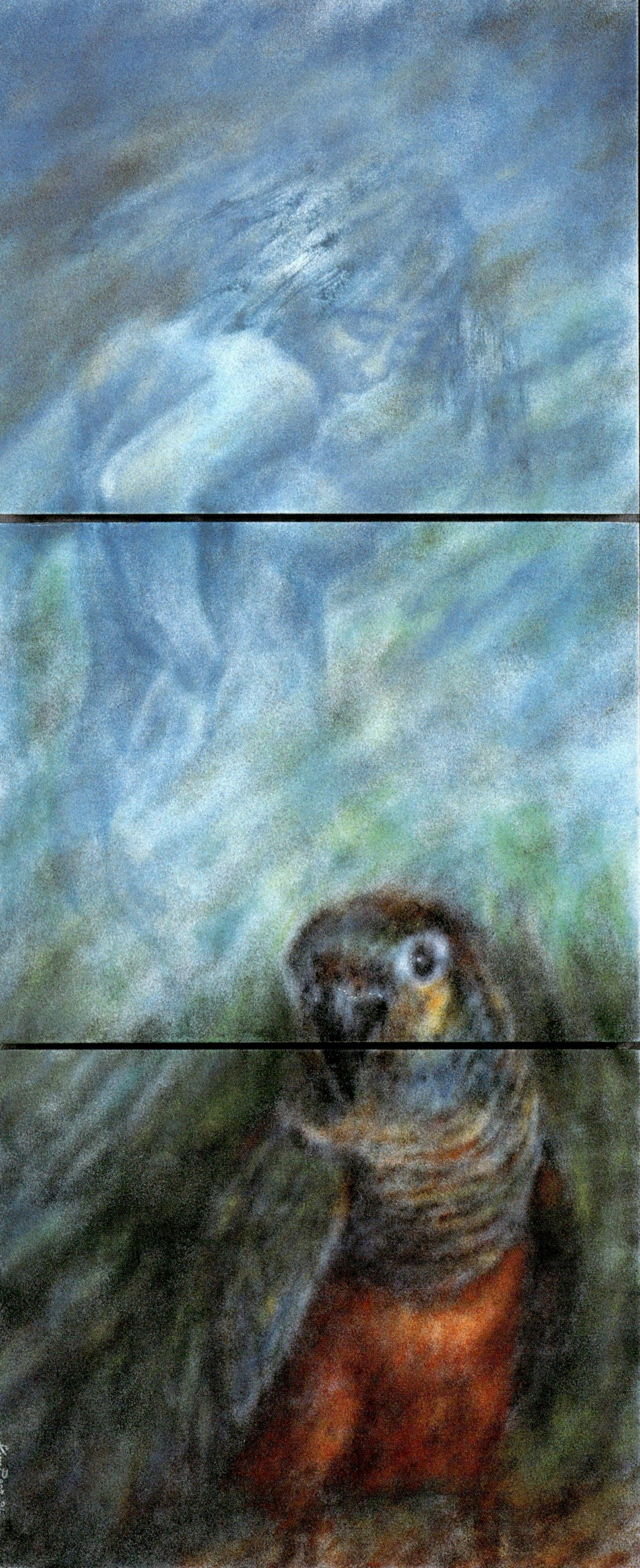

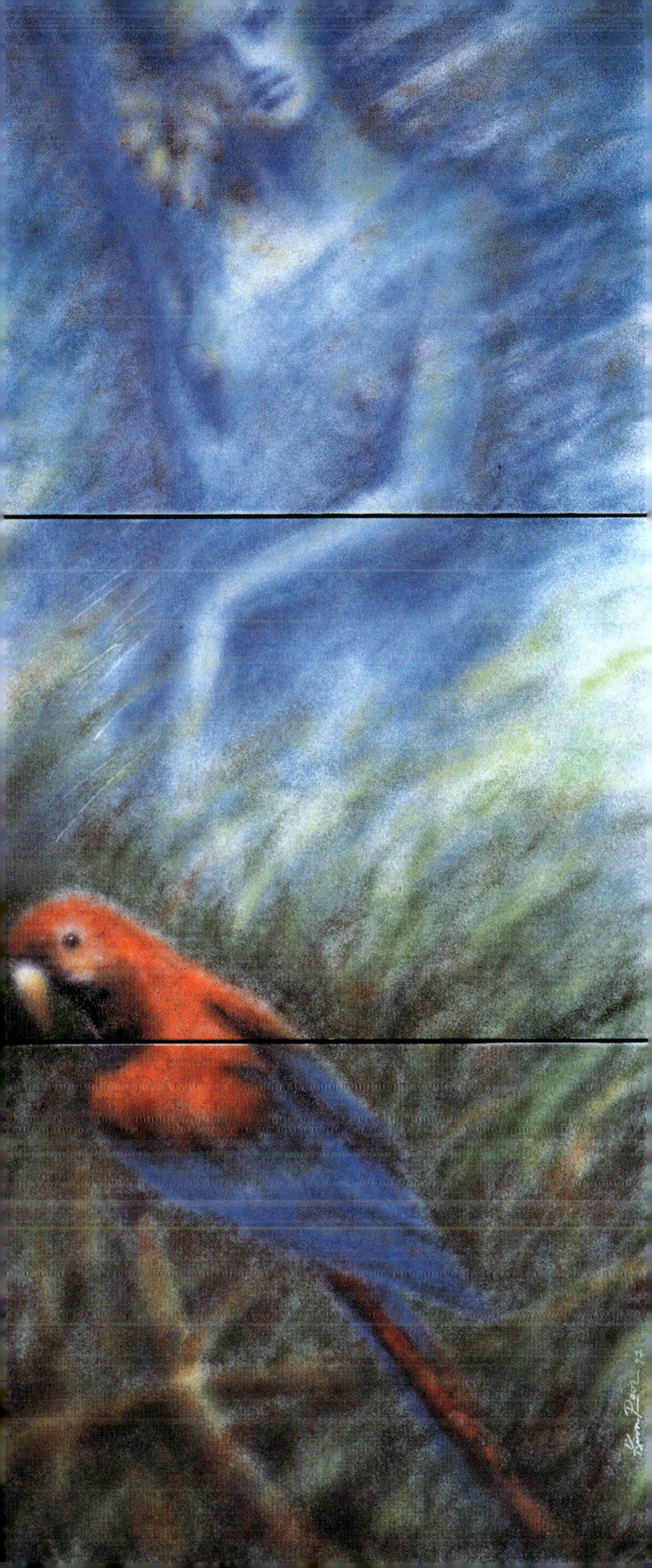

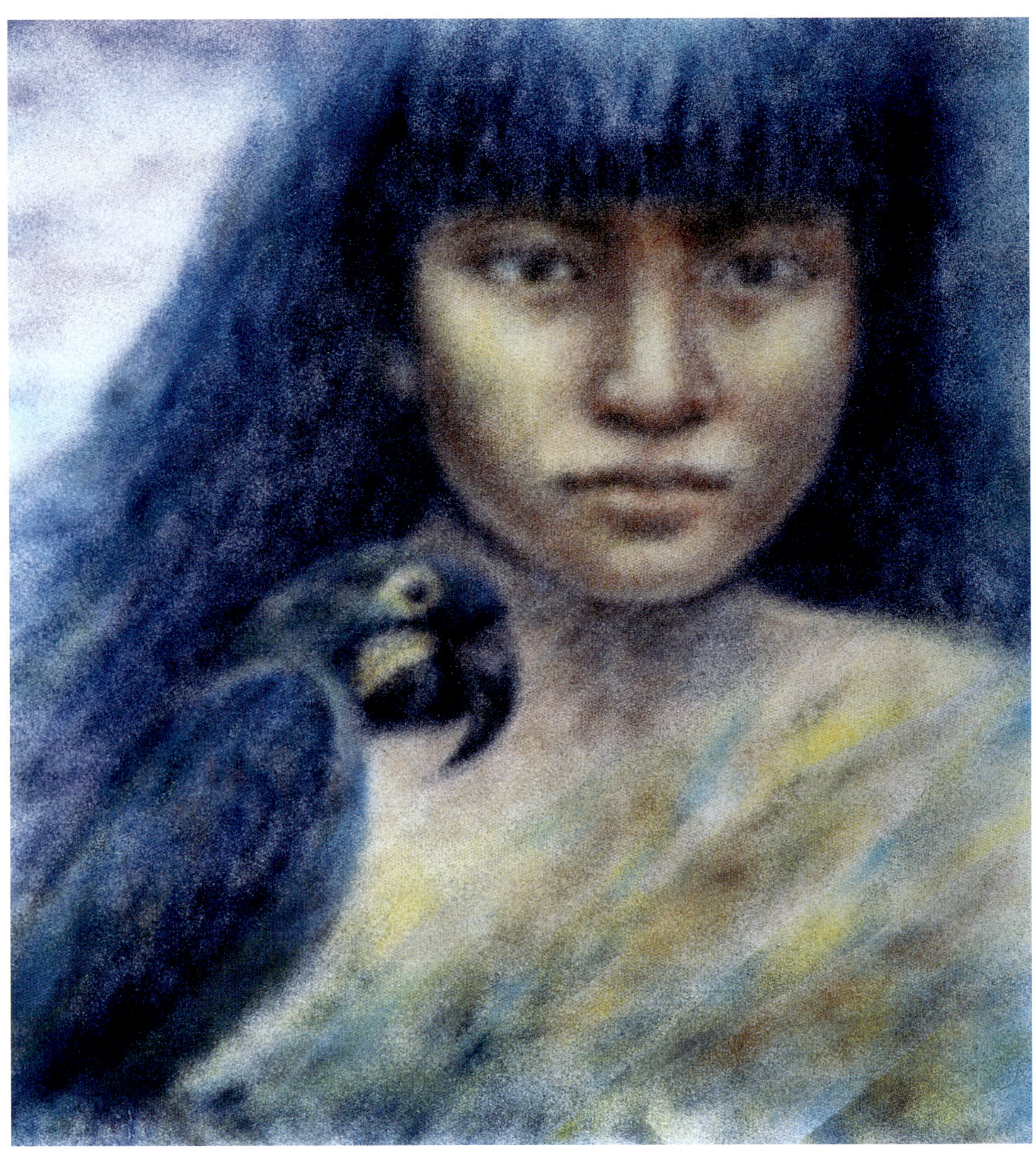

Sun
The Two Parrots

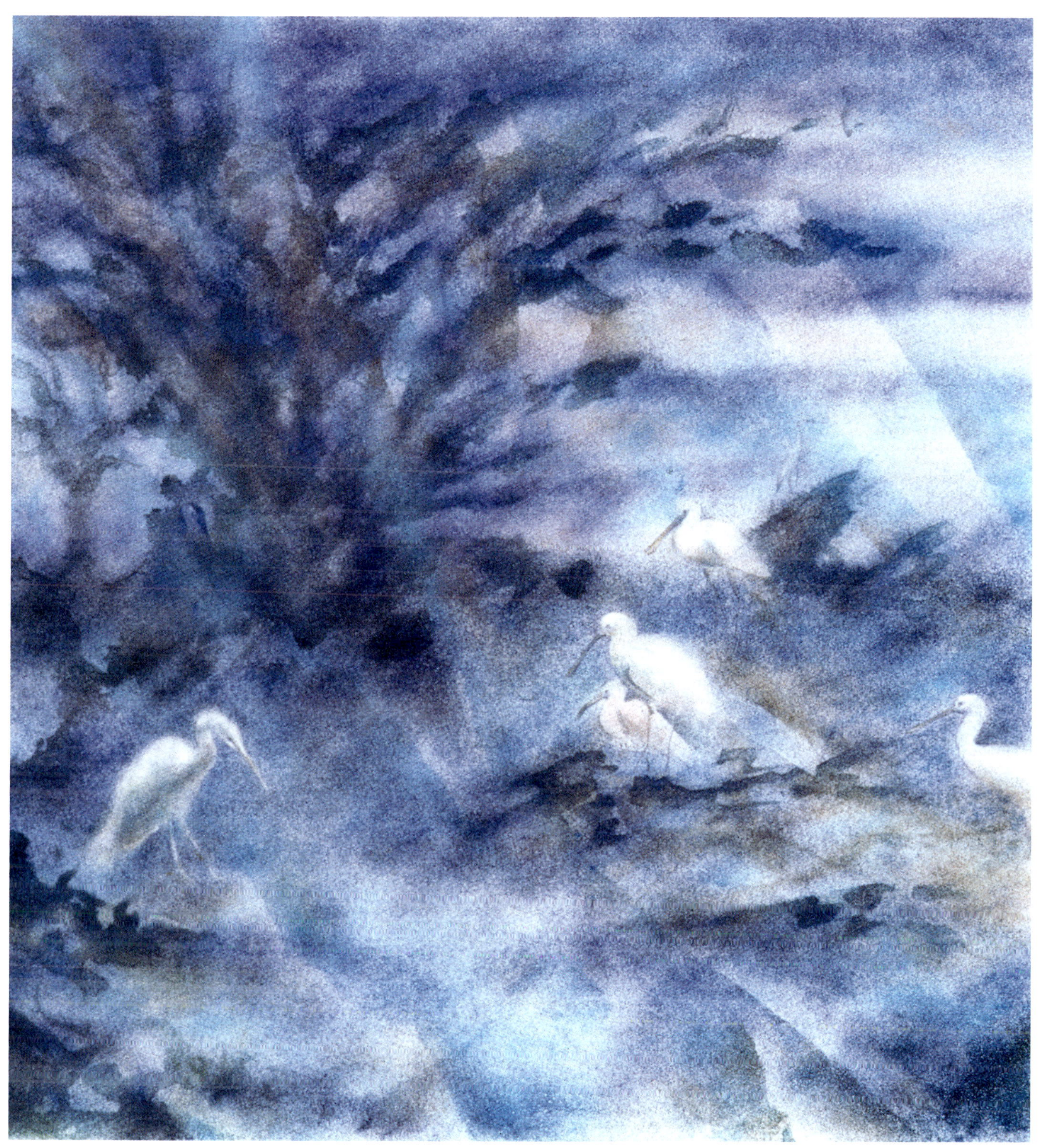

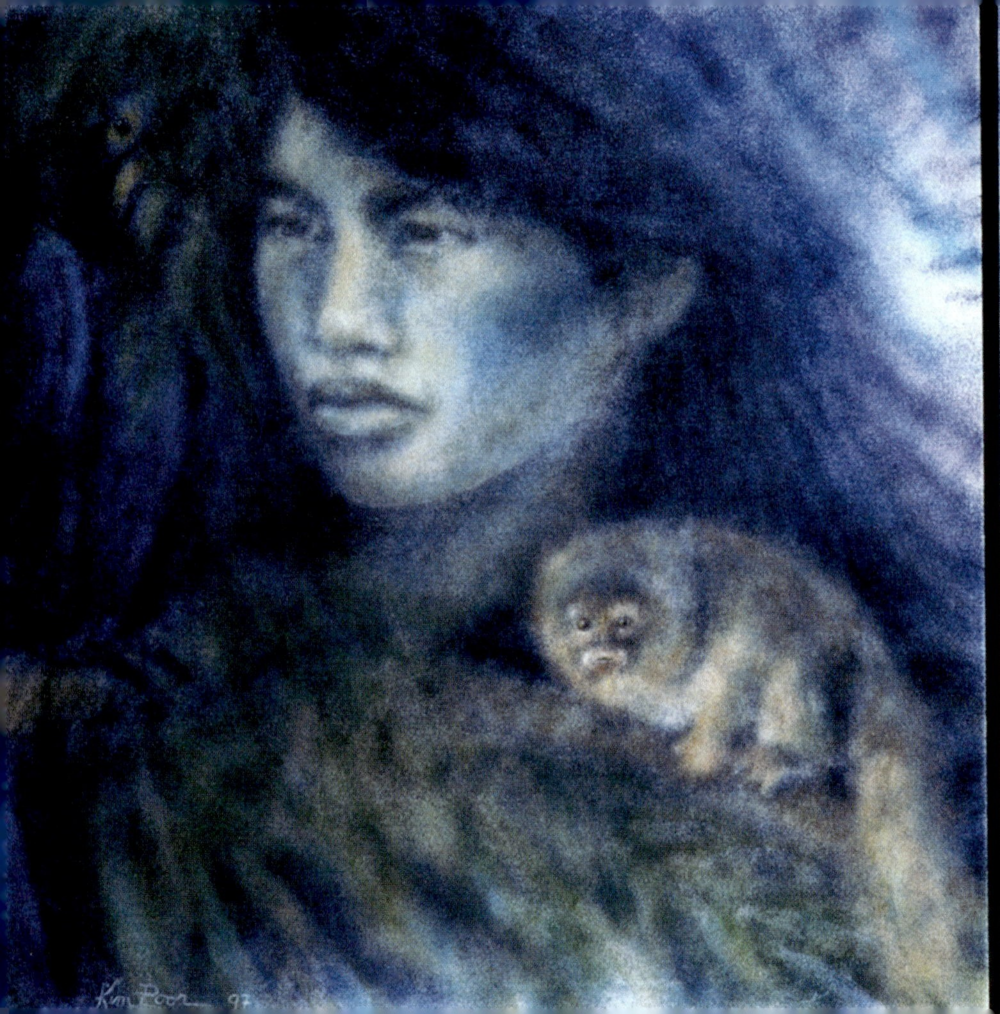

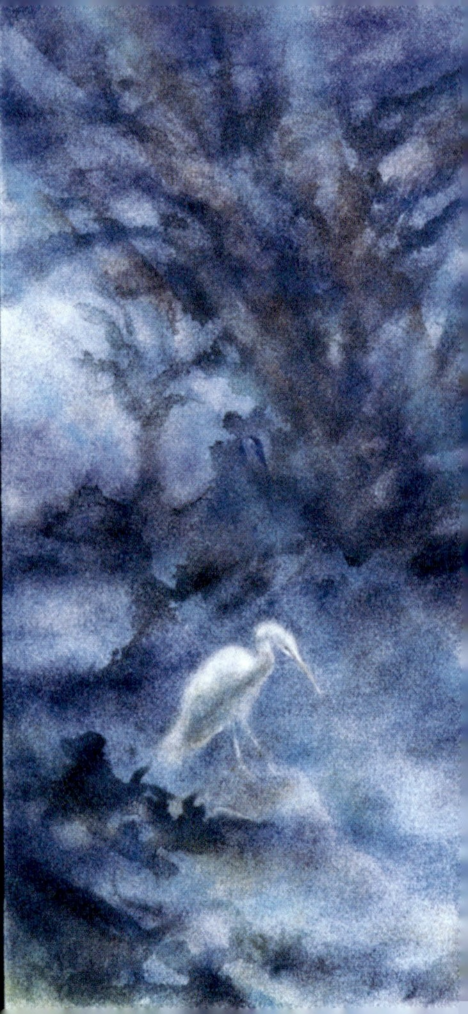

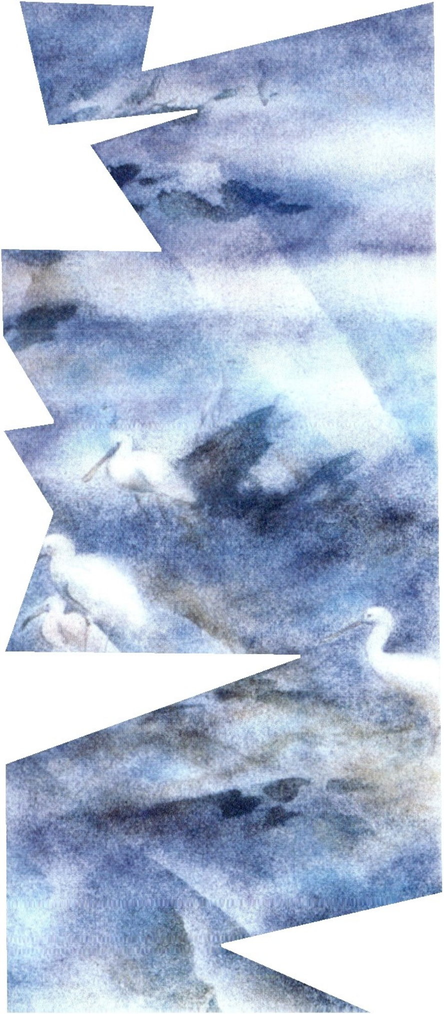

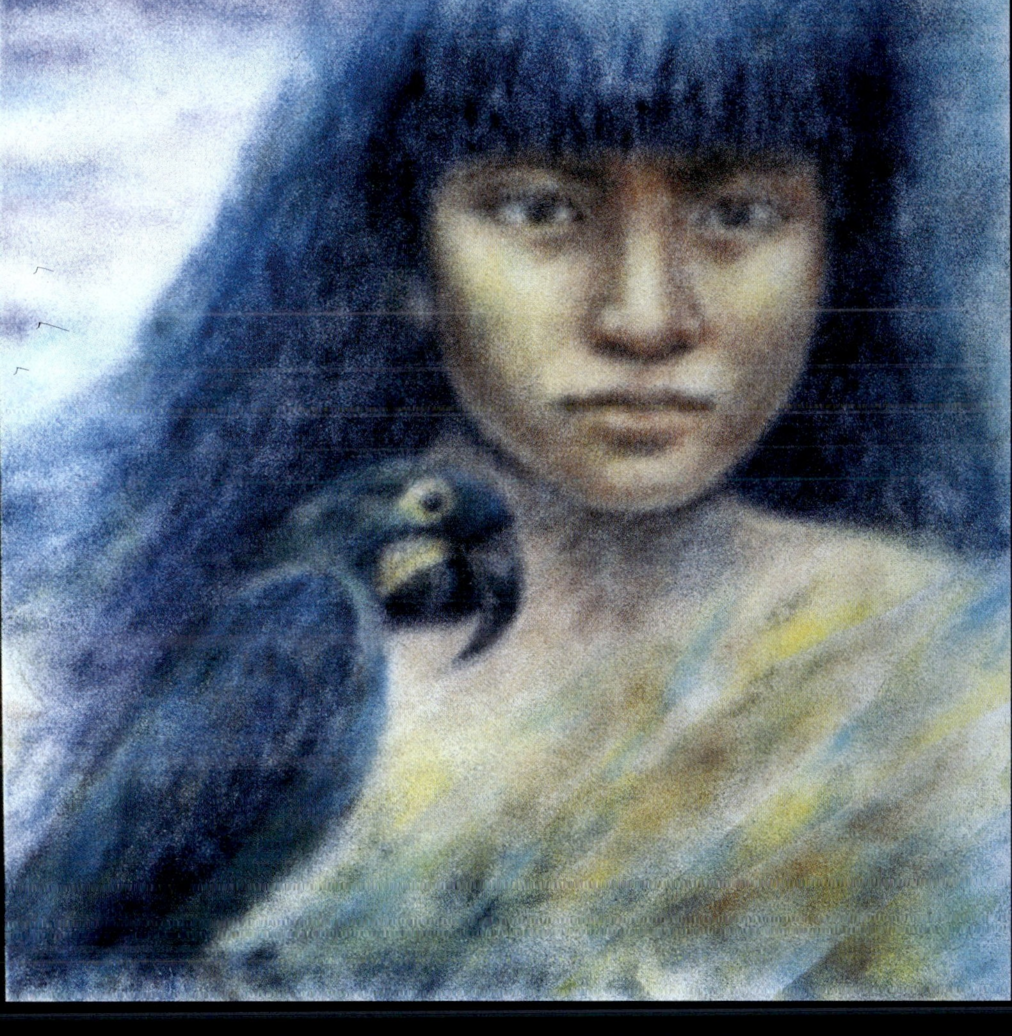

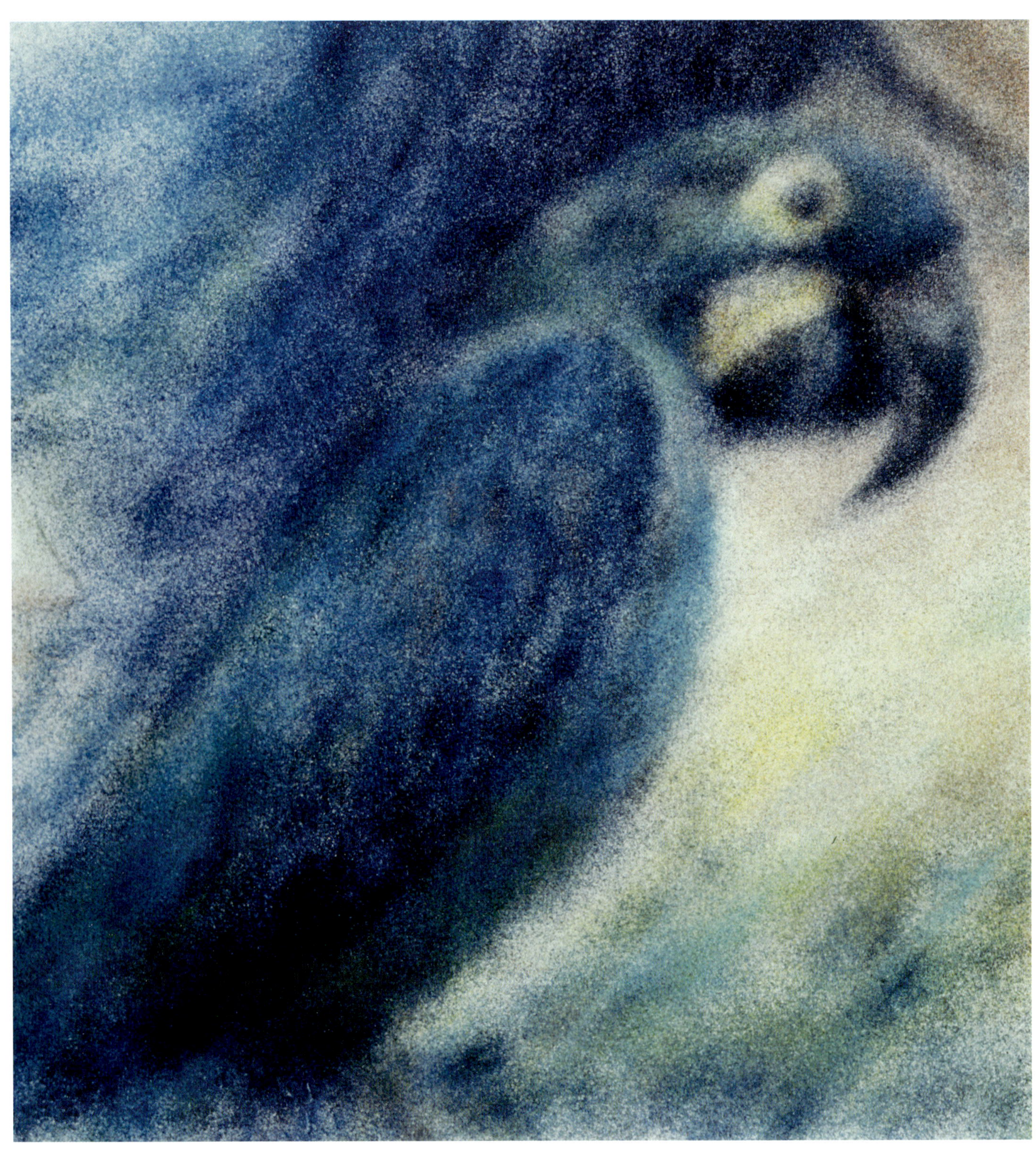

"IN NO TIME THE PARROTS HAD TRANSFORMED THEMSELVES INTO BEAUTIFUL WOMEN ..."

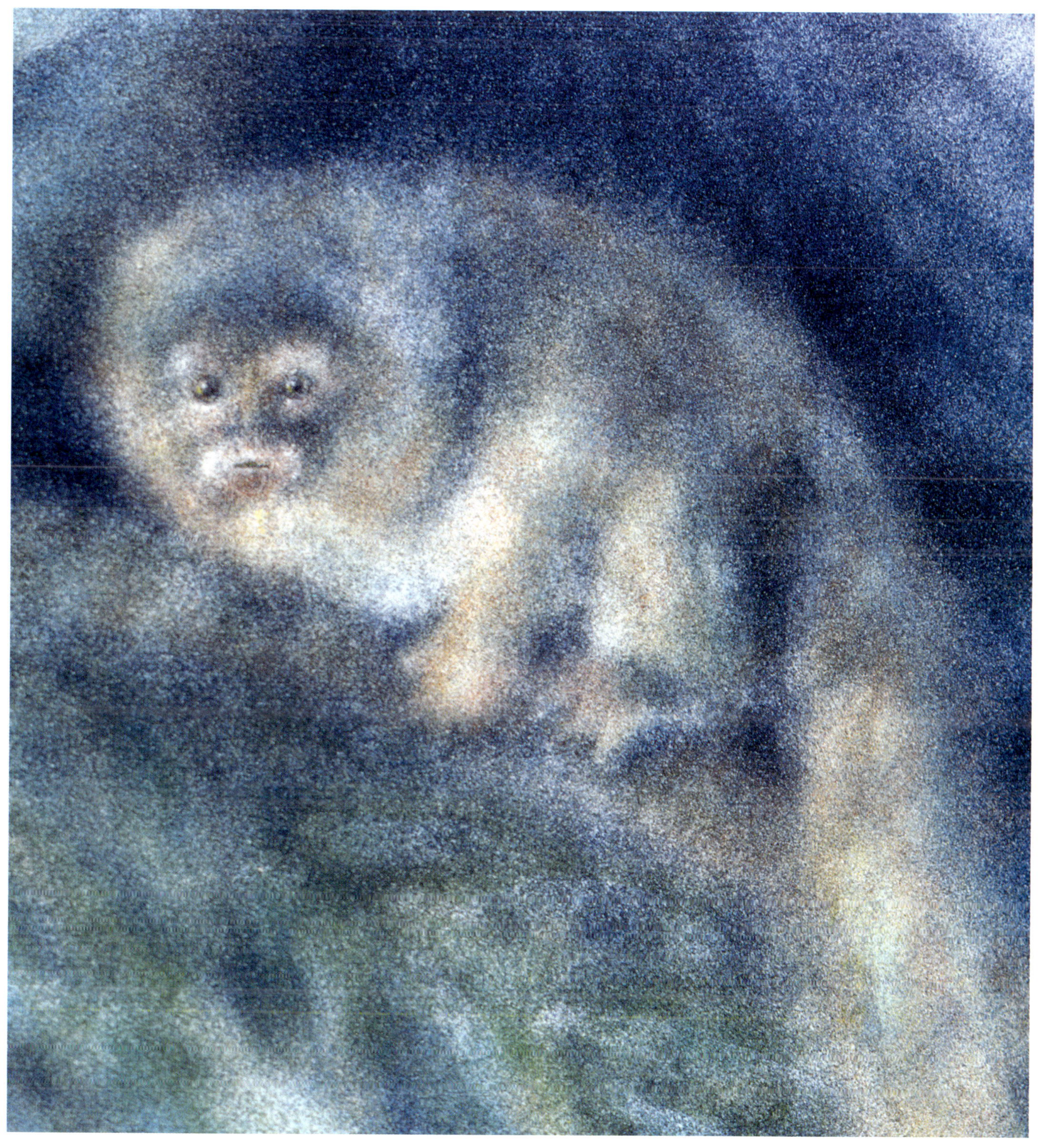

"… BY DOING SO THEY COULD BOTH BECOME PARROTS AGAIN AND NOT GIVE THEIR SECRET AWAY"

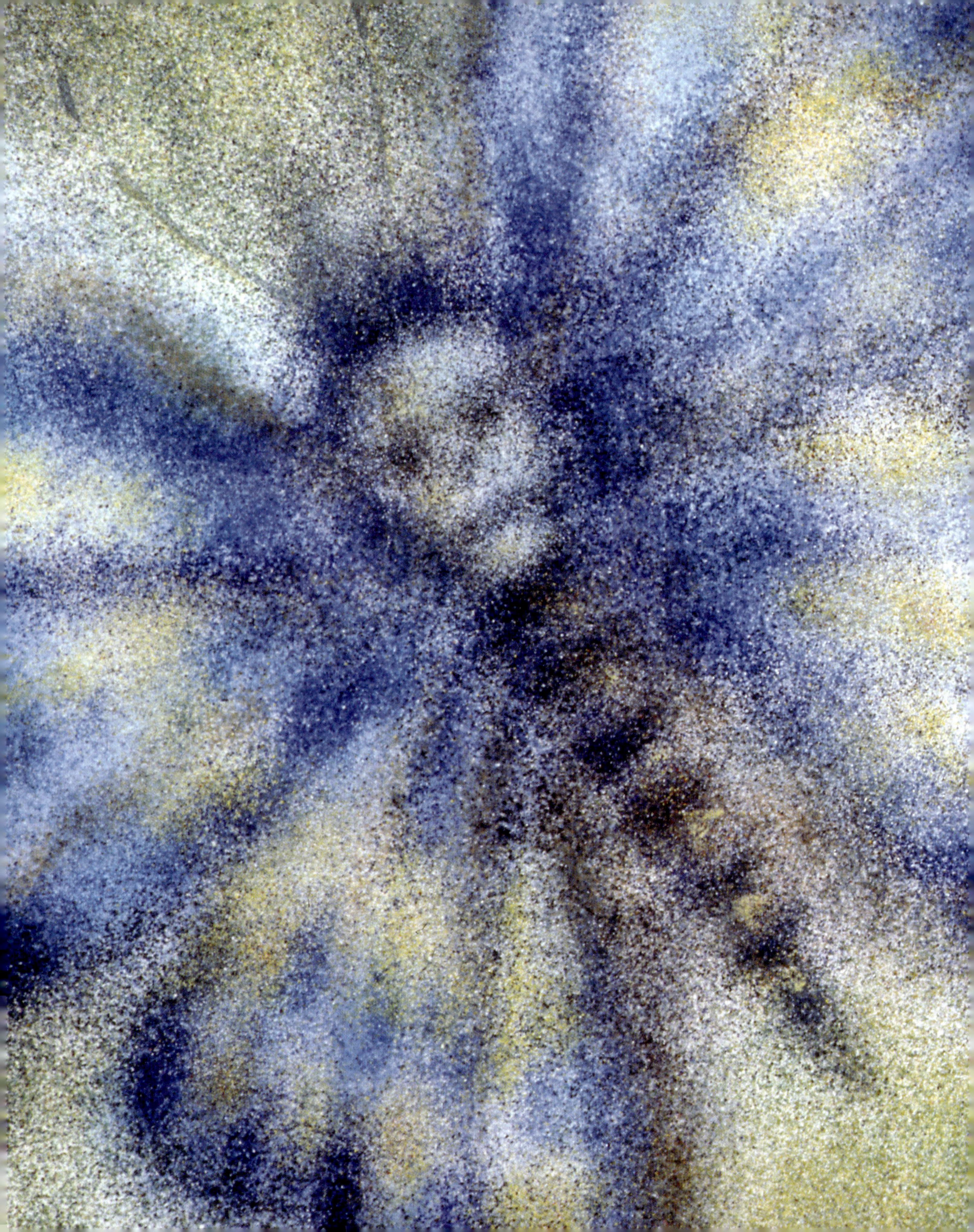

"A LONG TIME AGO THE BUTTERFLIES RESEMBLED HUMAN BEINGS ..."

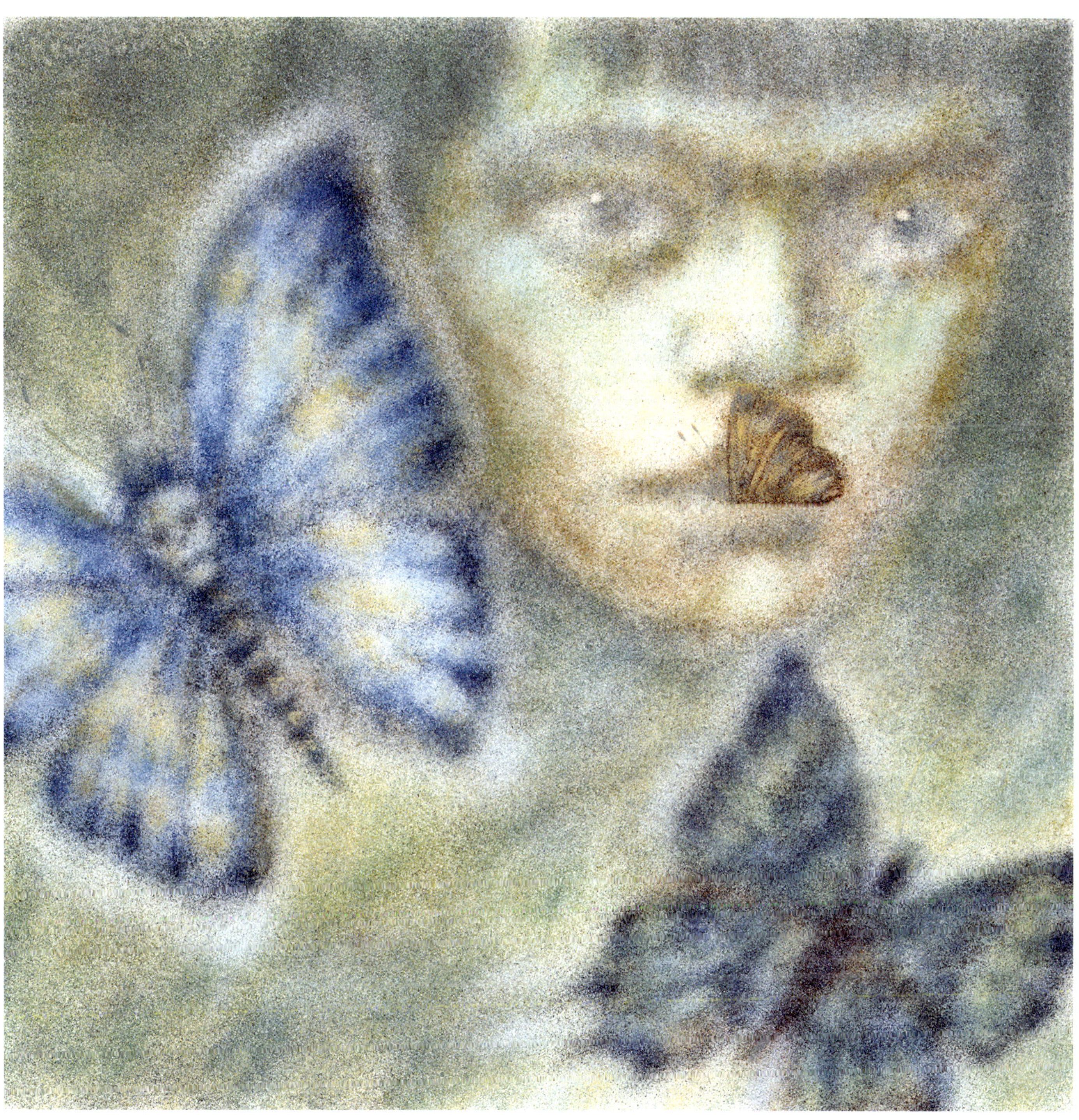

Green Butterfly
The Butterflies

LEGEND: THE BUTTERFLIES

"THEY STARTED TO FLY AND TRANSFORMED THEMSELVES BACK INTO REAL BUTTERFLIES."

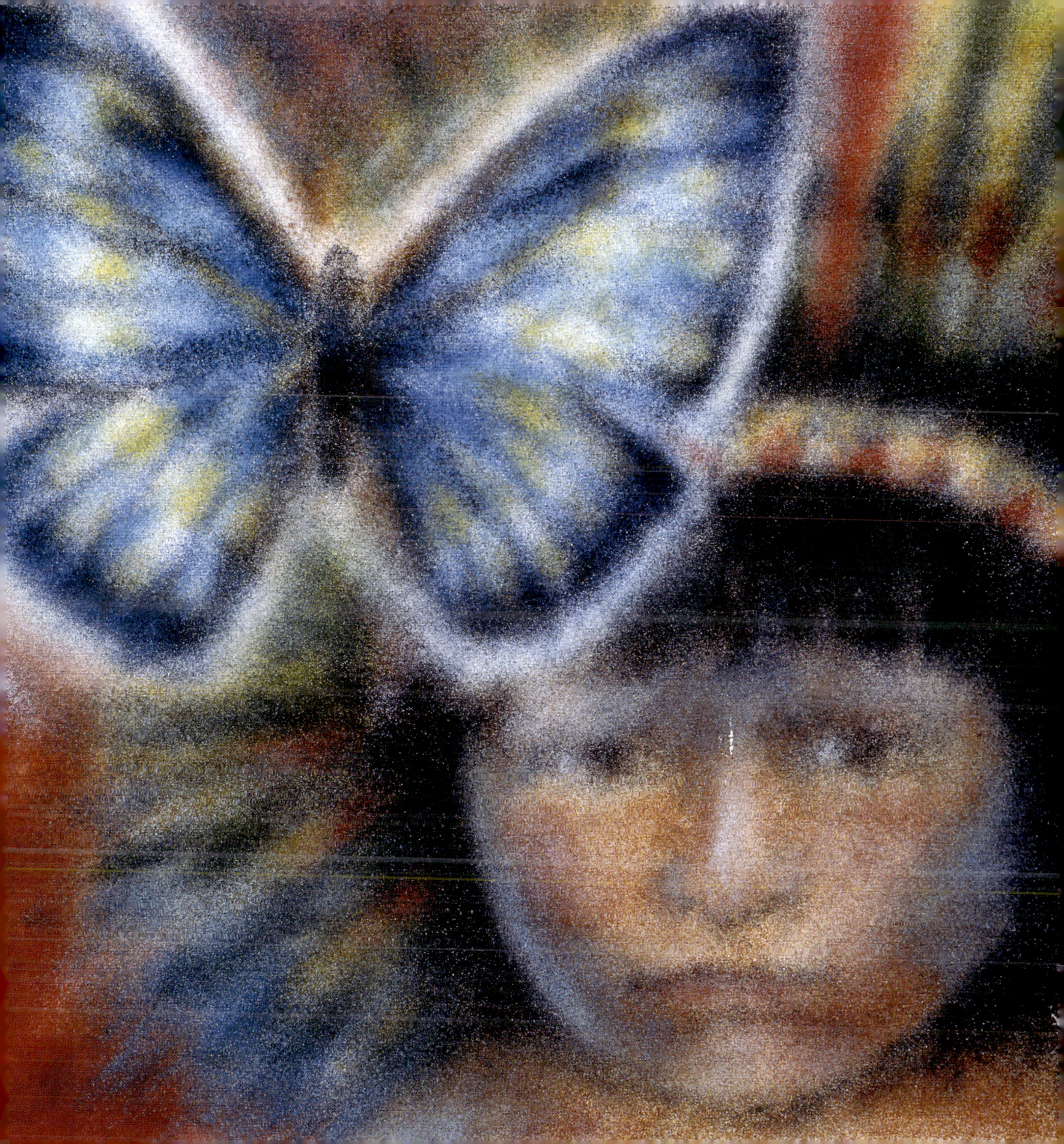

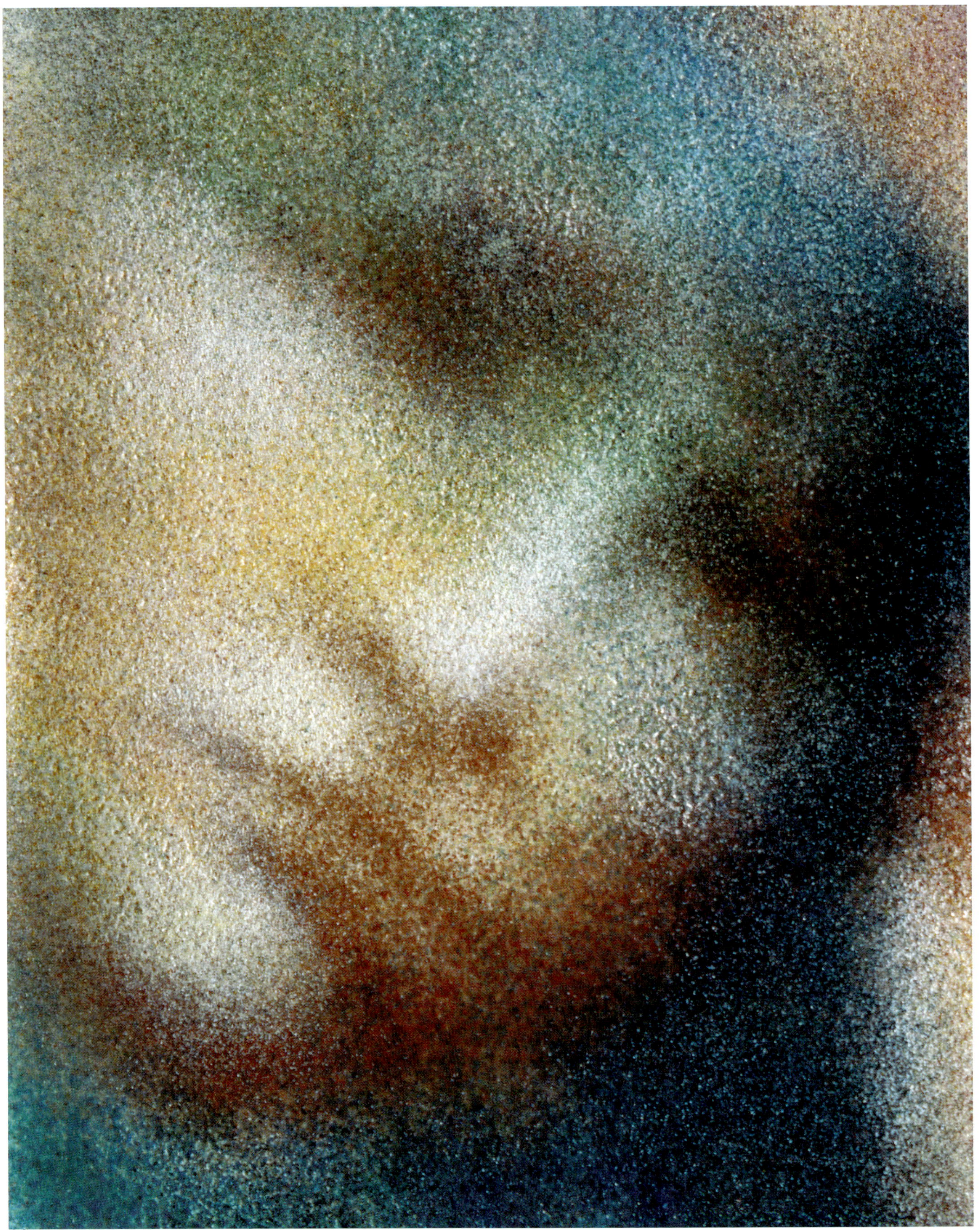

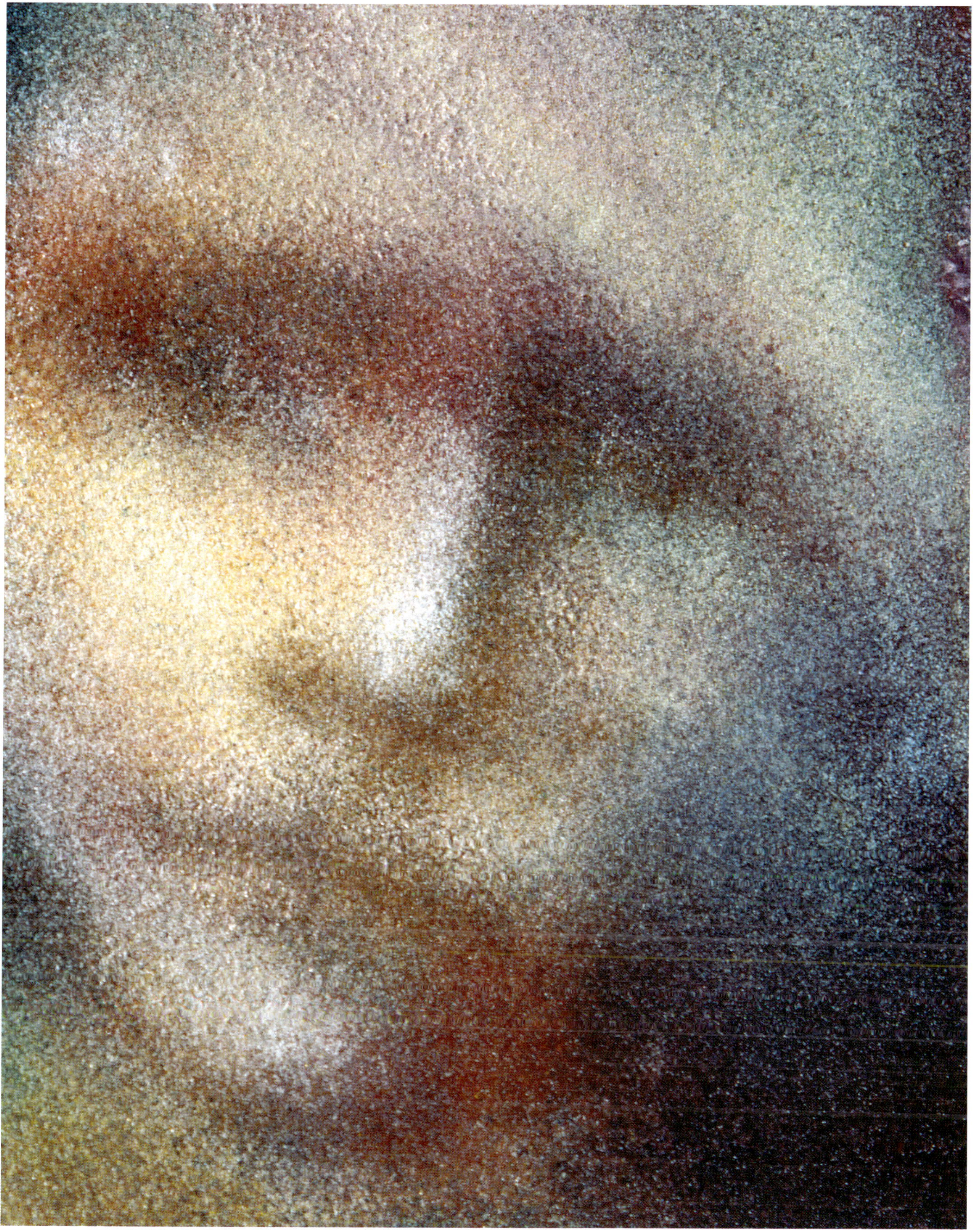

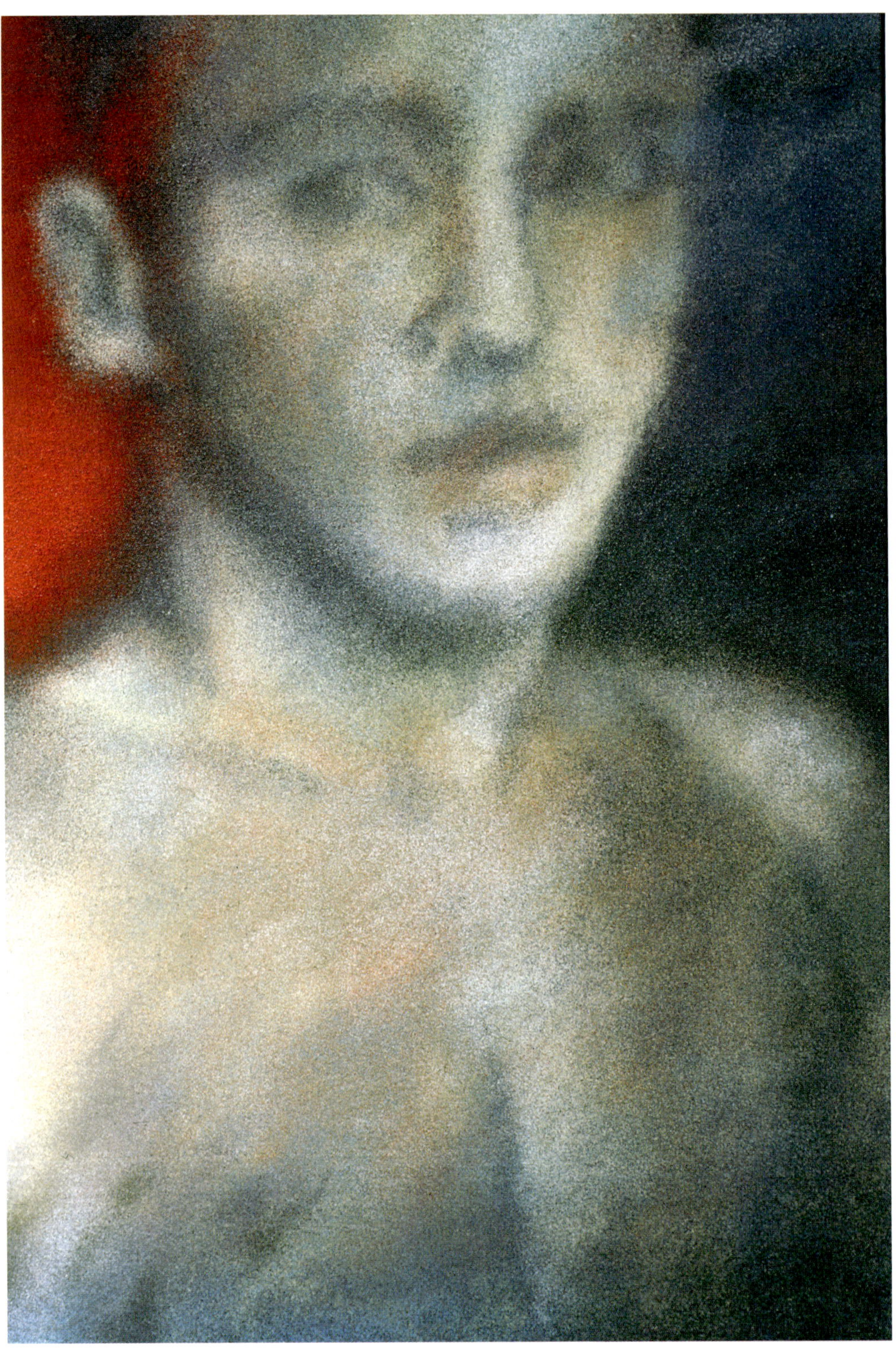

“BAIRA WAS A BRAVE AND INTELLIGENT PARINTIM INDIAN.”
“BAIRA TAUGHT HIS PEOPLE MANY THINGS ...”

The Legend Of Mandioca
Baira

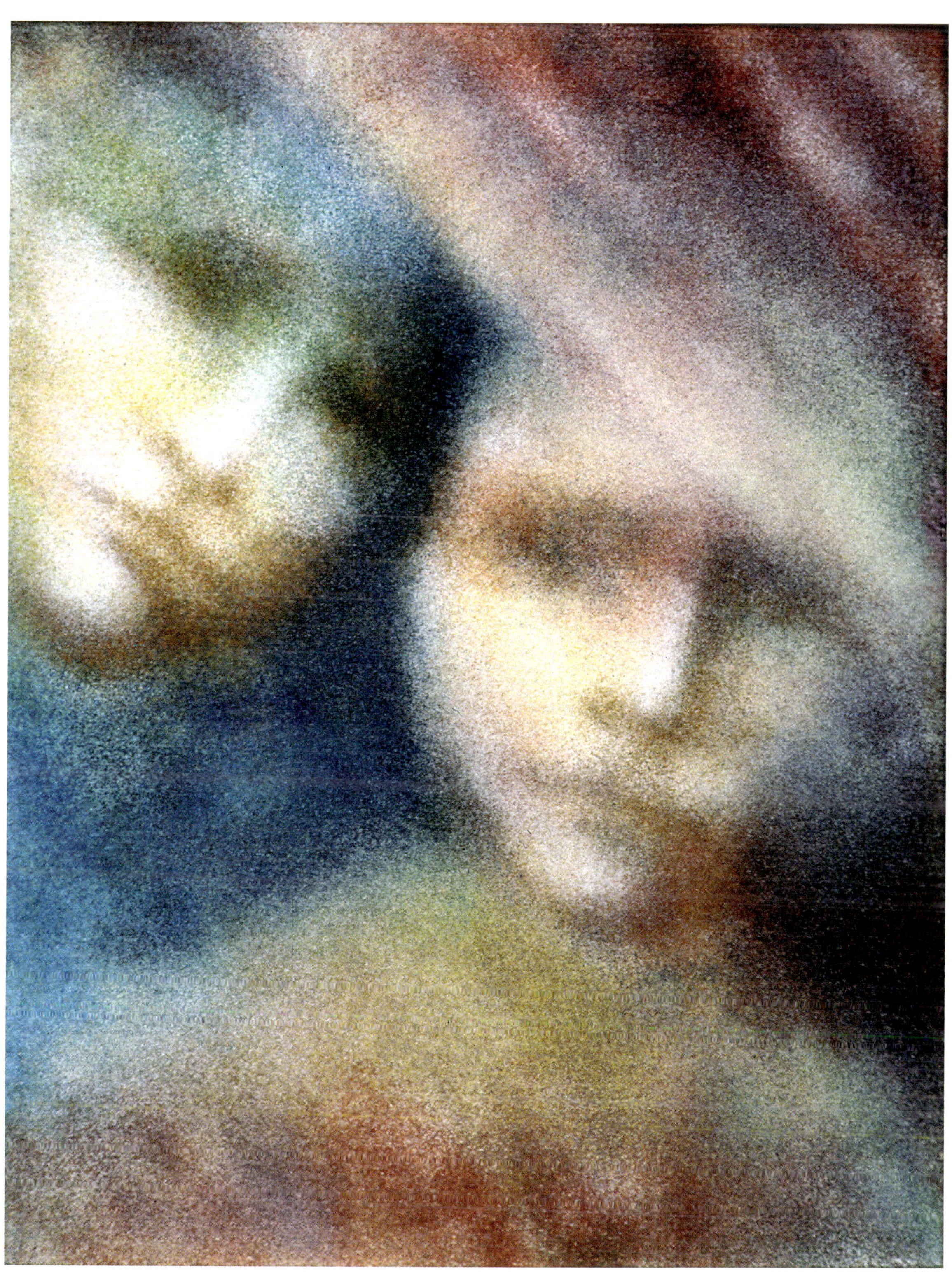

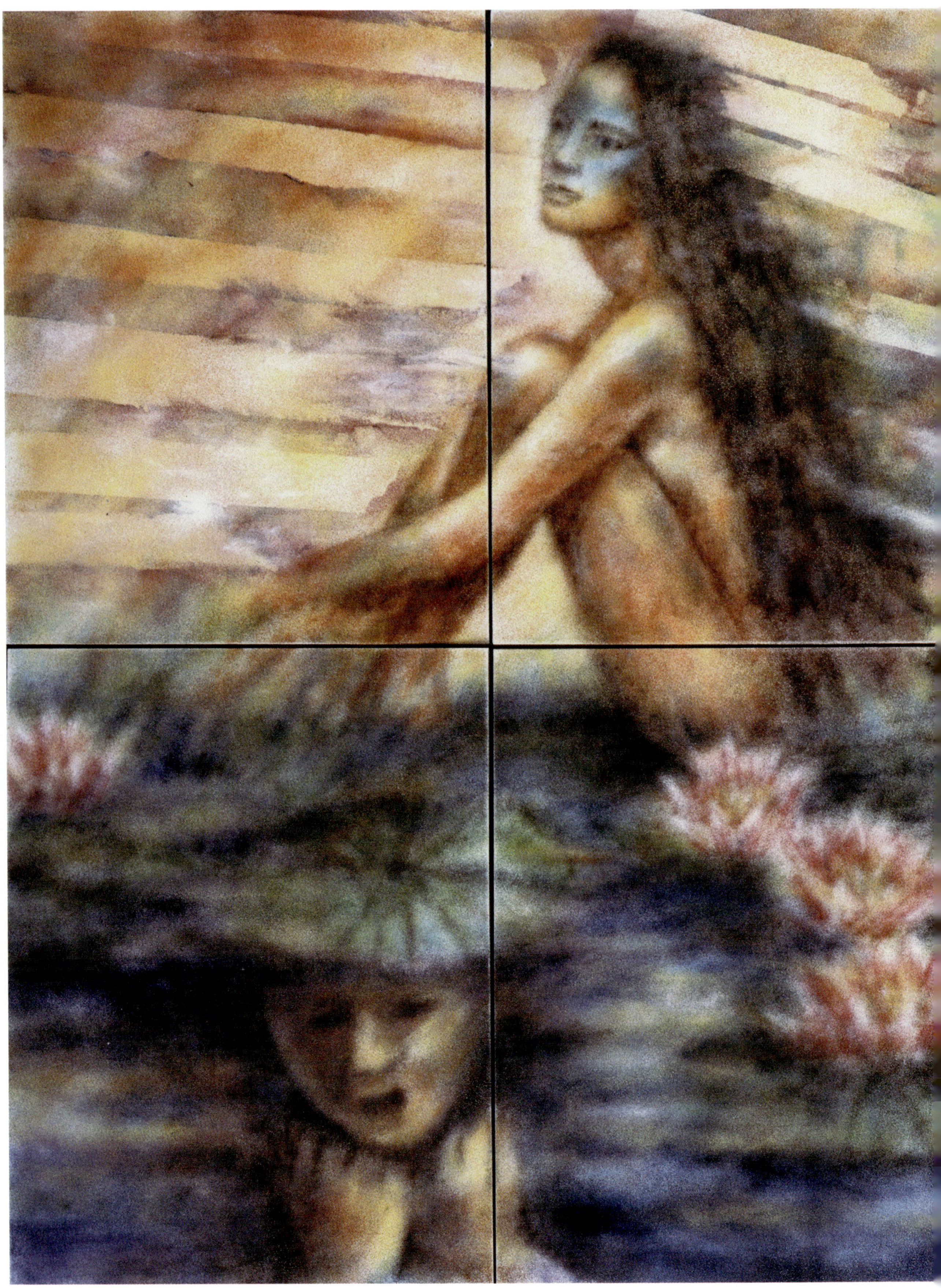

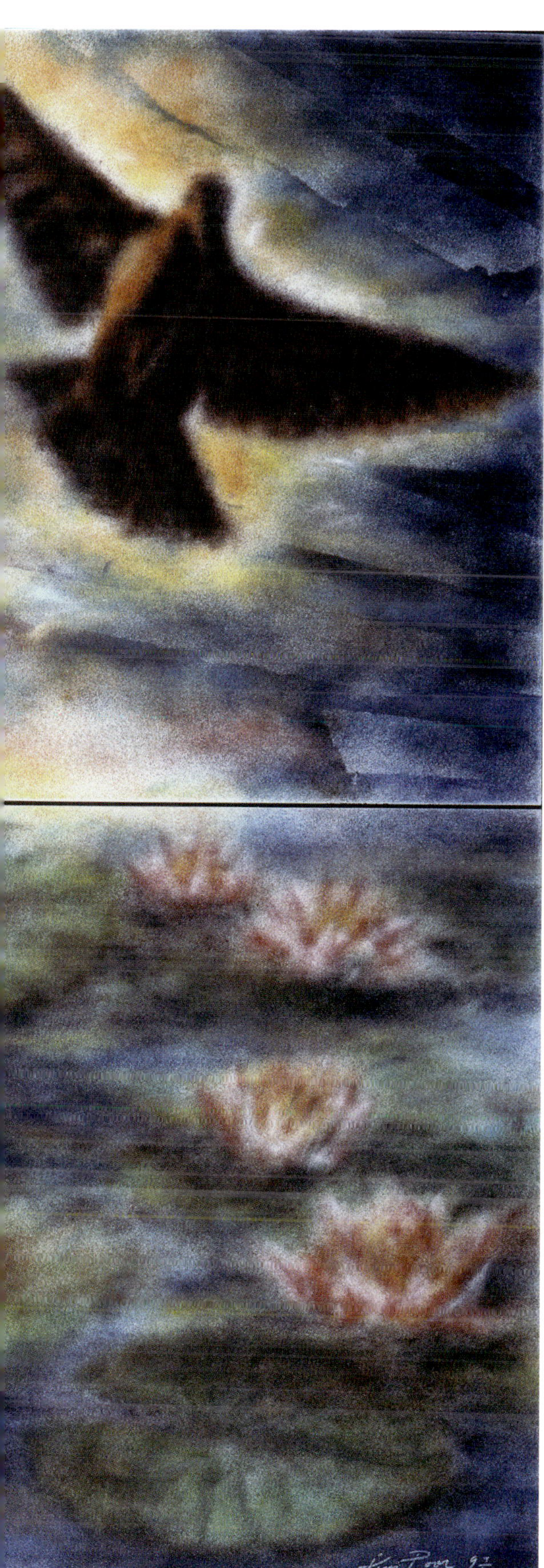

Vitoria Régia
Iara, Goddess Of The River

“IARA SANG … AND WAITED … THE BOY WOULD HAVE TO RETURN”

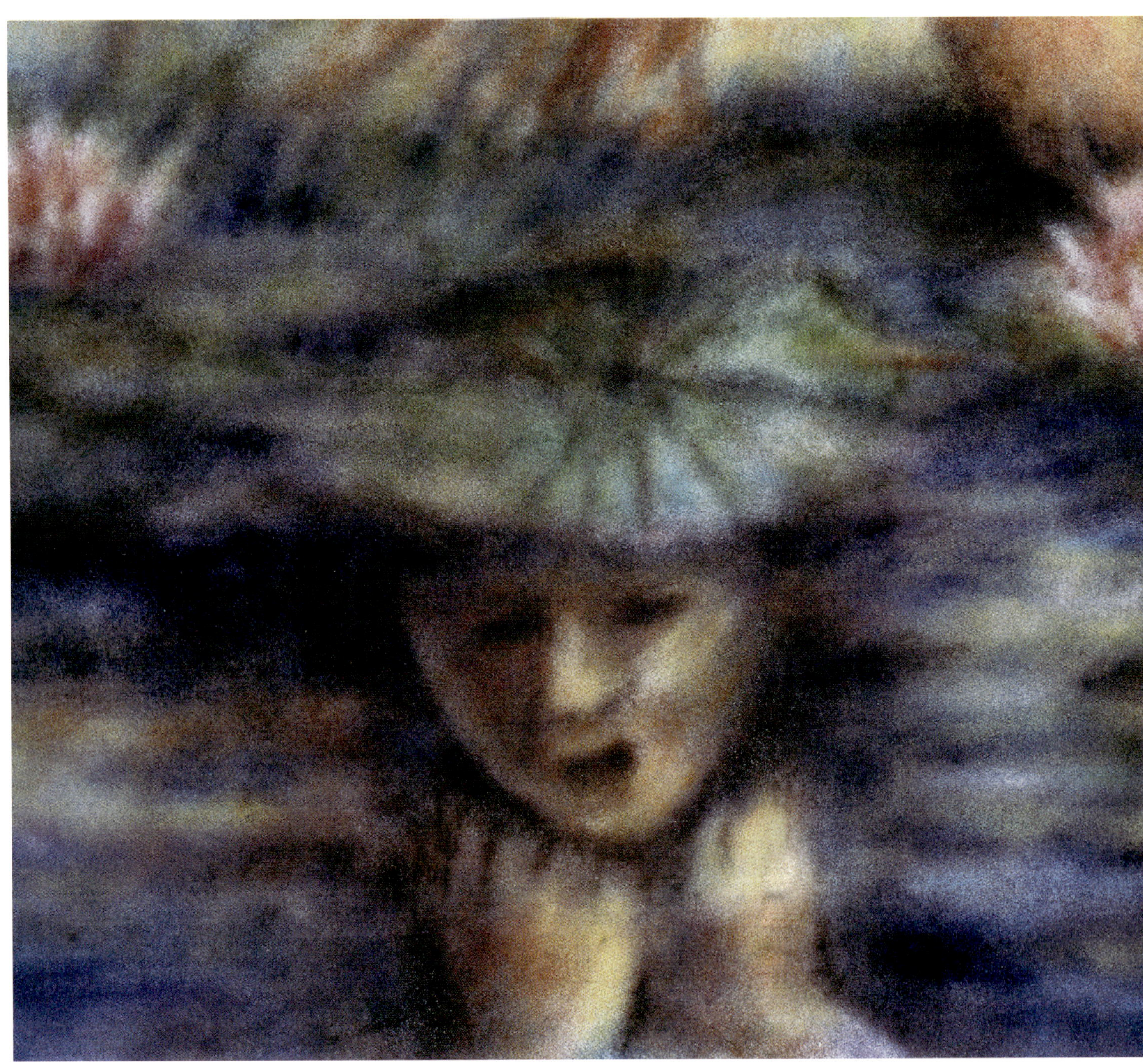

"AND IARA, AS SHE SANG, TOOK THE BRAVE INDIAN BOY WITH HER TO THE BOTTOM OF THE RIVER."

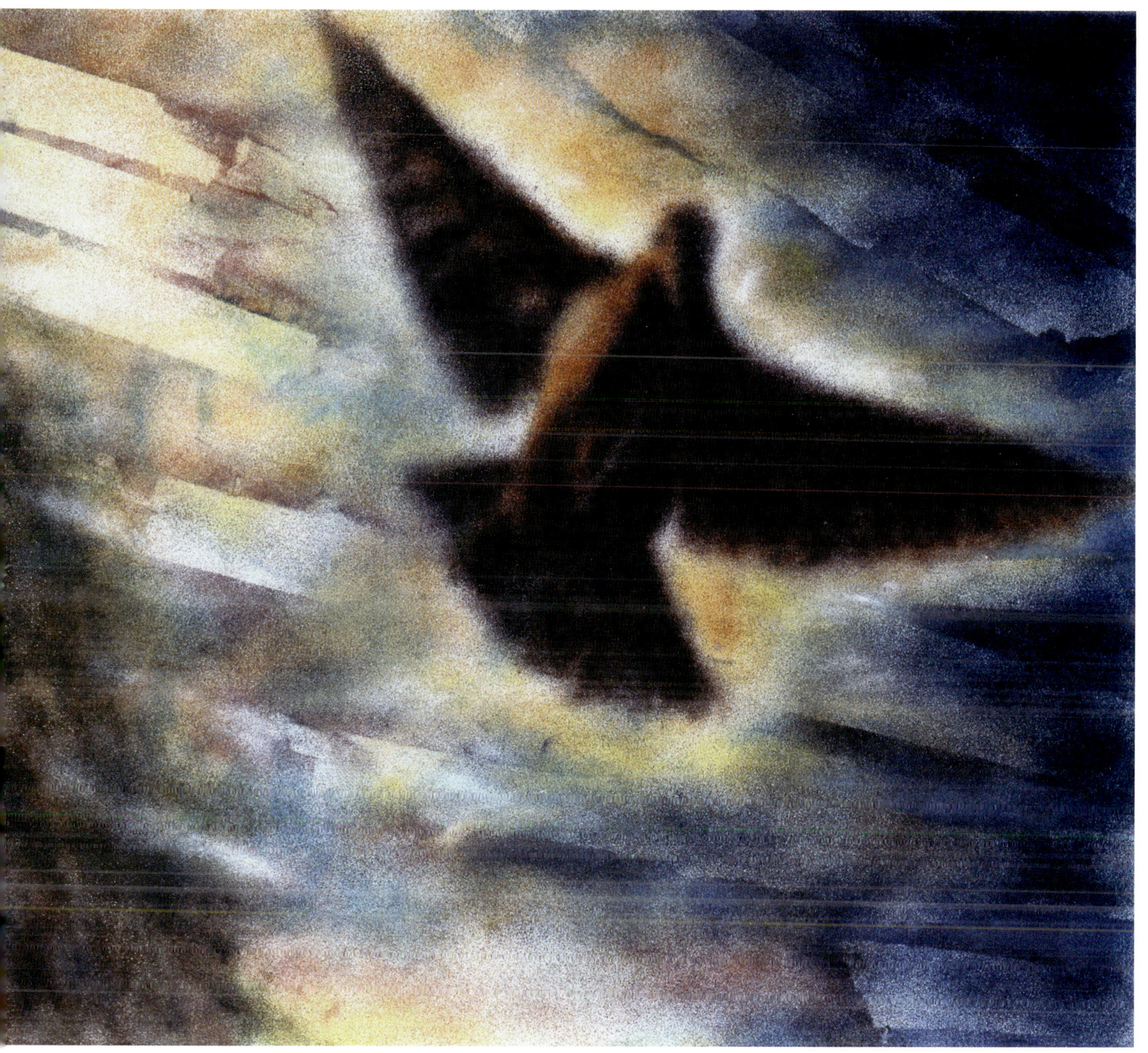

THE LEGEND OF MANDIOCA

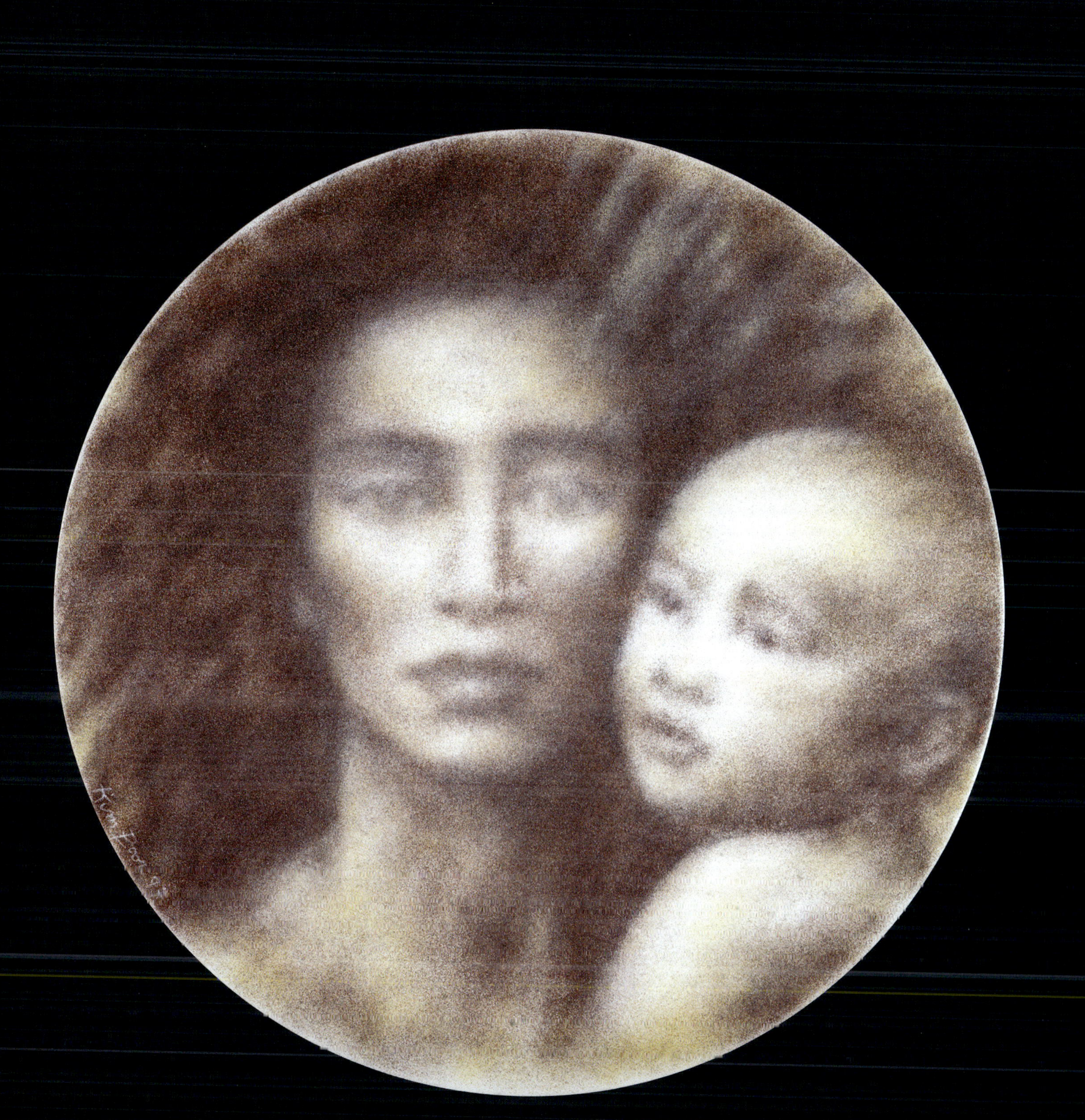

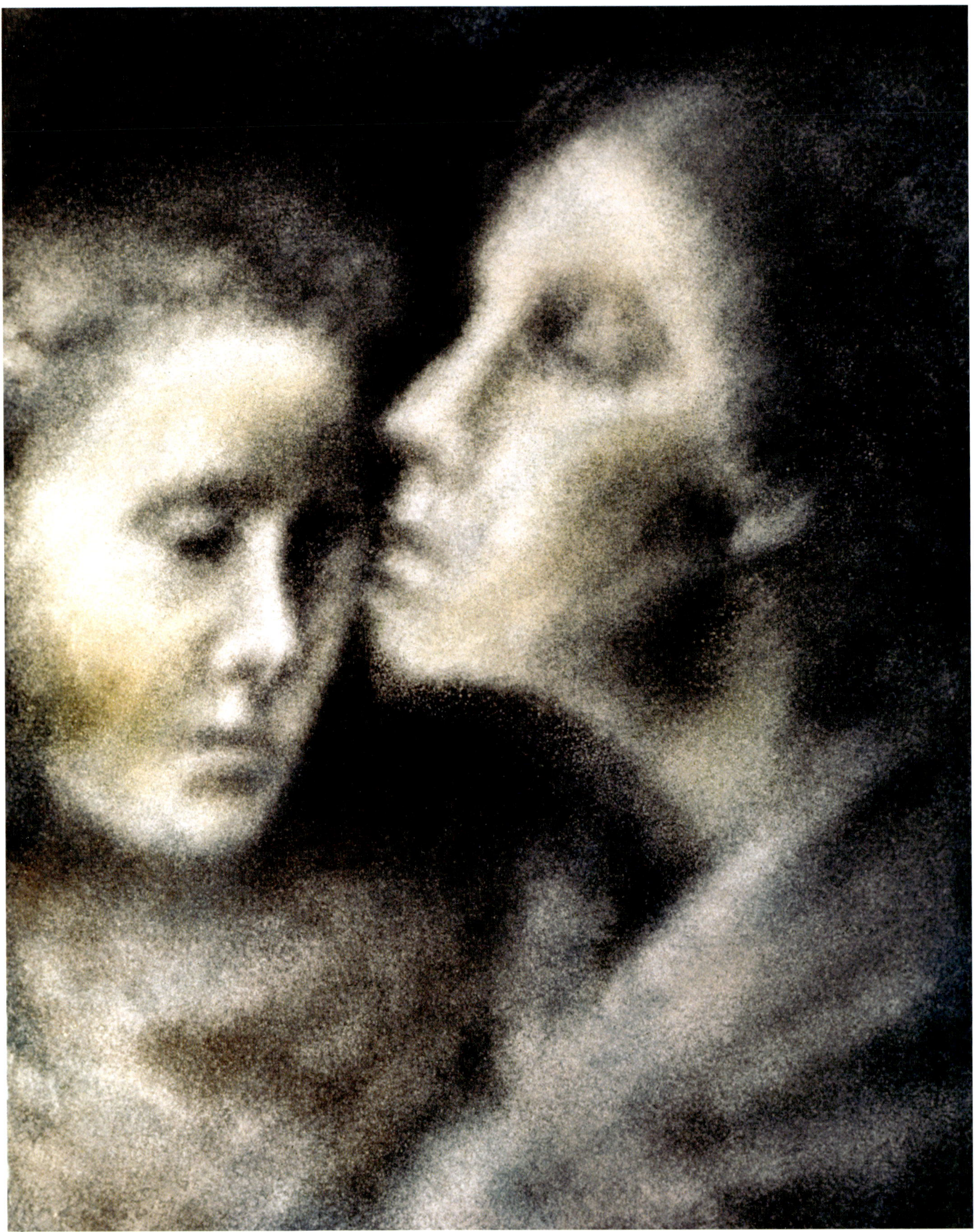

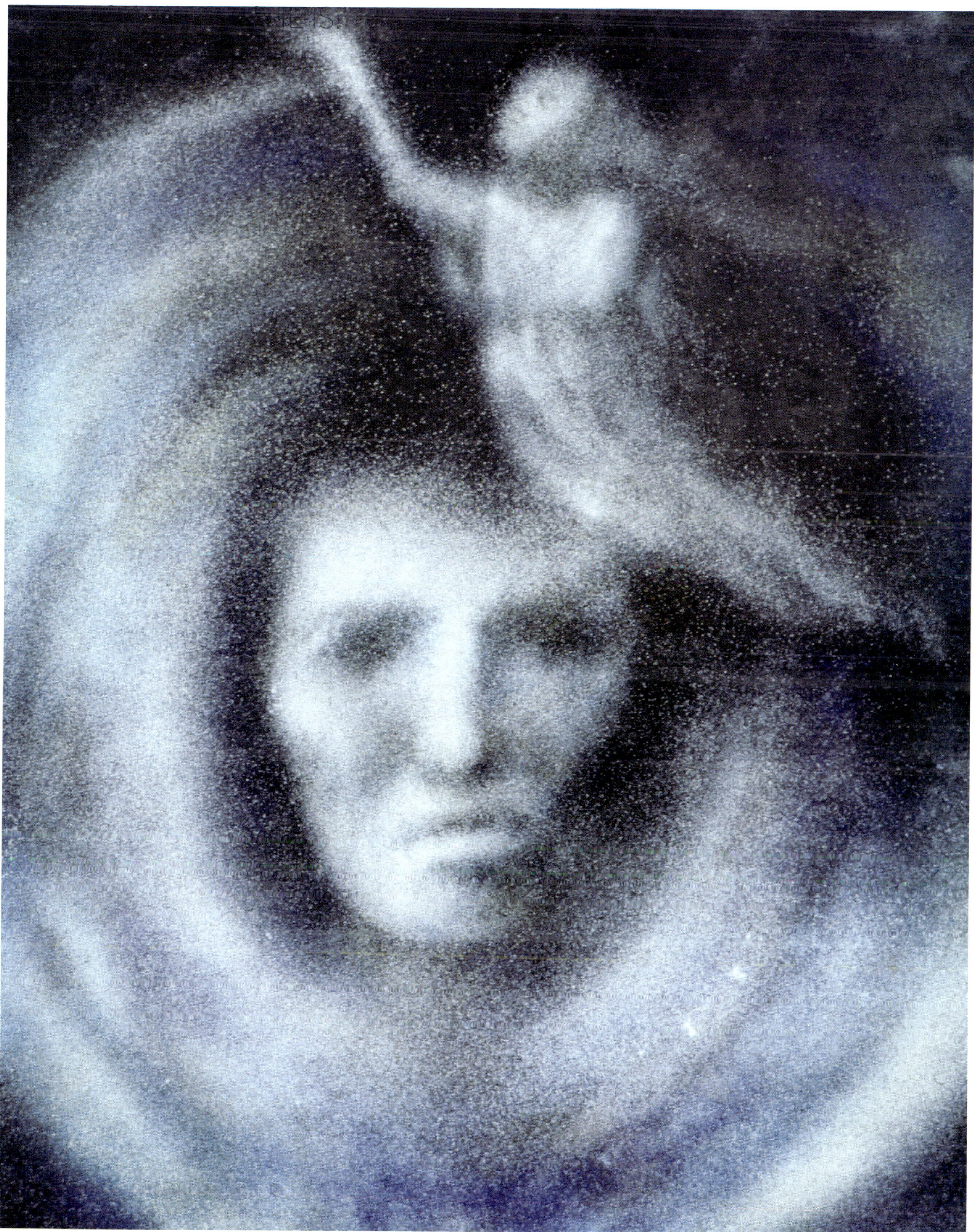

Previous page, left
Mandioca
The Legend Of Mandioca

Previous page, right
Moon's Dew

Above
The Birth of Mani
The Legend Of Mandioca

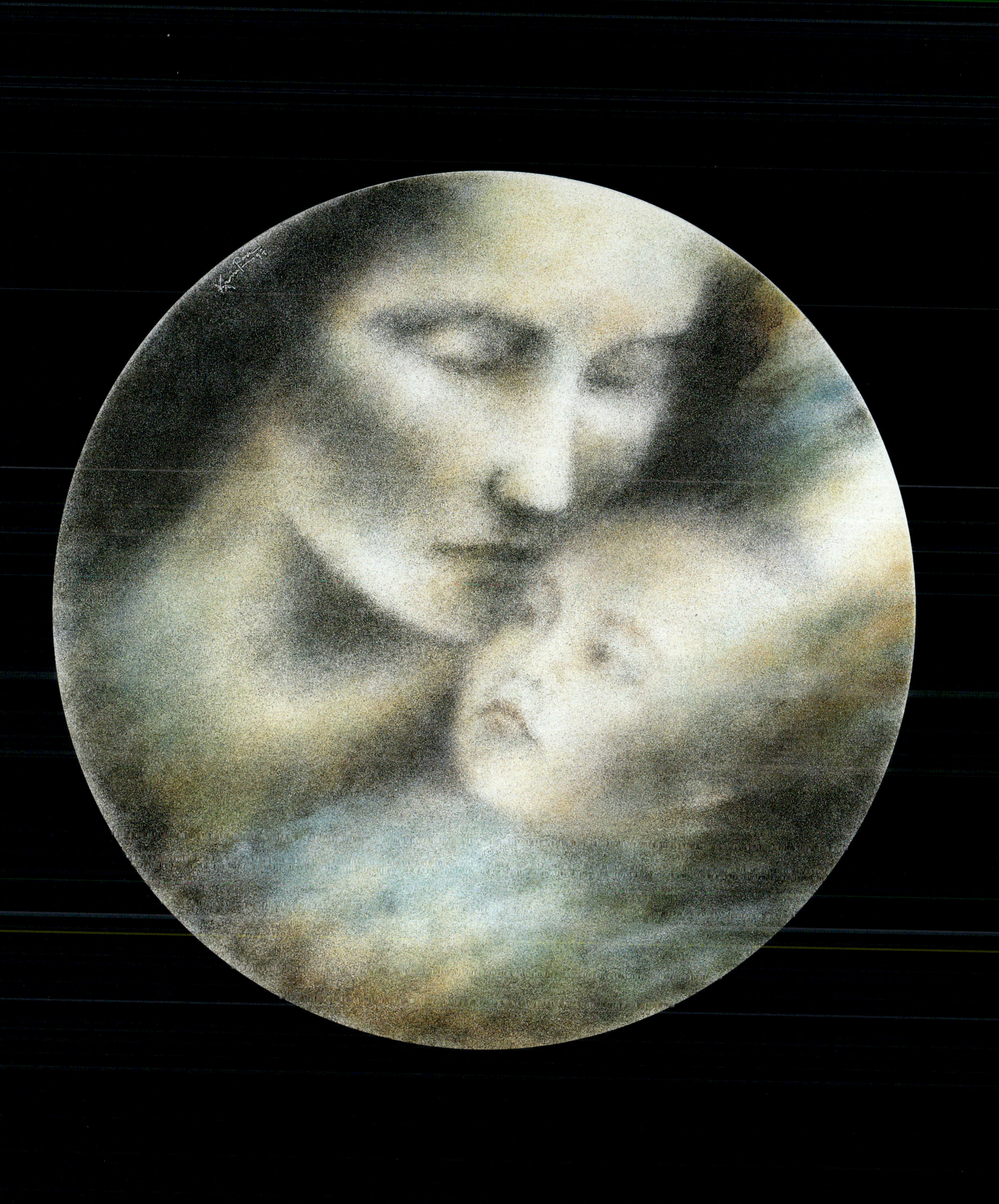

"BECAUSE IT HAD GROWN FROM MANI'S OCA THE TRIBE DECIDED TO NAME THE NEW PLANT 'MANI-OCA' IN HER HONOUR"

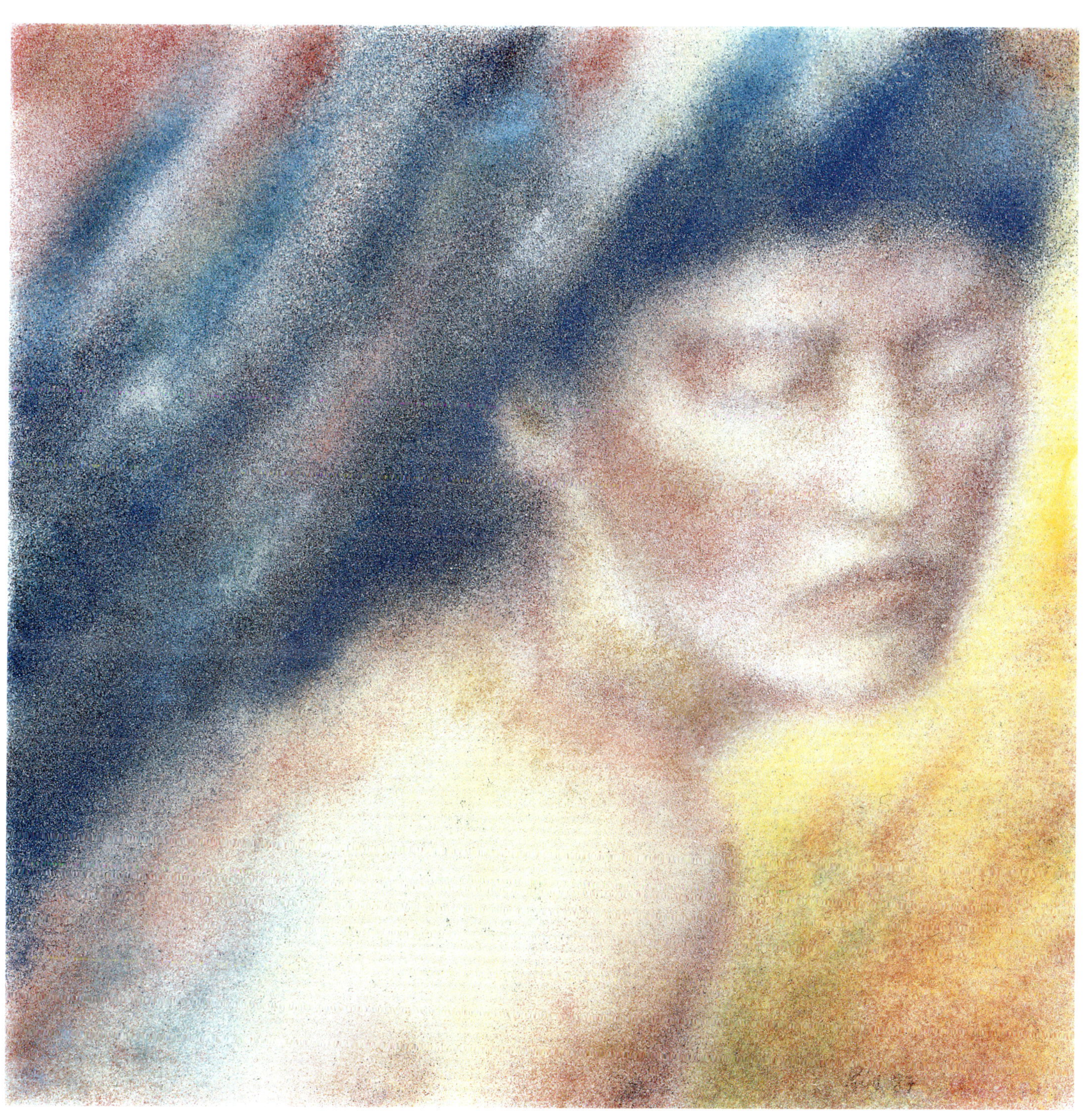

Mani

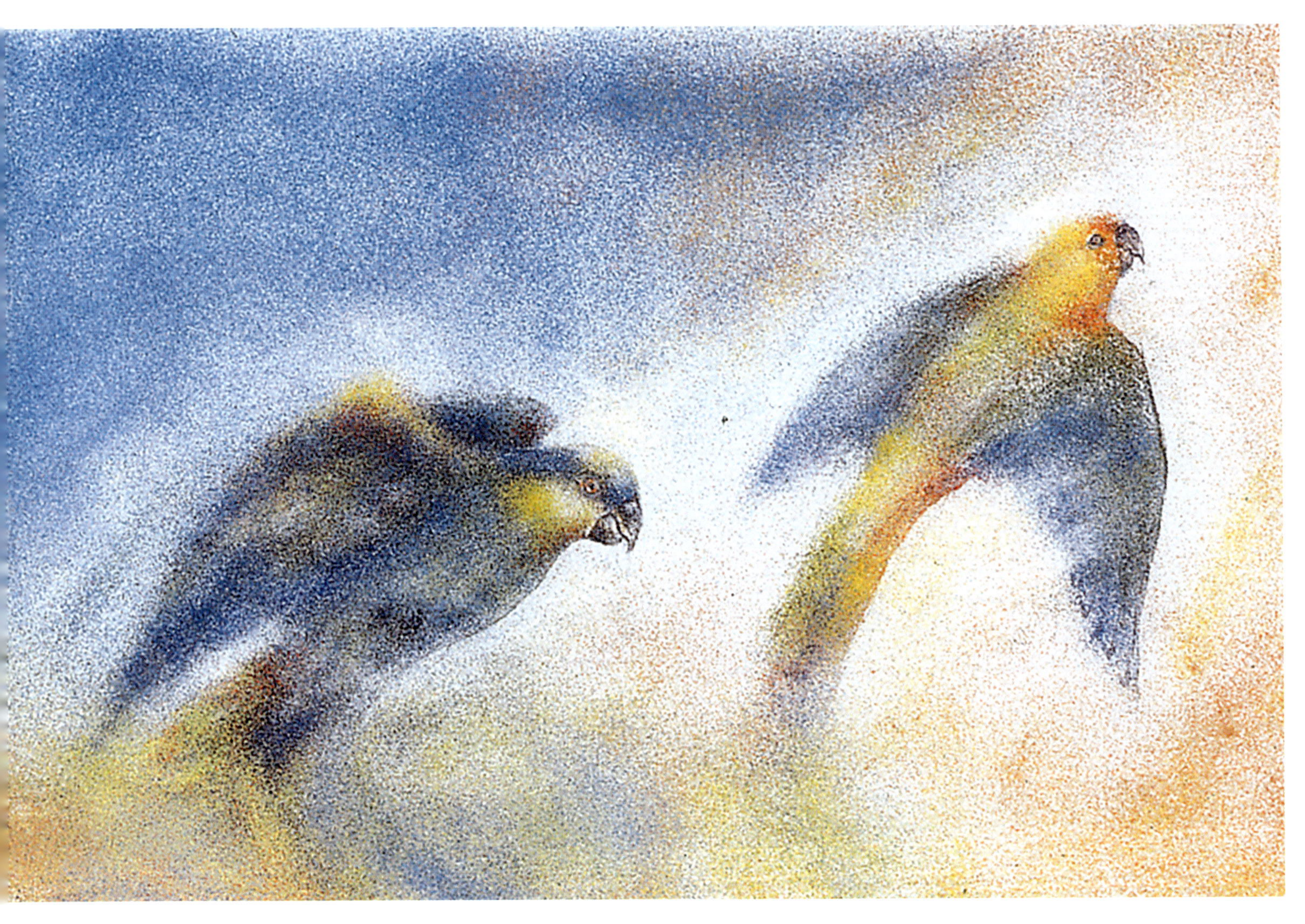

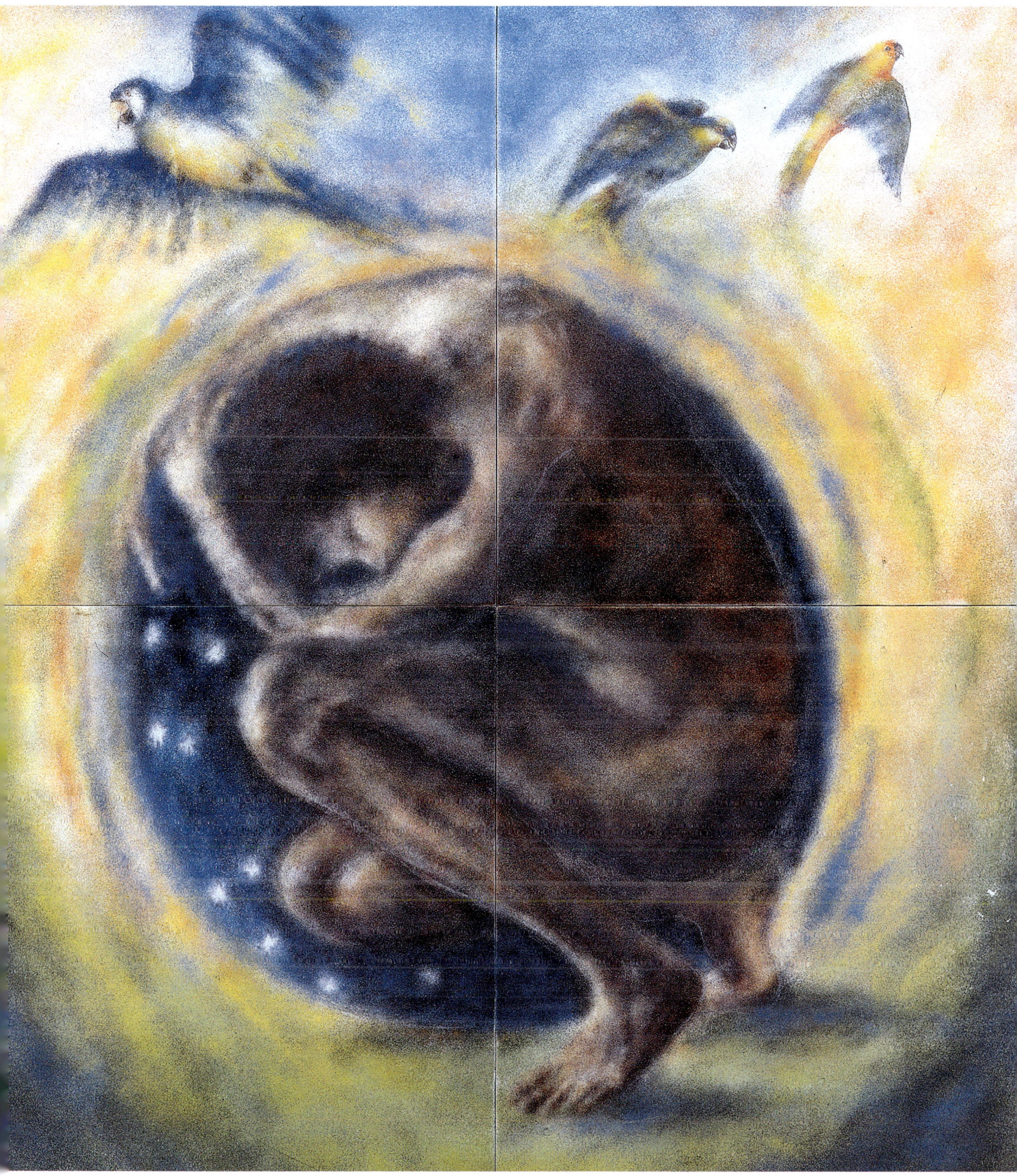

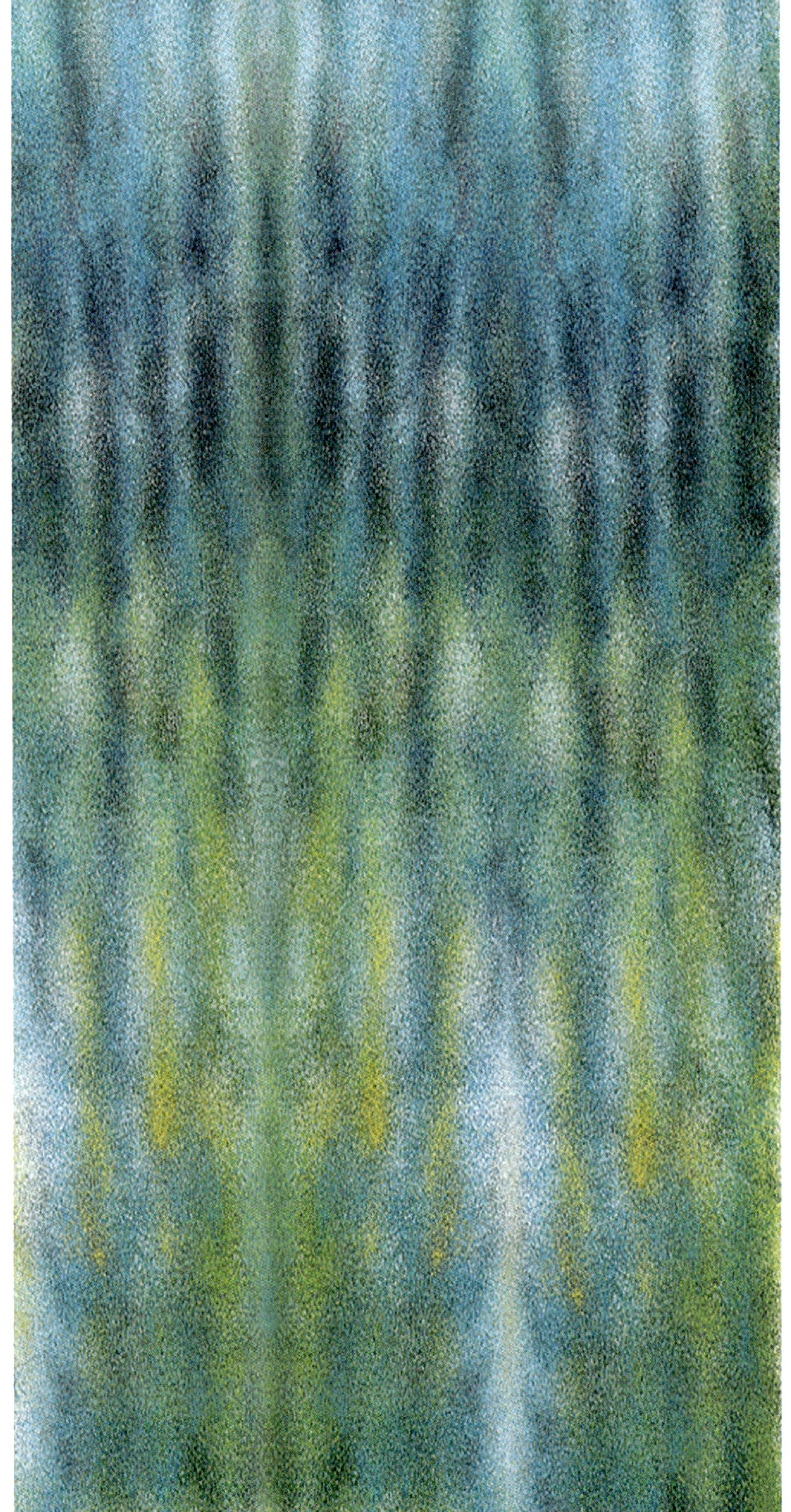

A RIVER OF TEARS WAS FORMED, WHICH THE ANCIENT KIÑA PEOPLE CALLED 'AIAKÁ-MAÉ' WHICH MEANS 'THE RIVER OF LOVE'. TODAY THAT RIVER IS CALLED THE AMAZON

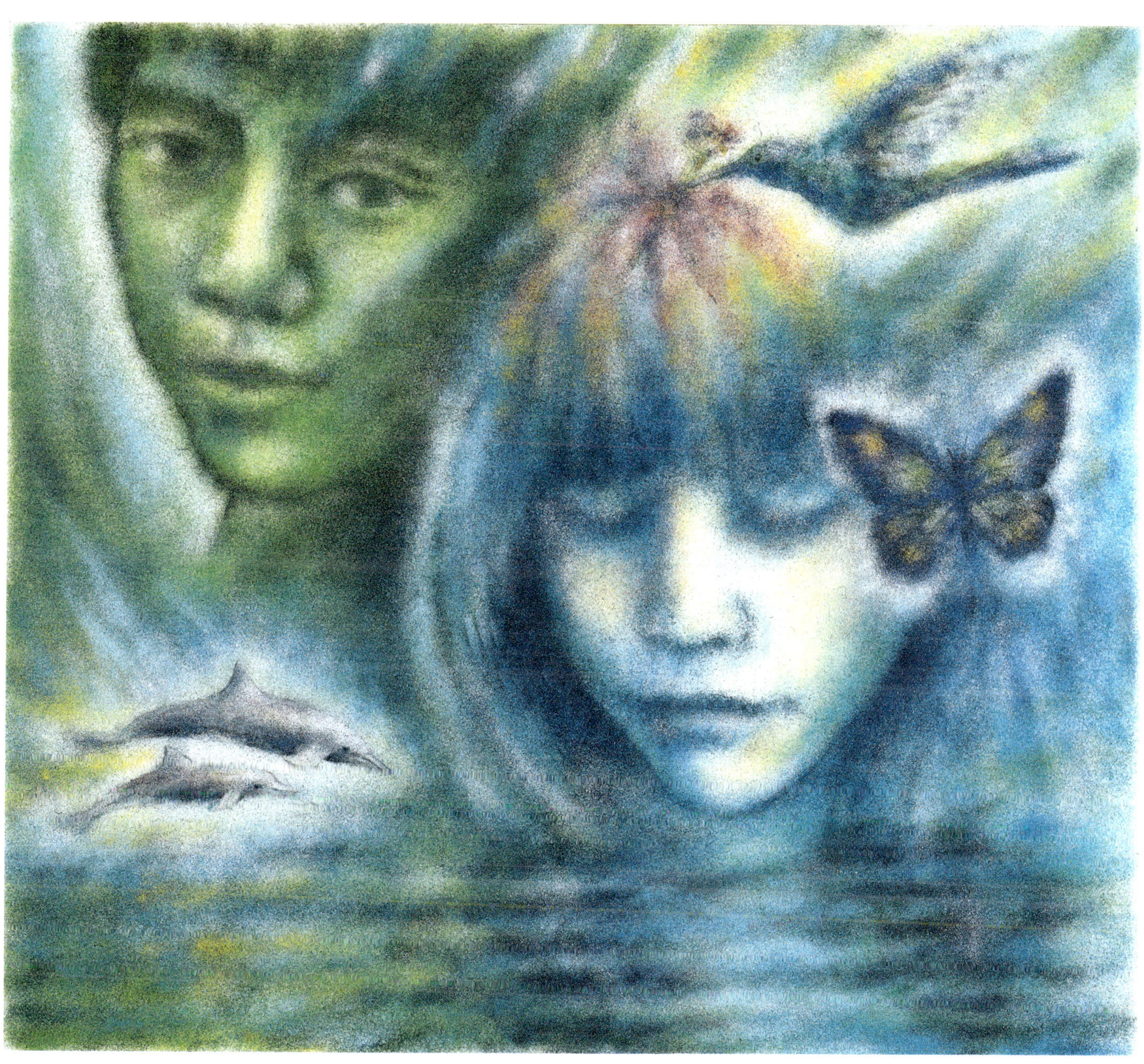

Aiaká-maé
The River Of Love

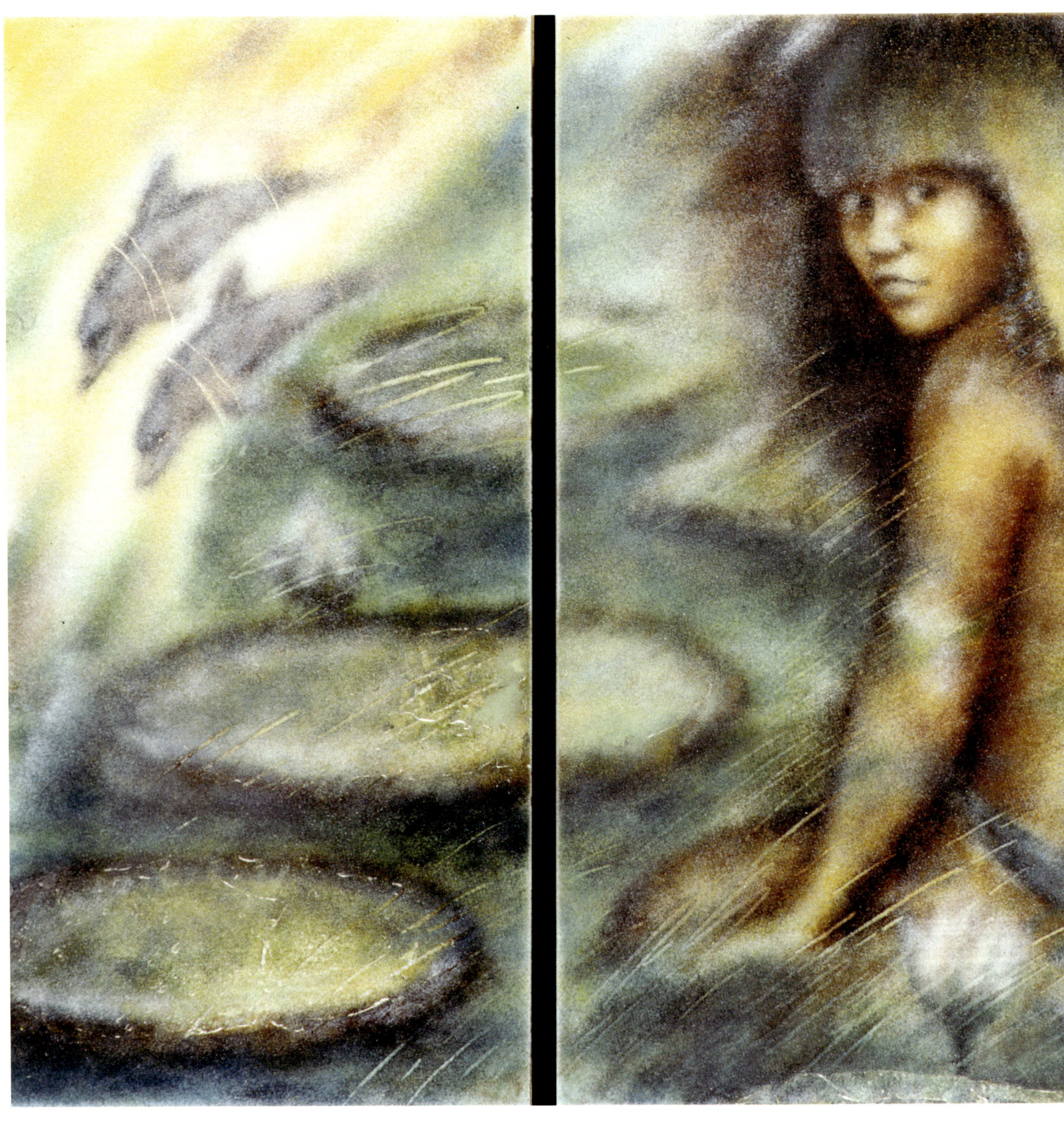

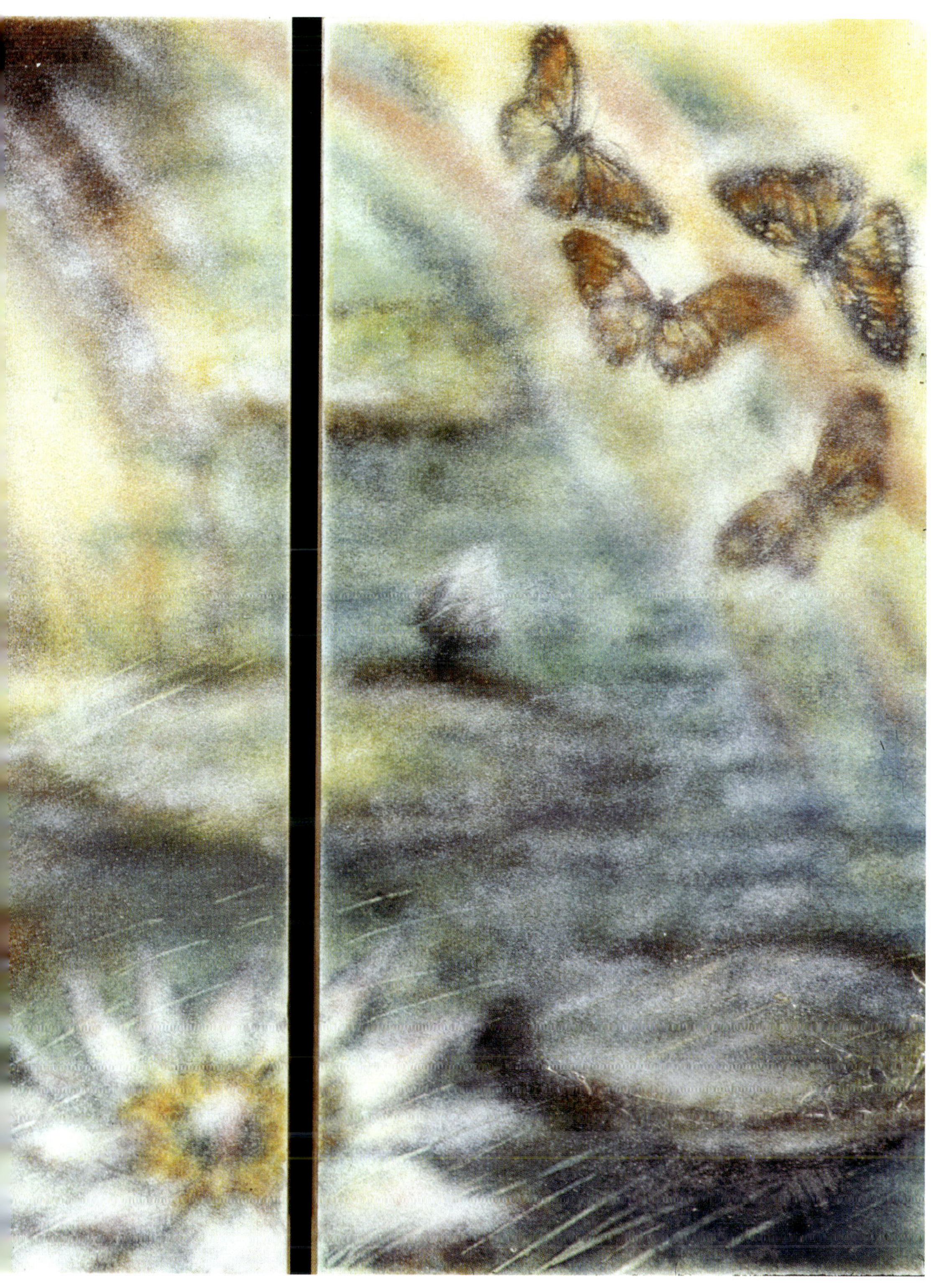

Mãe d'Água
Iara, Goddess Of The River

"SUNSET IS IARA'S TIME OF DAY ... "STAY AWAY FROM THE RIVER WHEN THE SUN IS GOING DOWN! IARA LOOKS FOR LITTLE BOYS TO KEEP!"

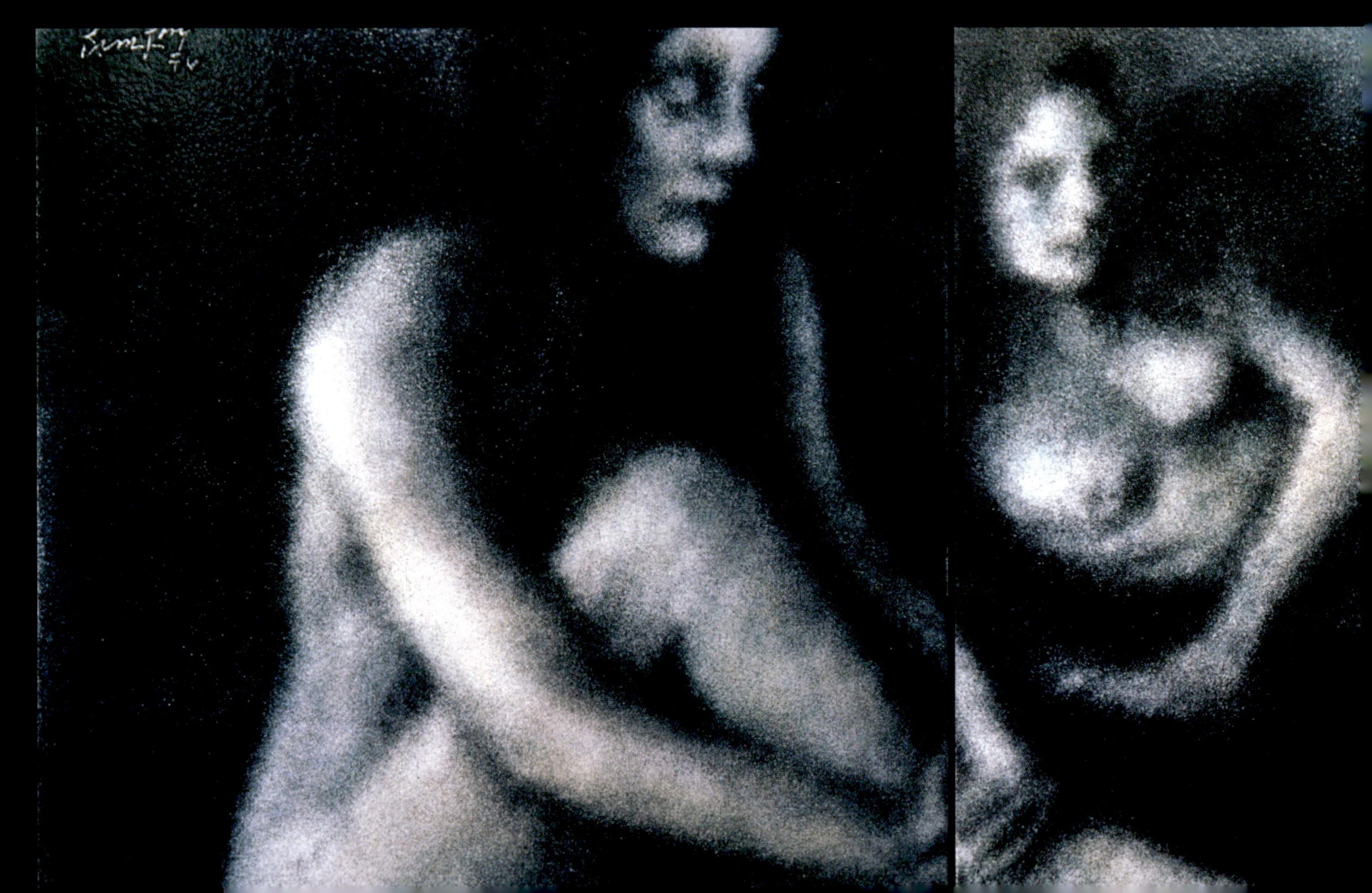

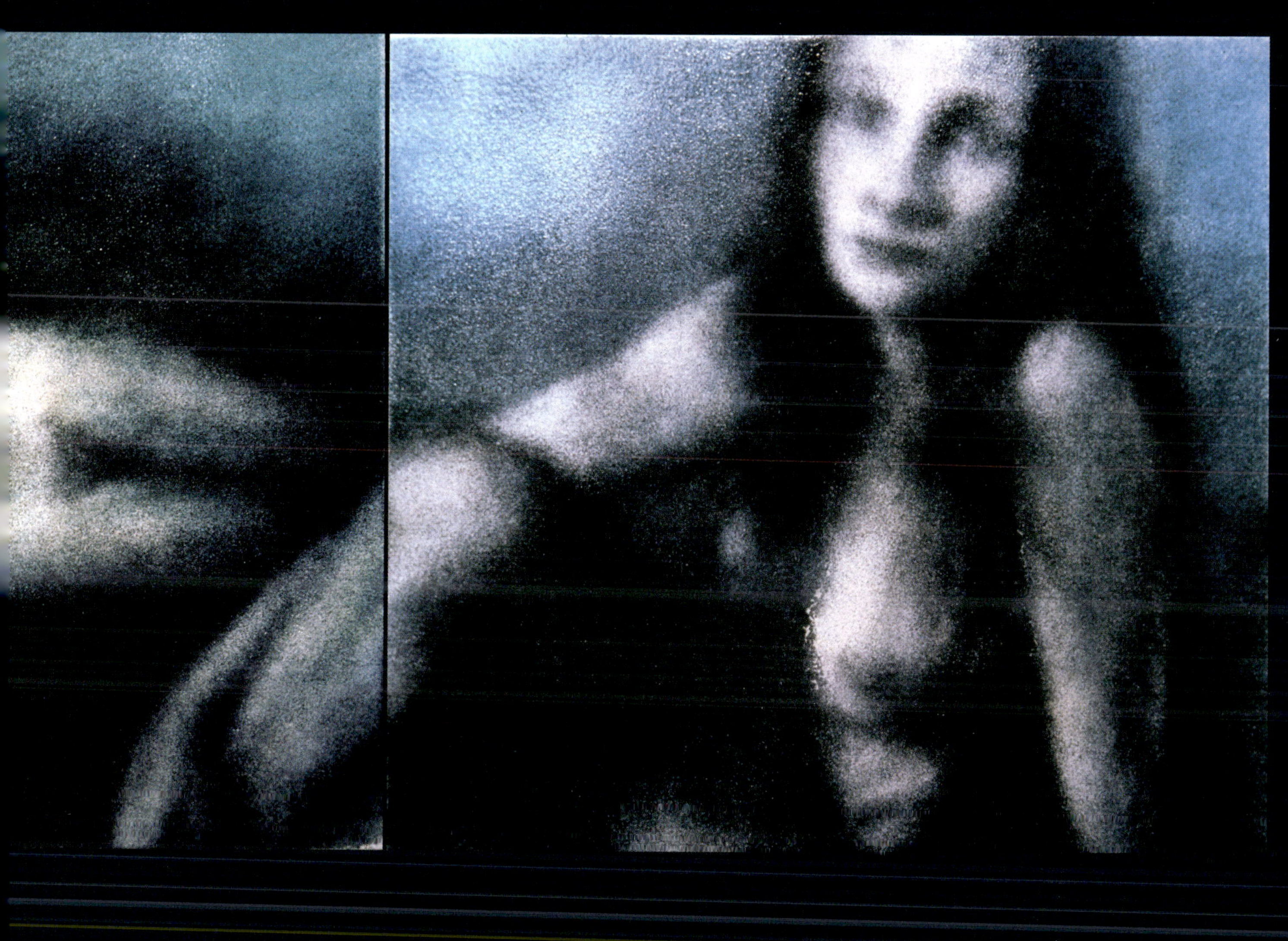

Iaras
Iara, Goddess Of The River

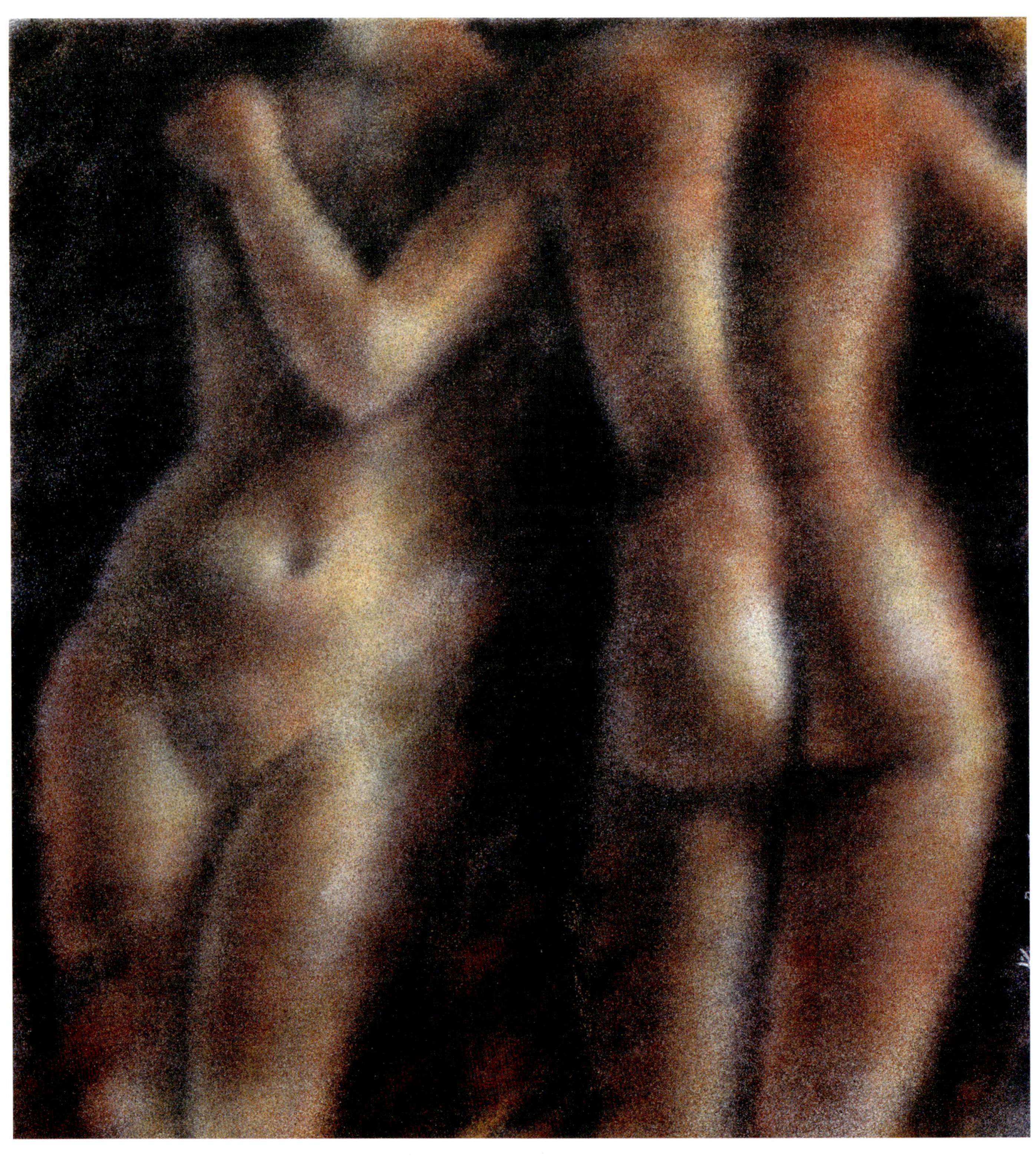

Songs of The Iaras
Iara, Goddess Of The River

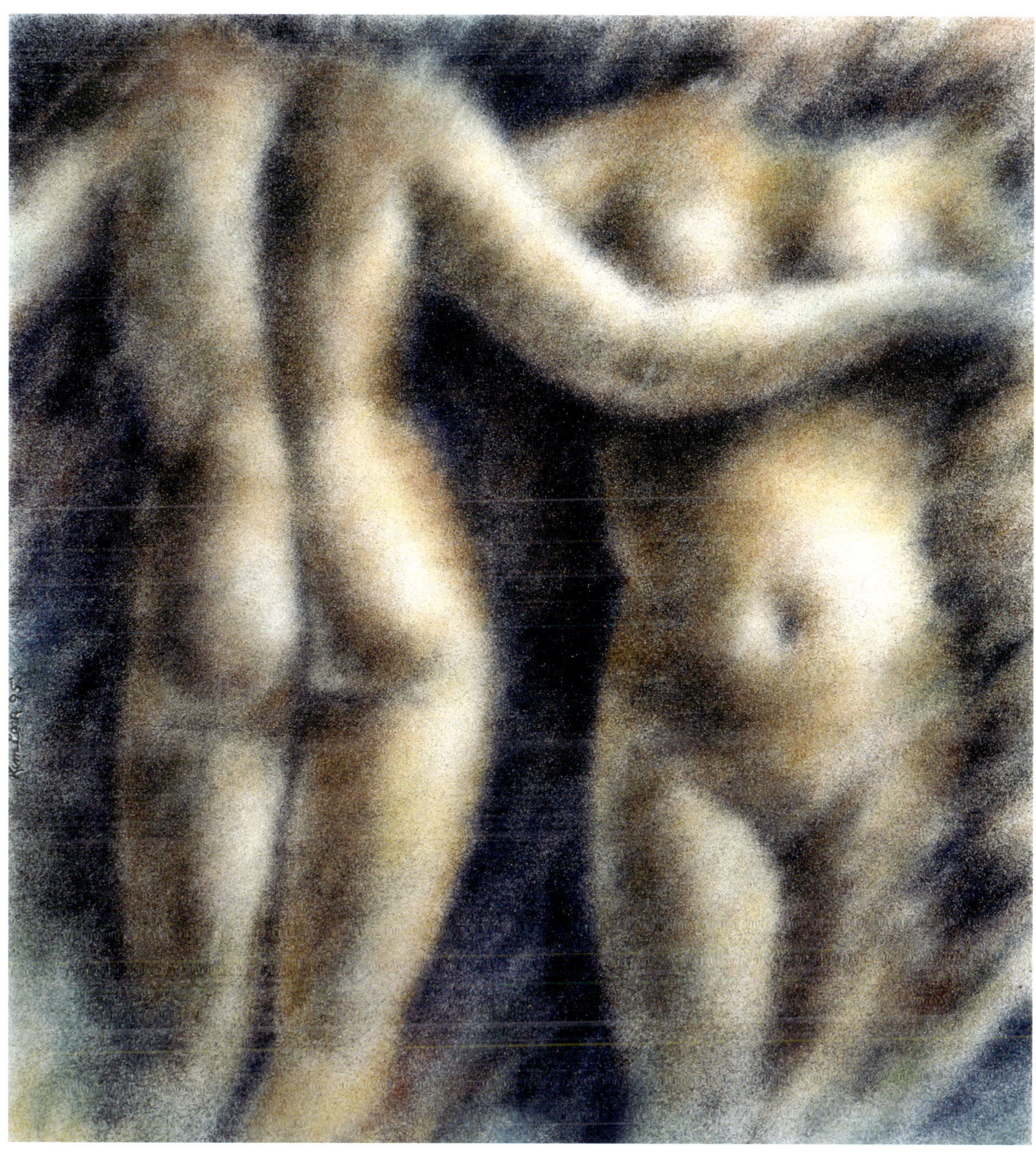

Sounds of The Iaras

Iara, Goddess Of The River

THE WARRIORS

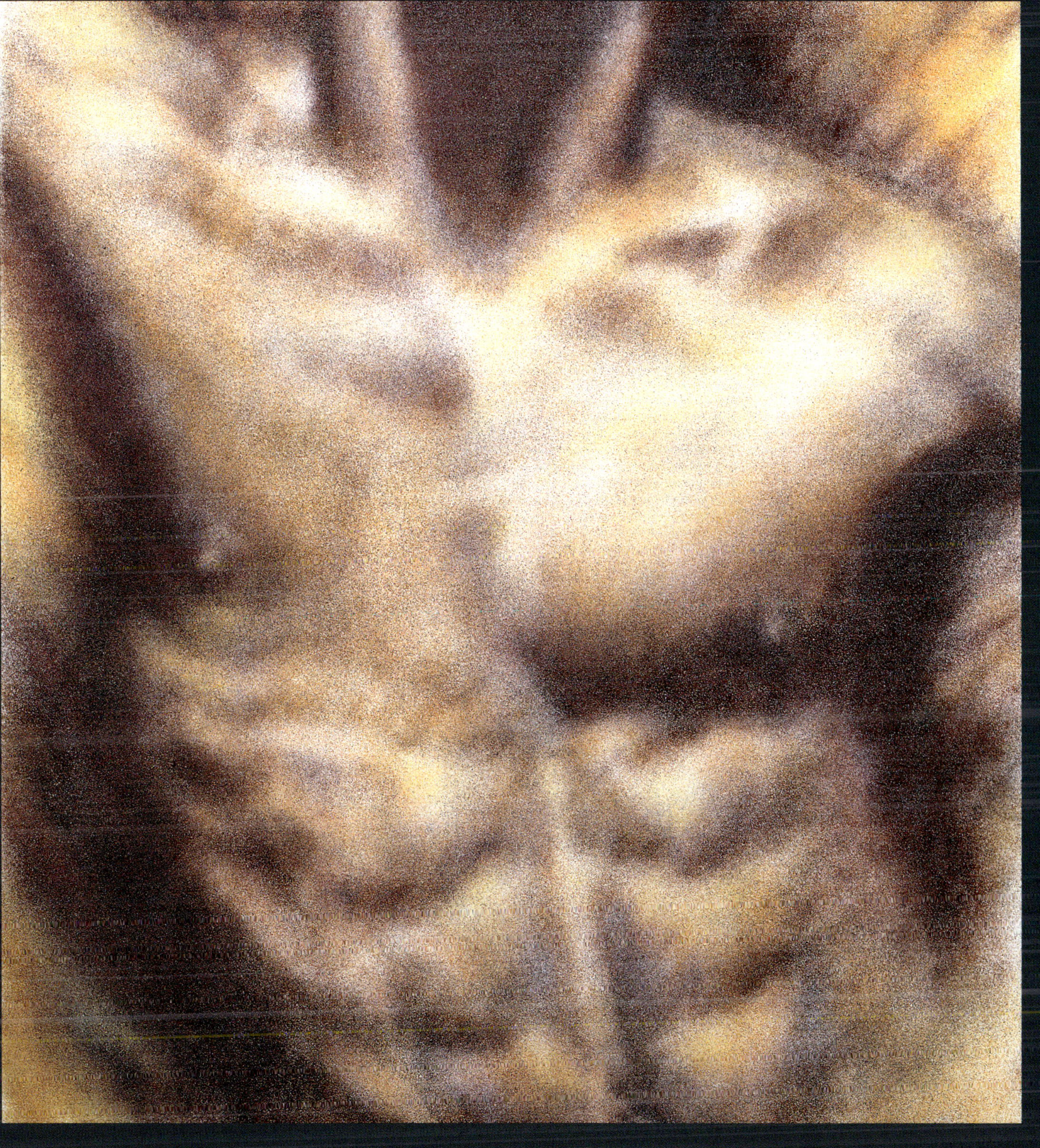

Gamep
The Butterflies

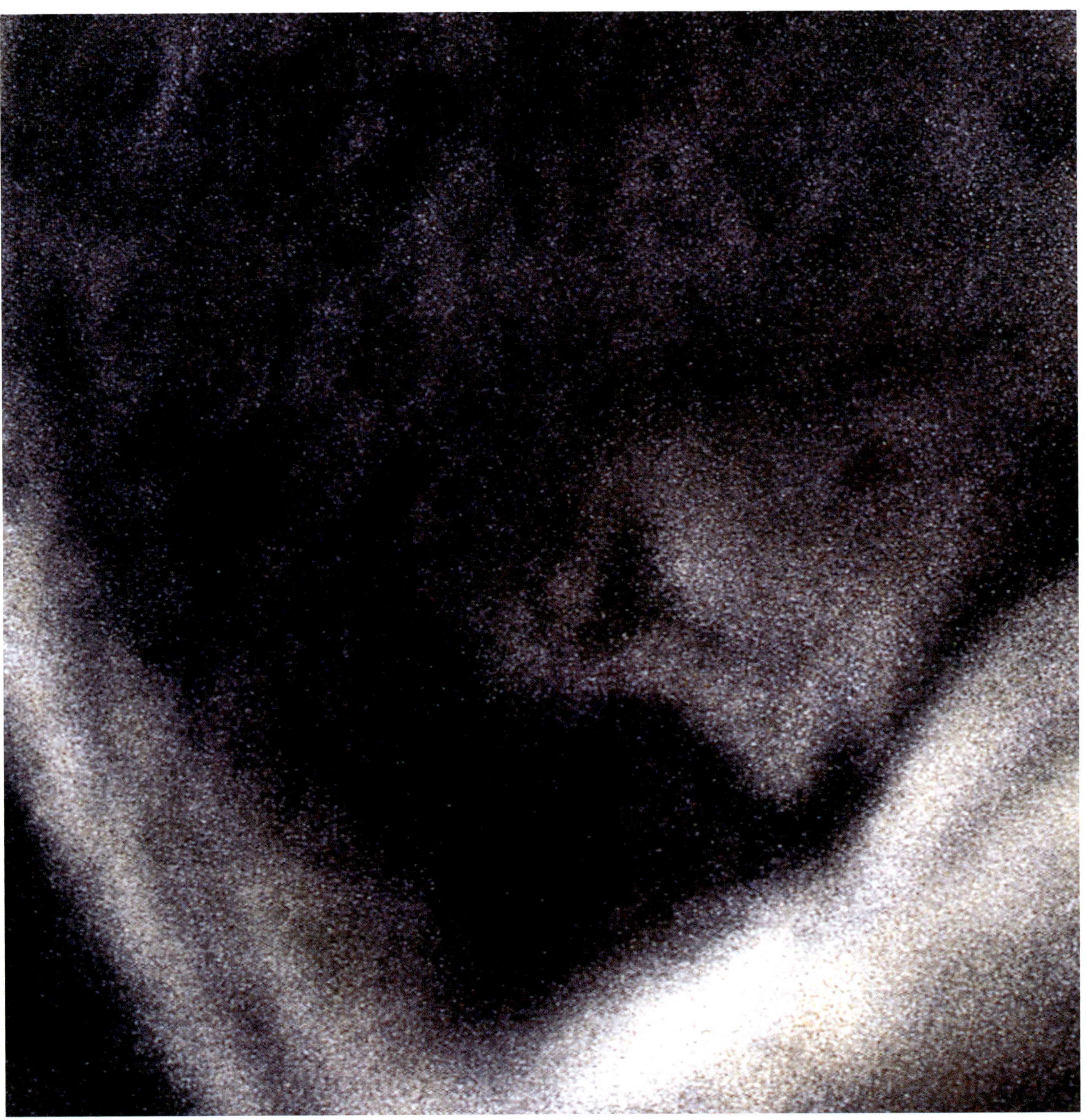

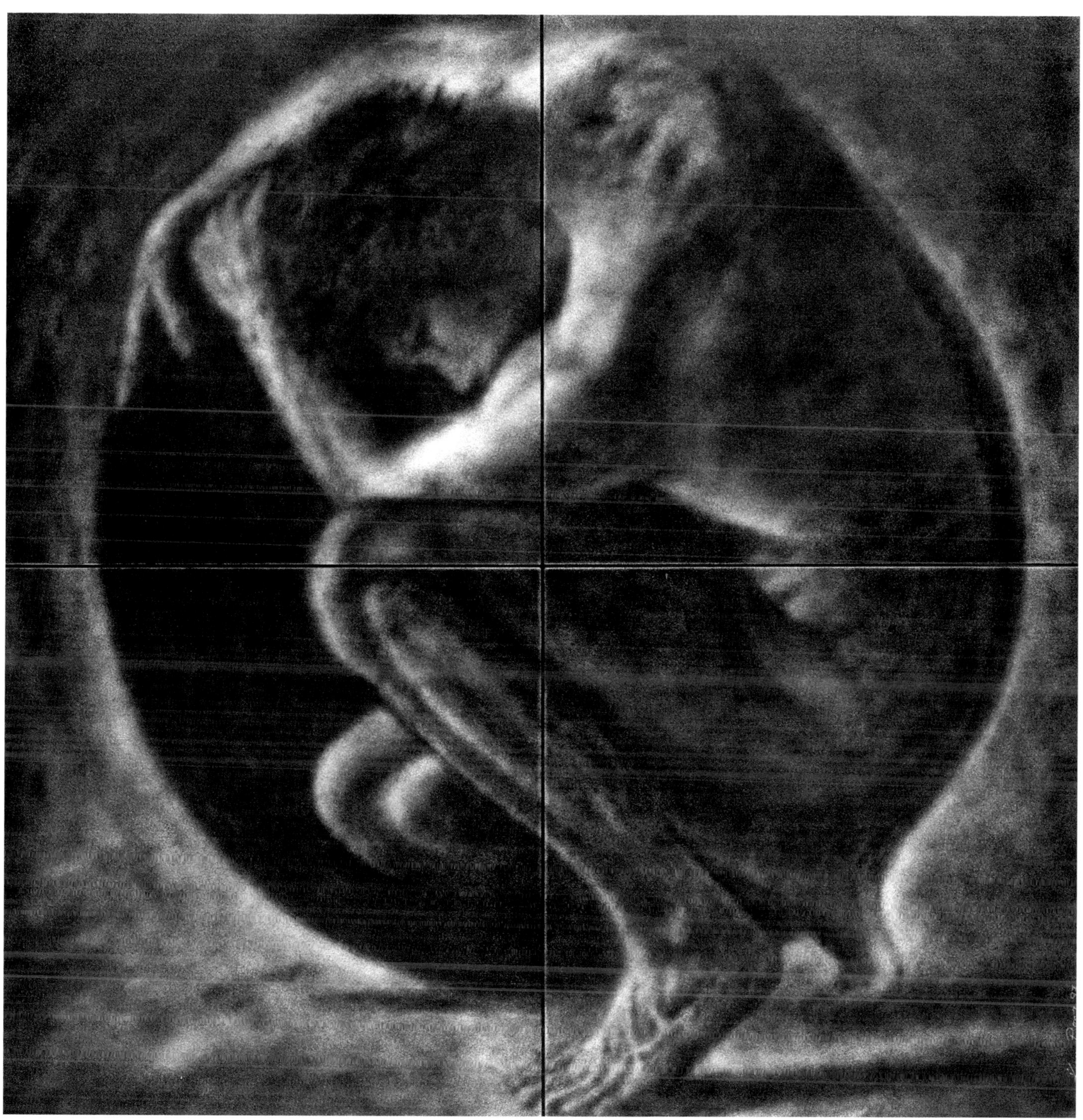

Creation

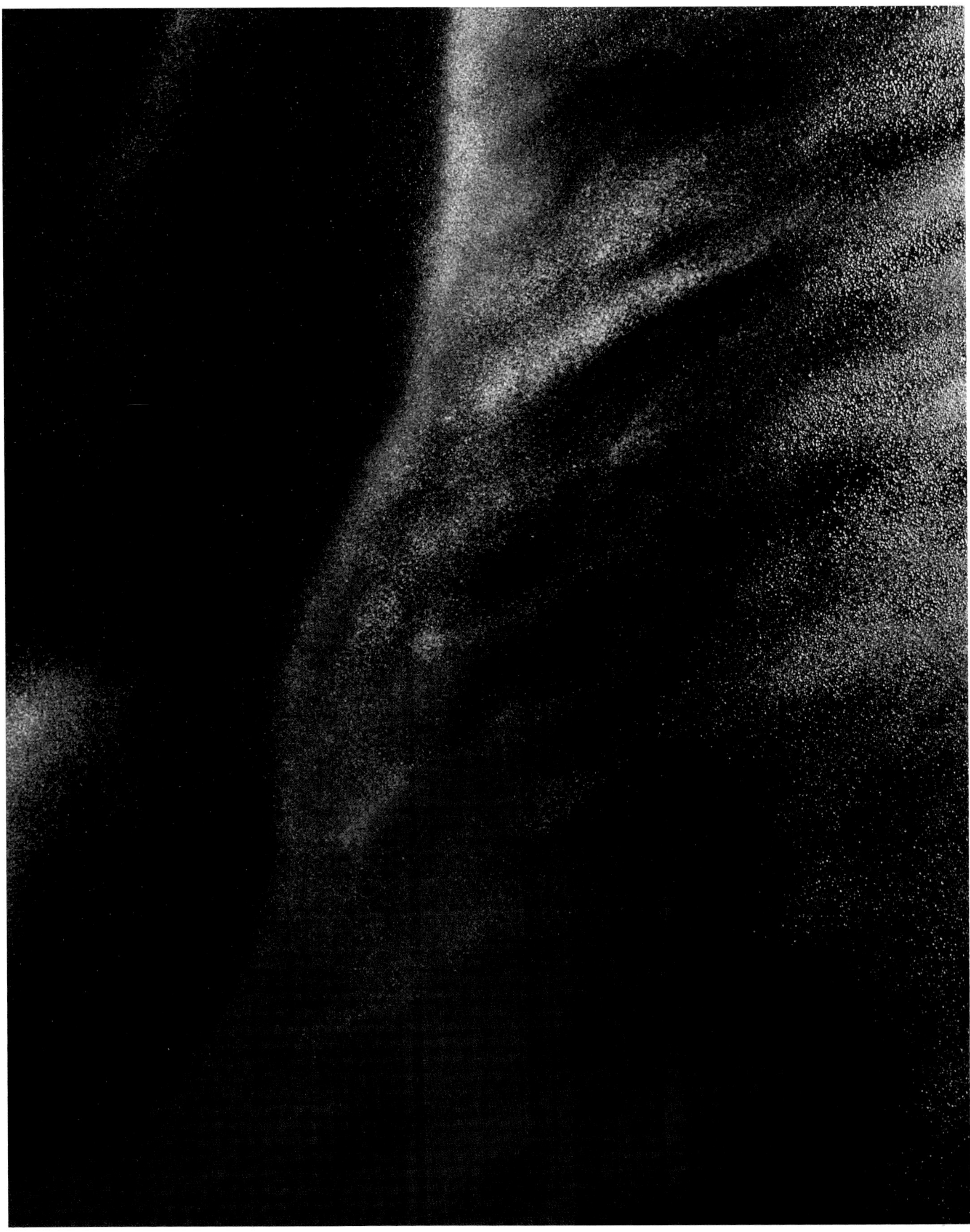

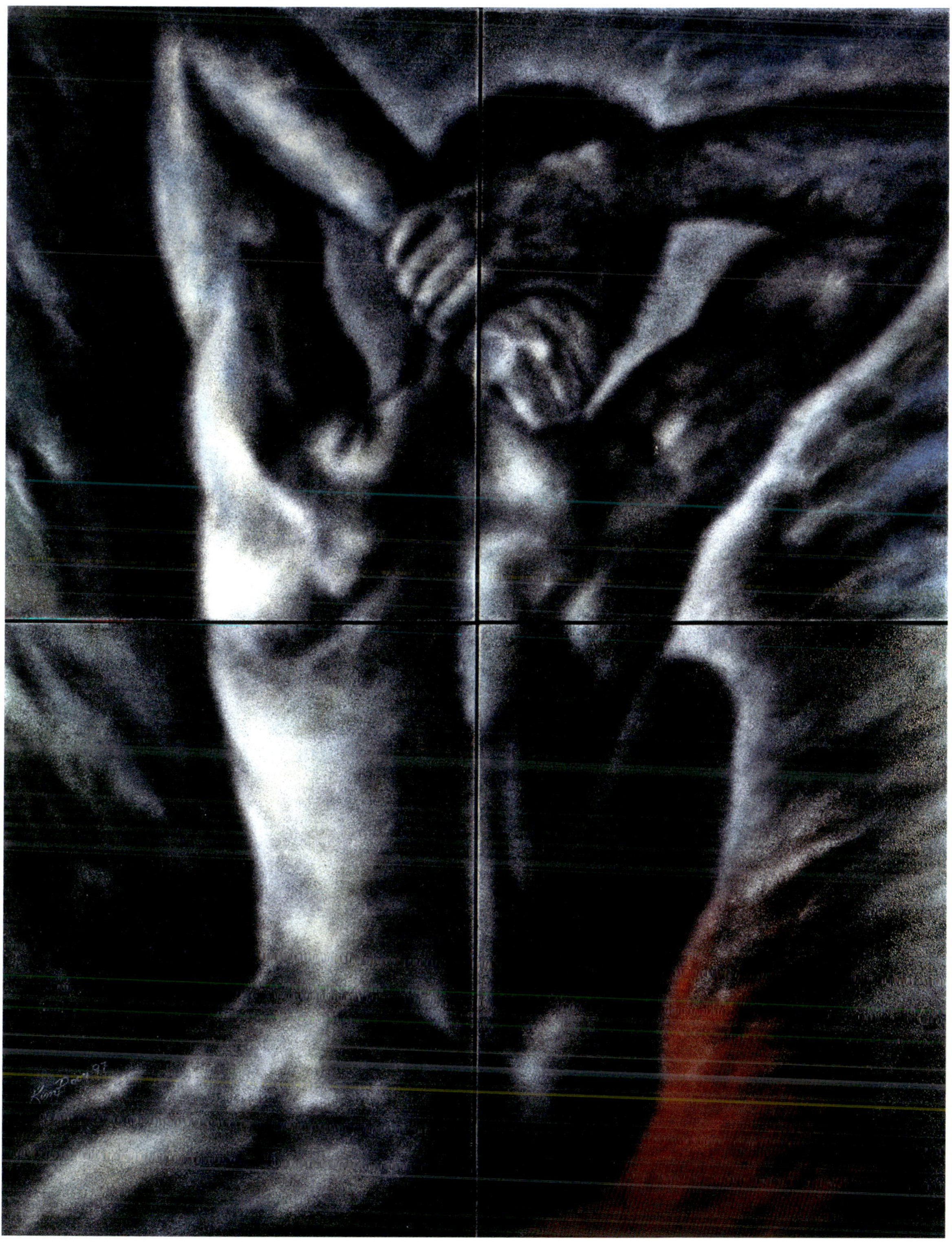

Tortured Warrior

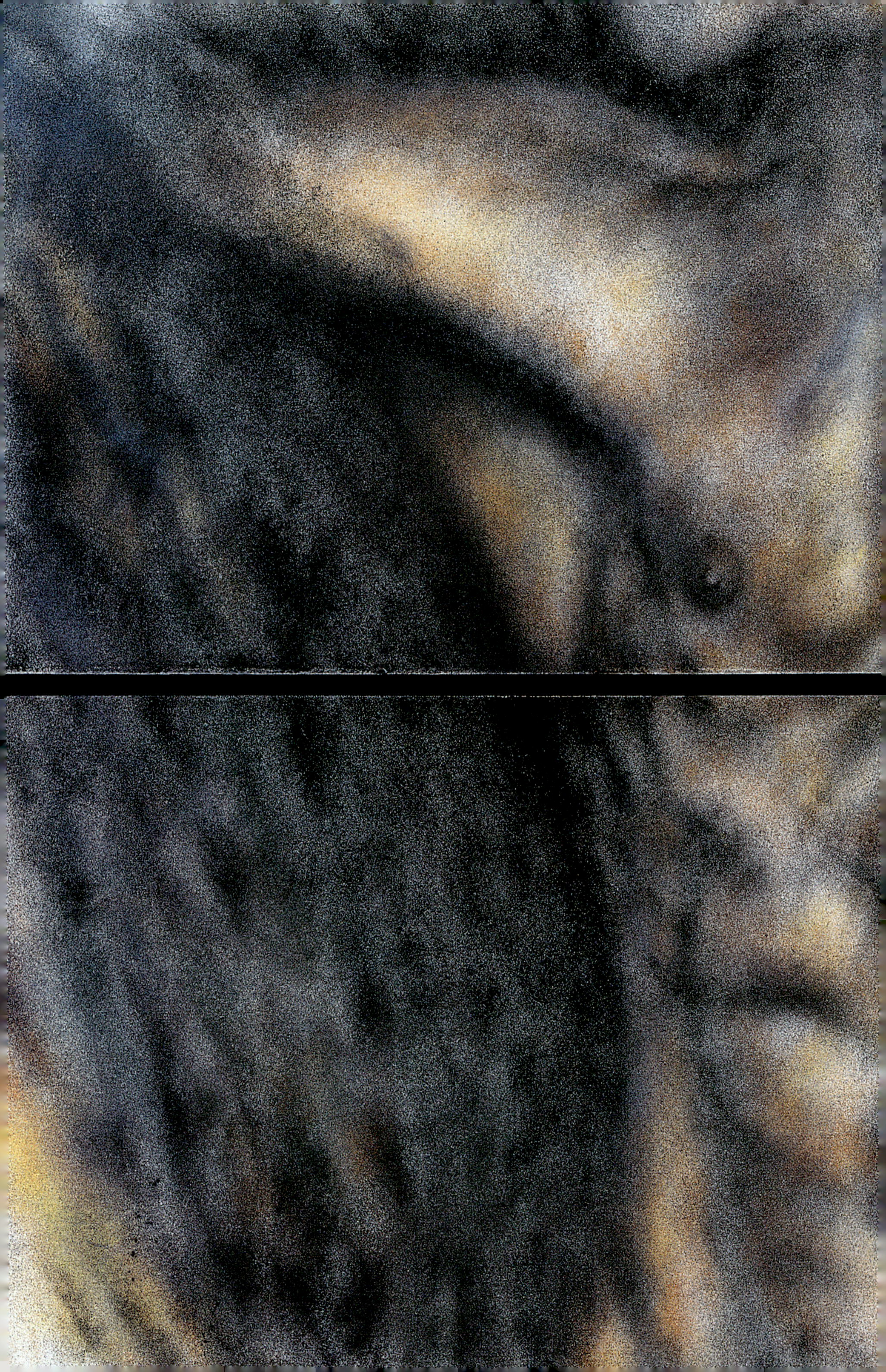

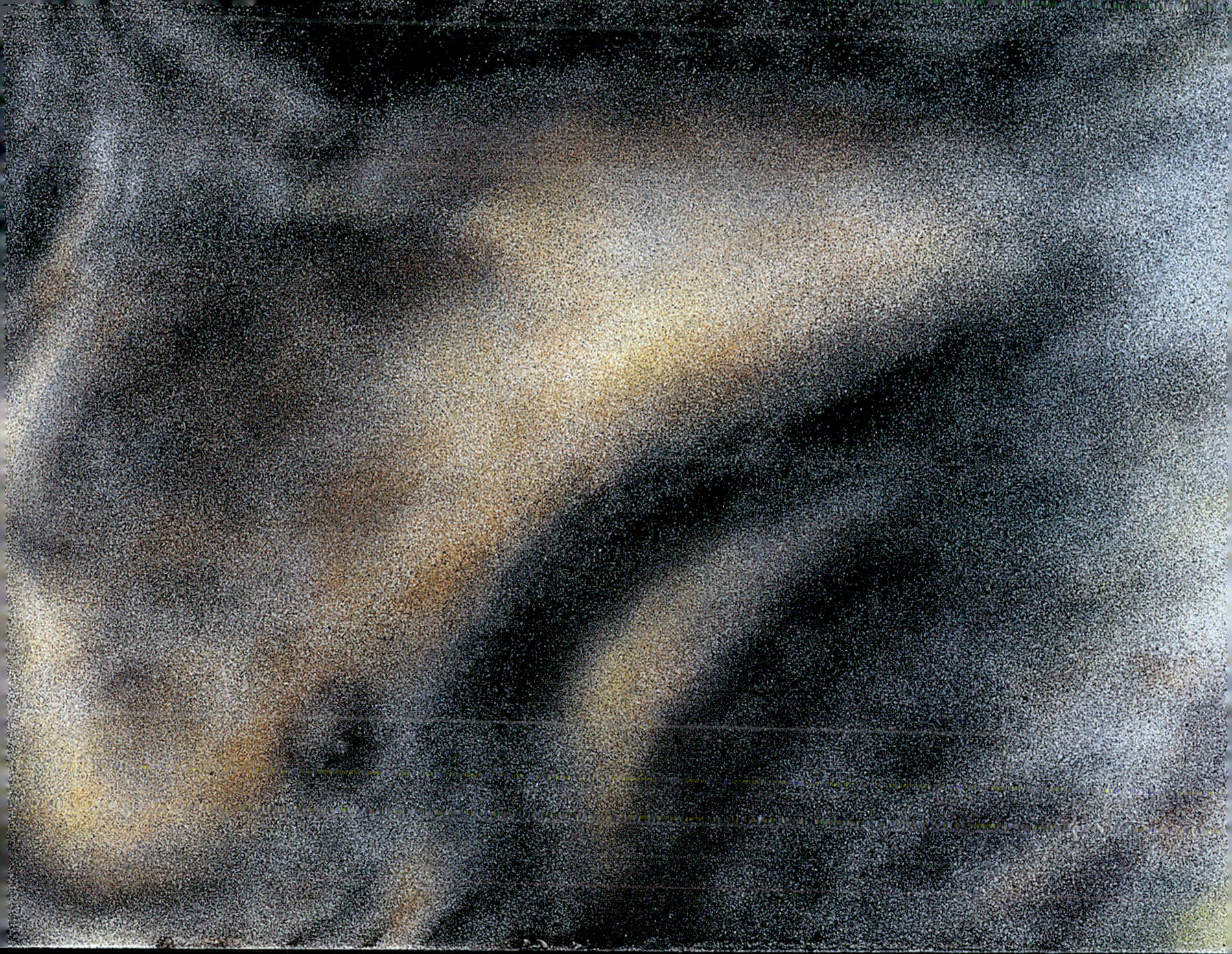

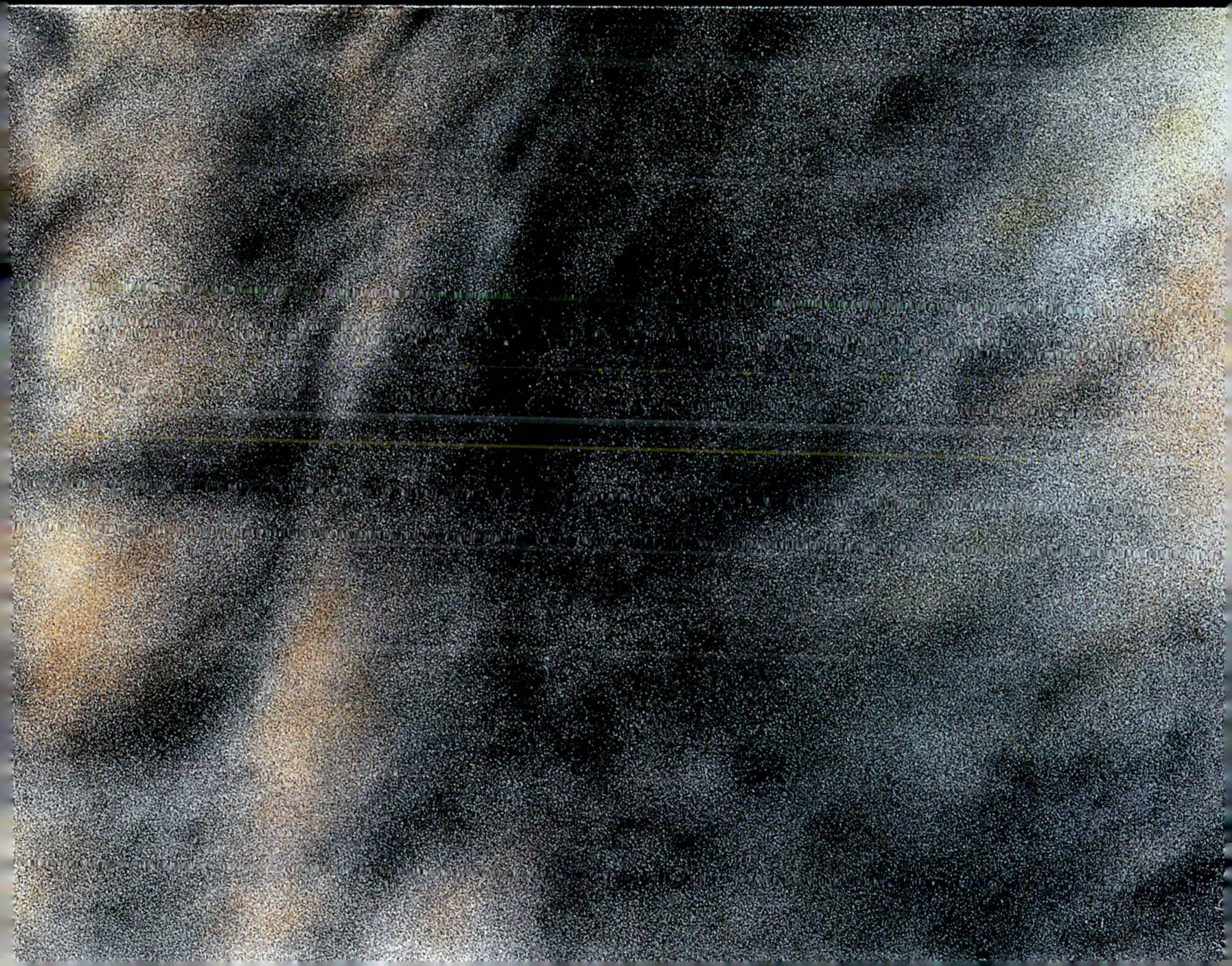

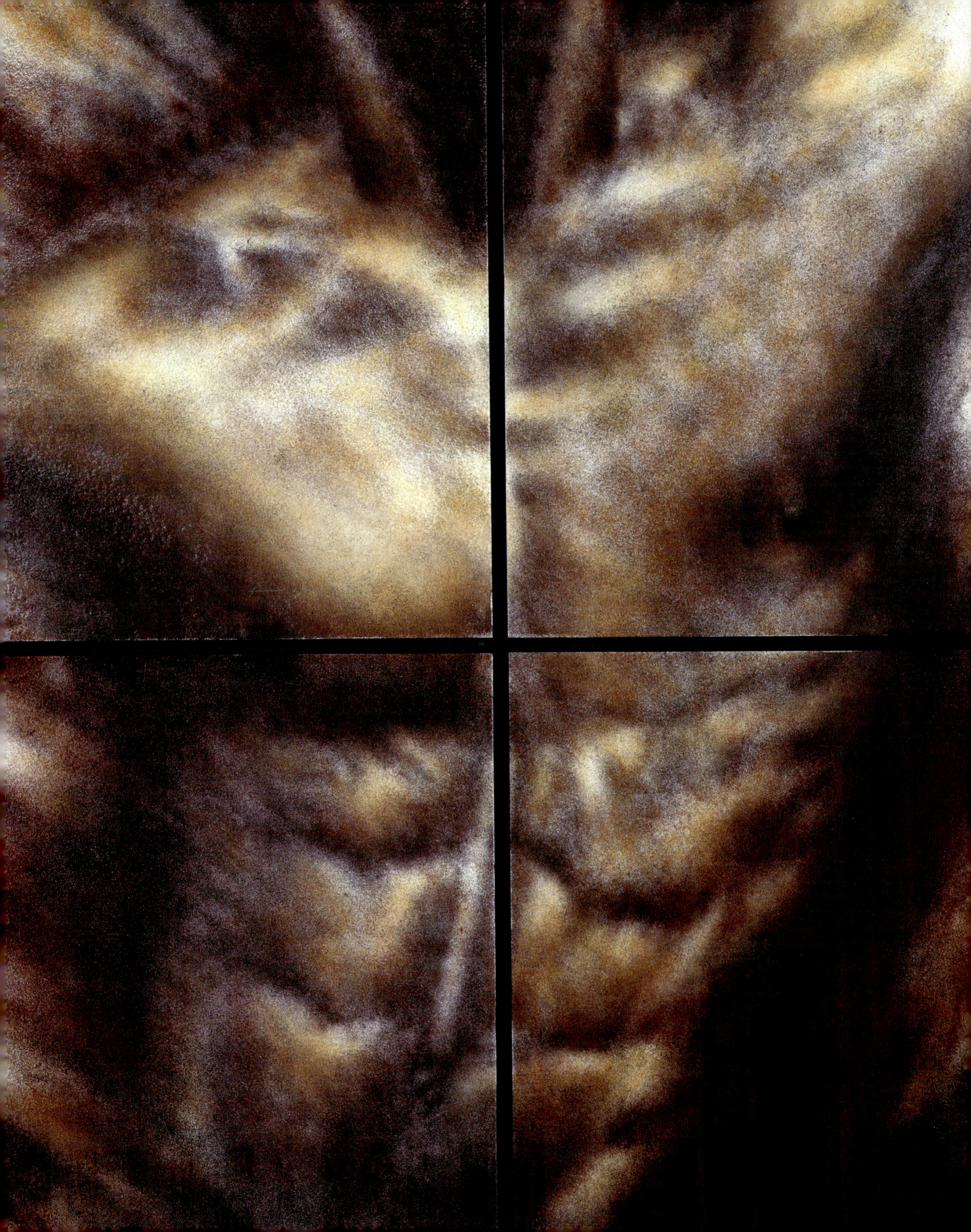

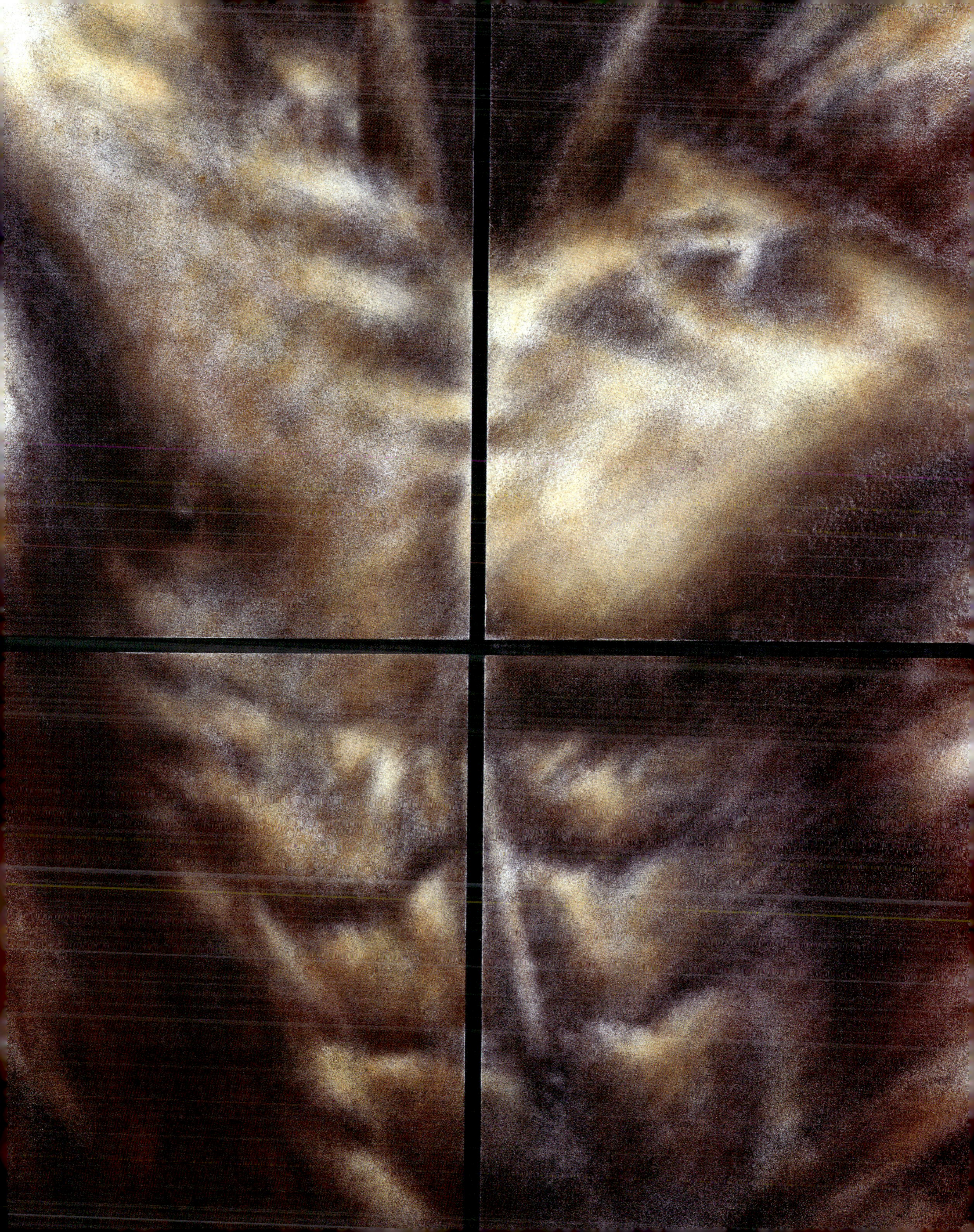

Previous pages
Crucified Warrior
Out Of The Earth

Tamacavi
The Butterflies

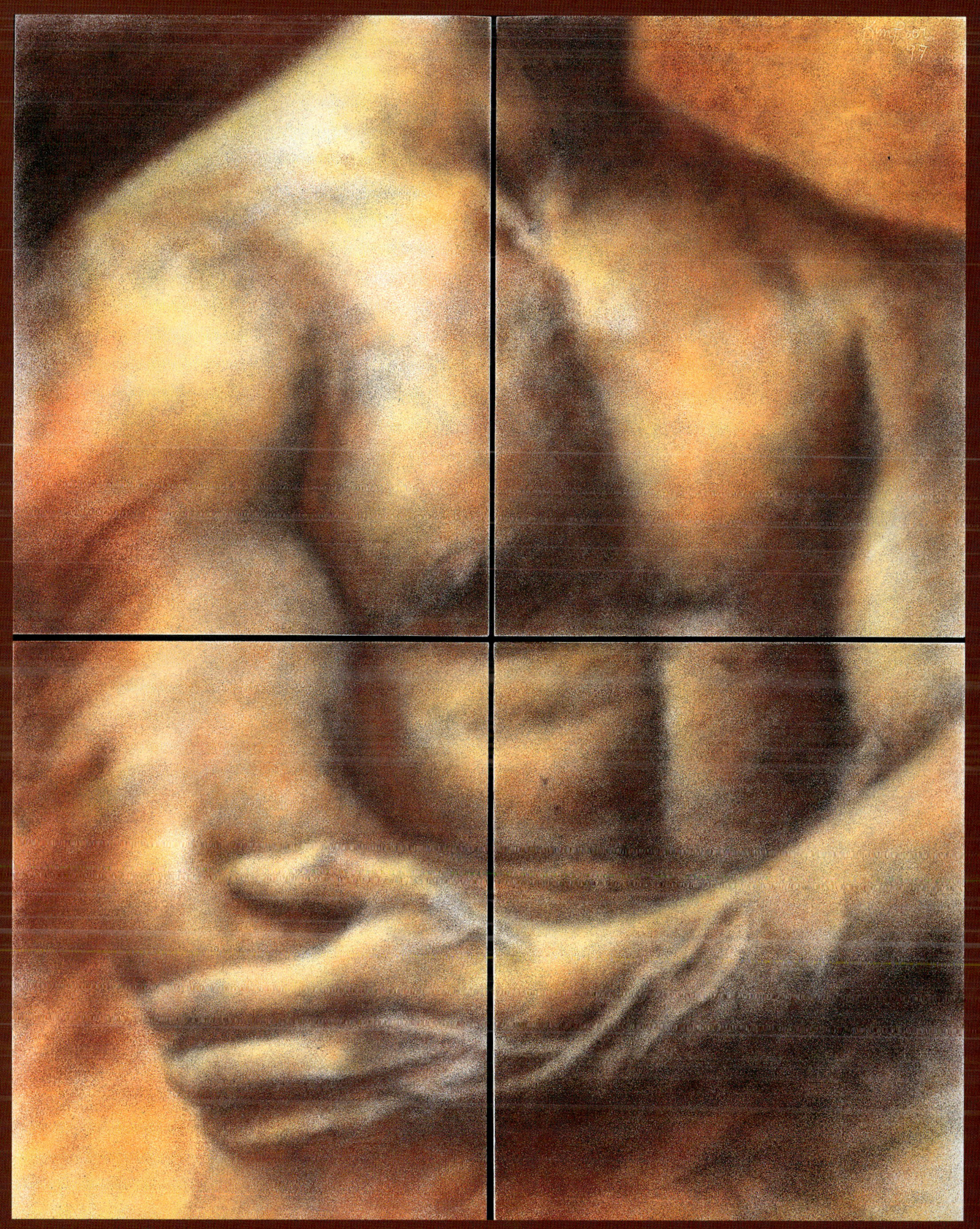

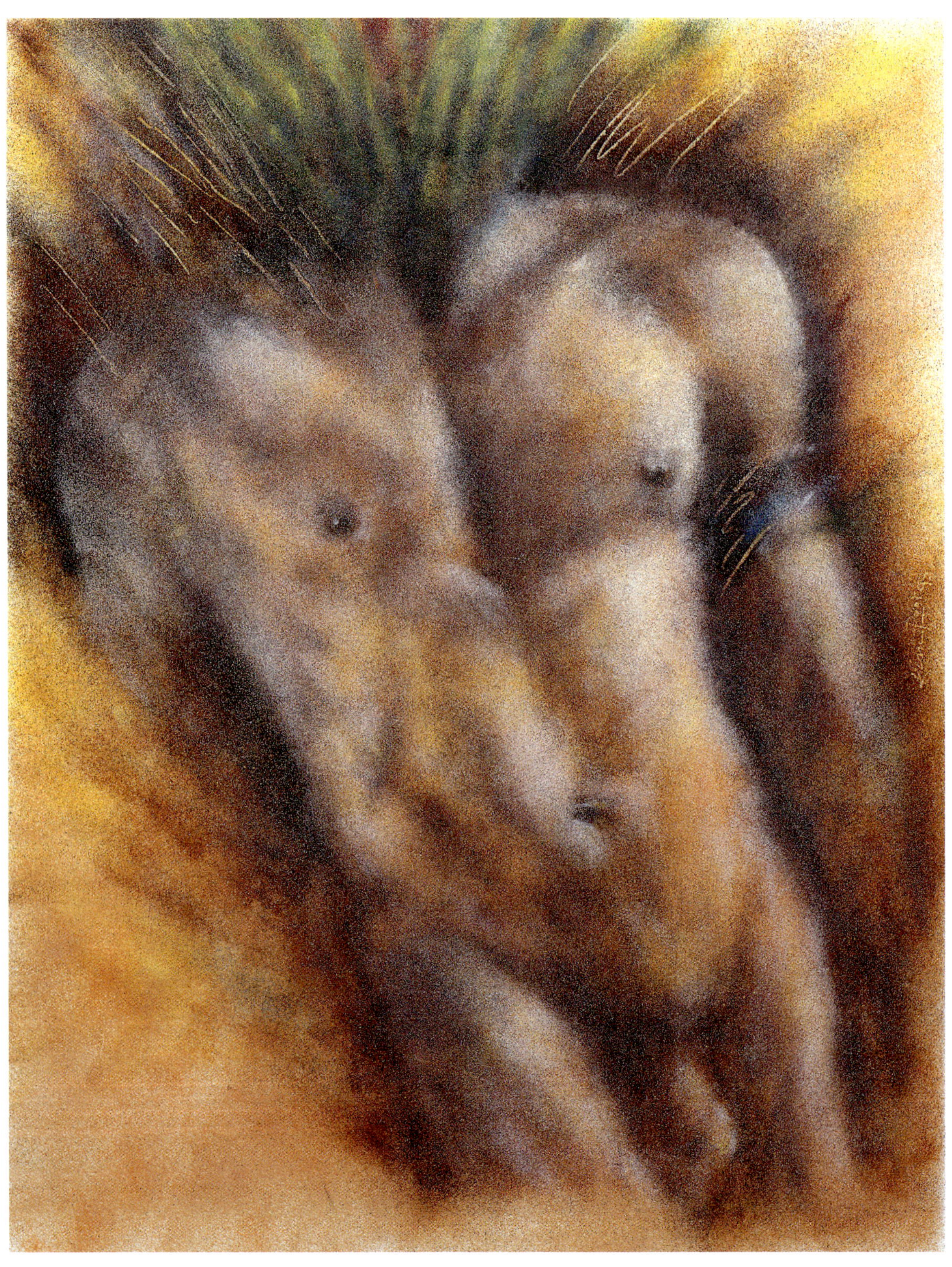

Sun Warrior
The Two Parrots

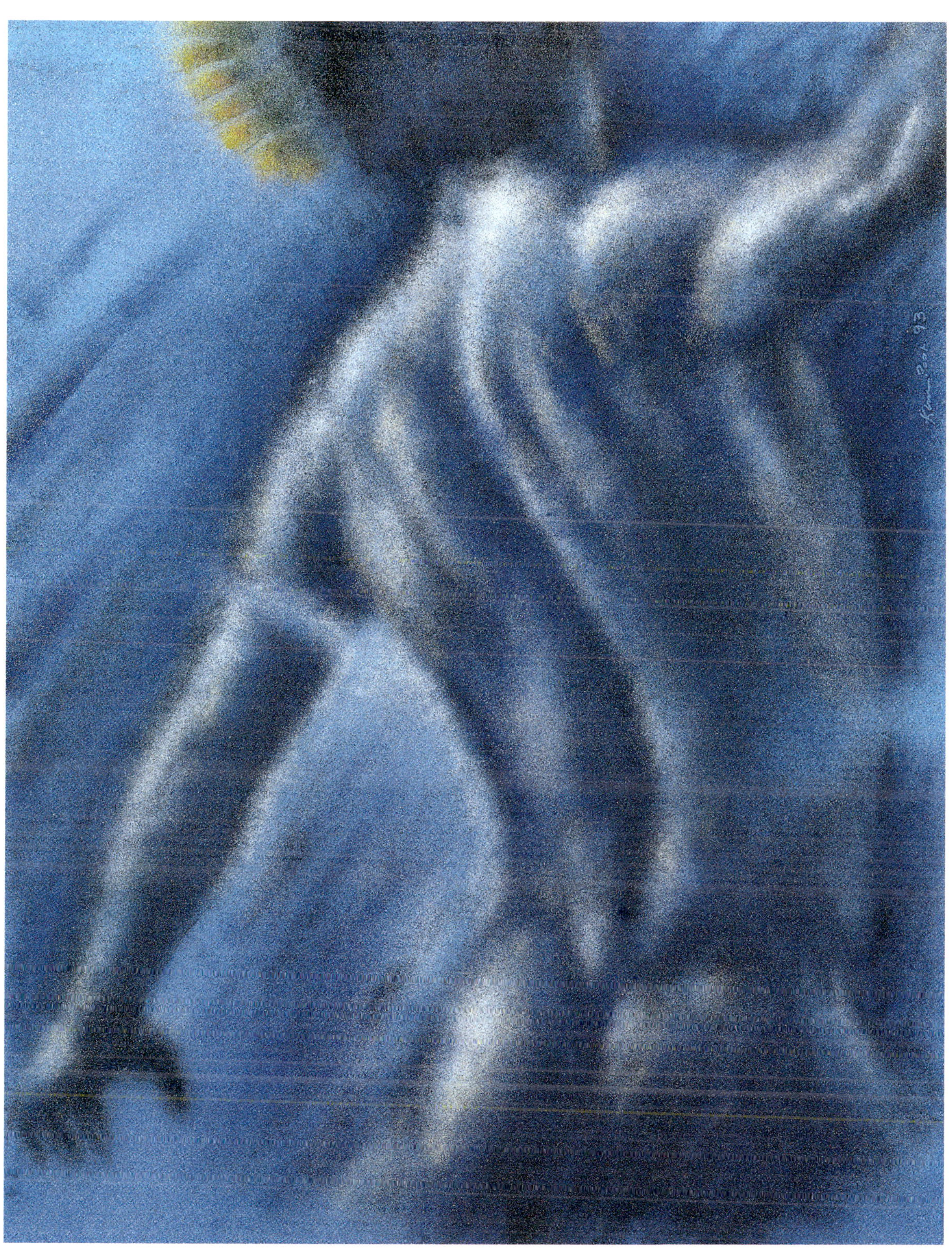

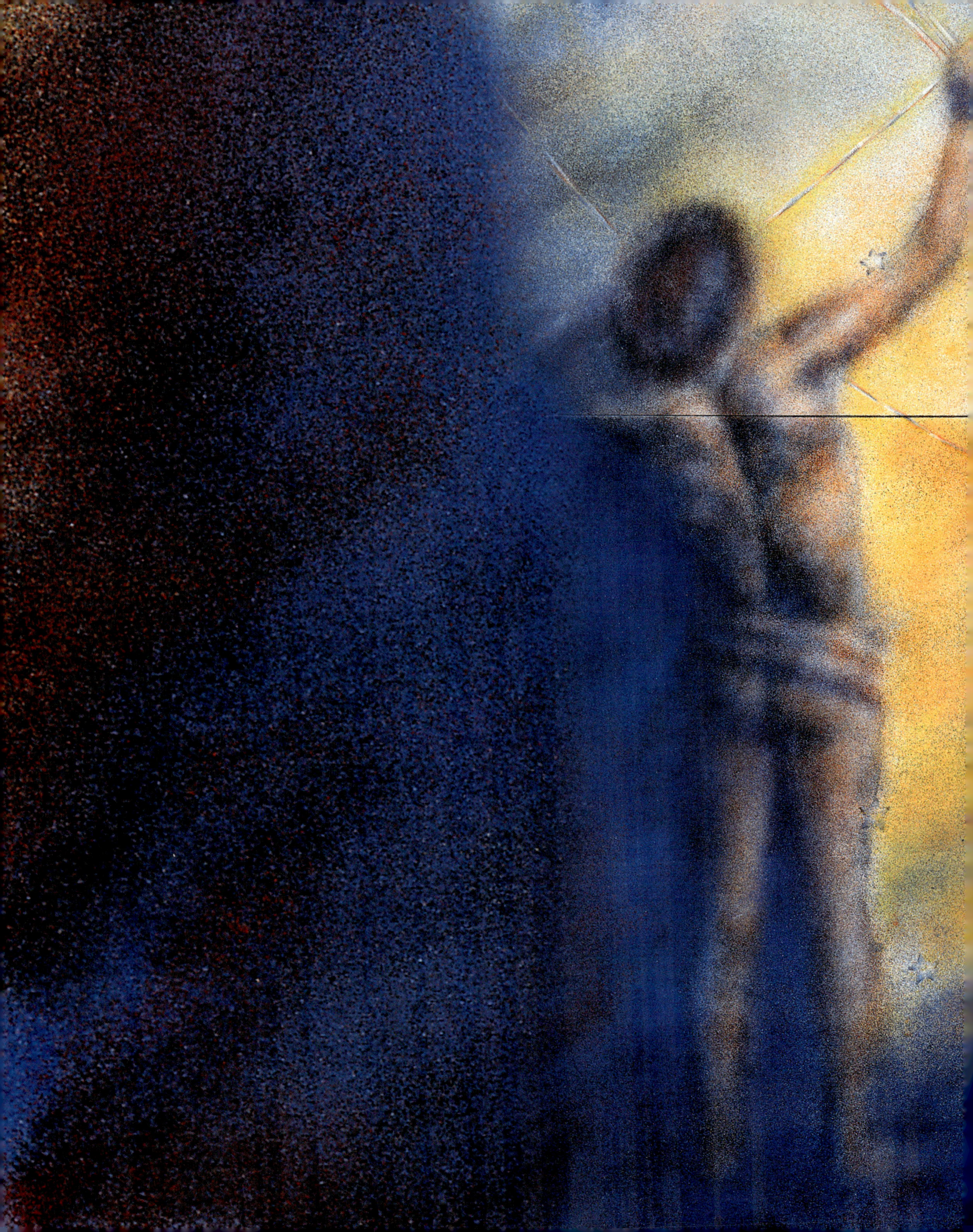

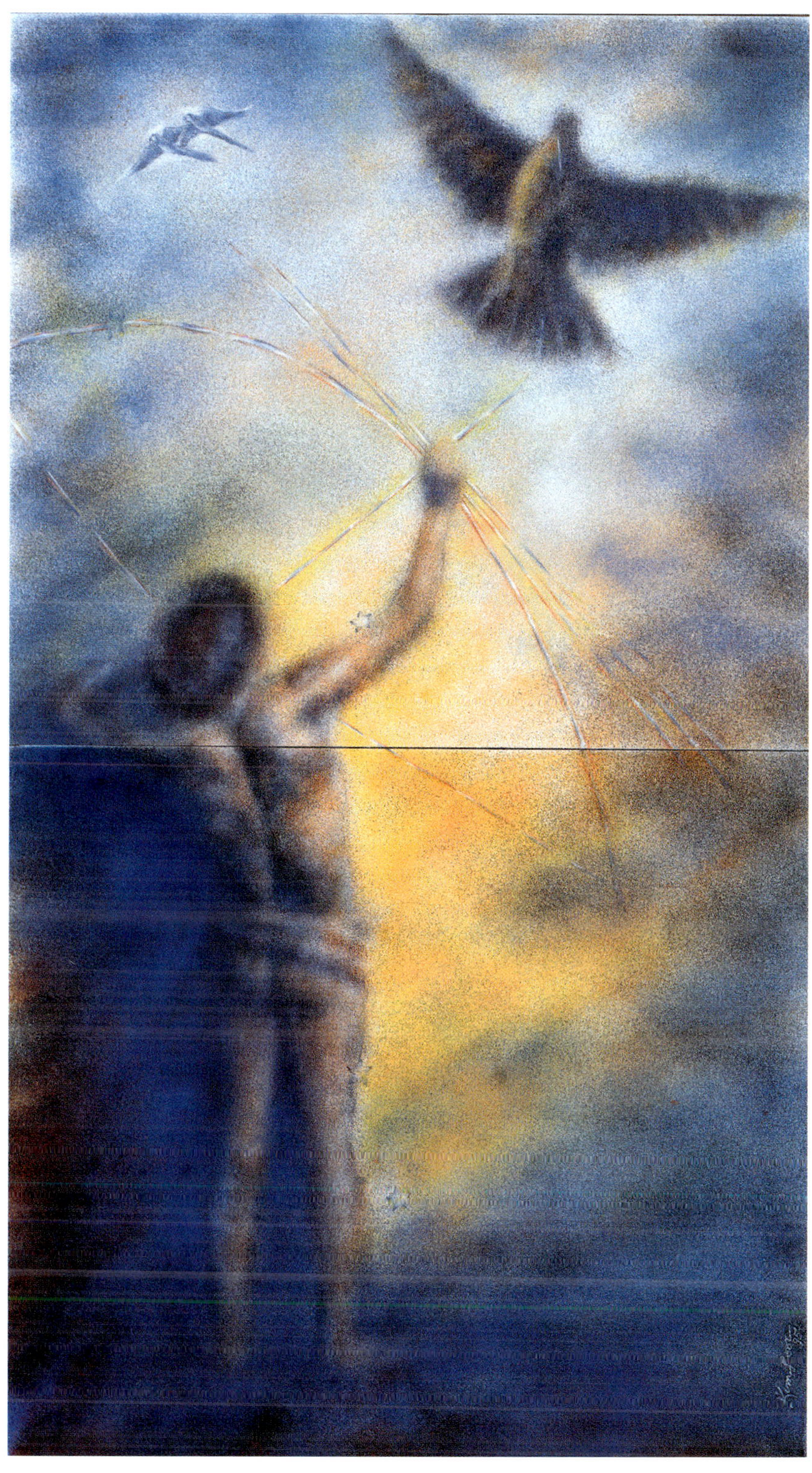

Magic Arrow

LEGENDS OF THE AMAZON

Exhibition at
The Museum of Modern Art
Rio de Janeiro

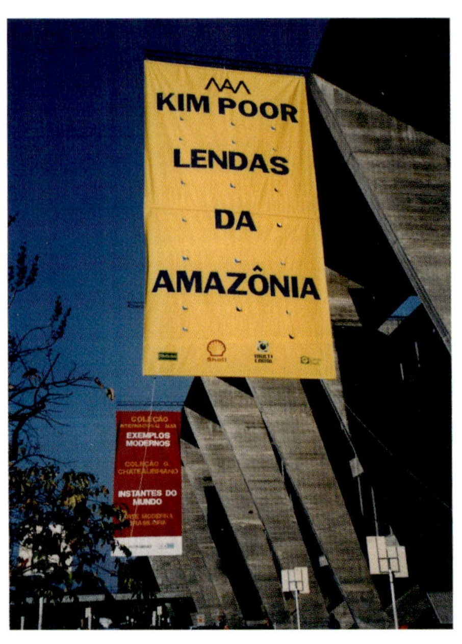

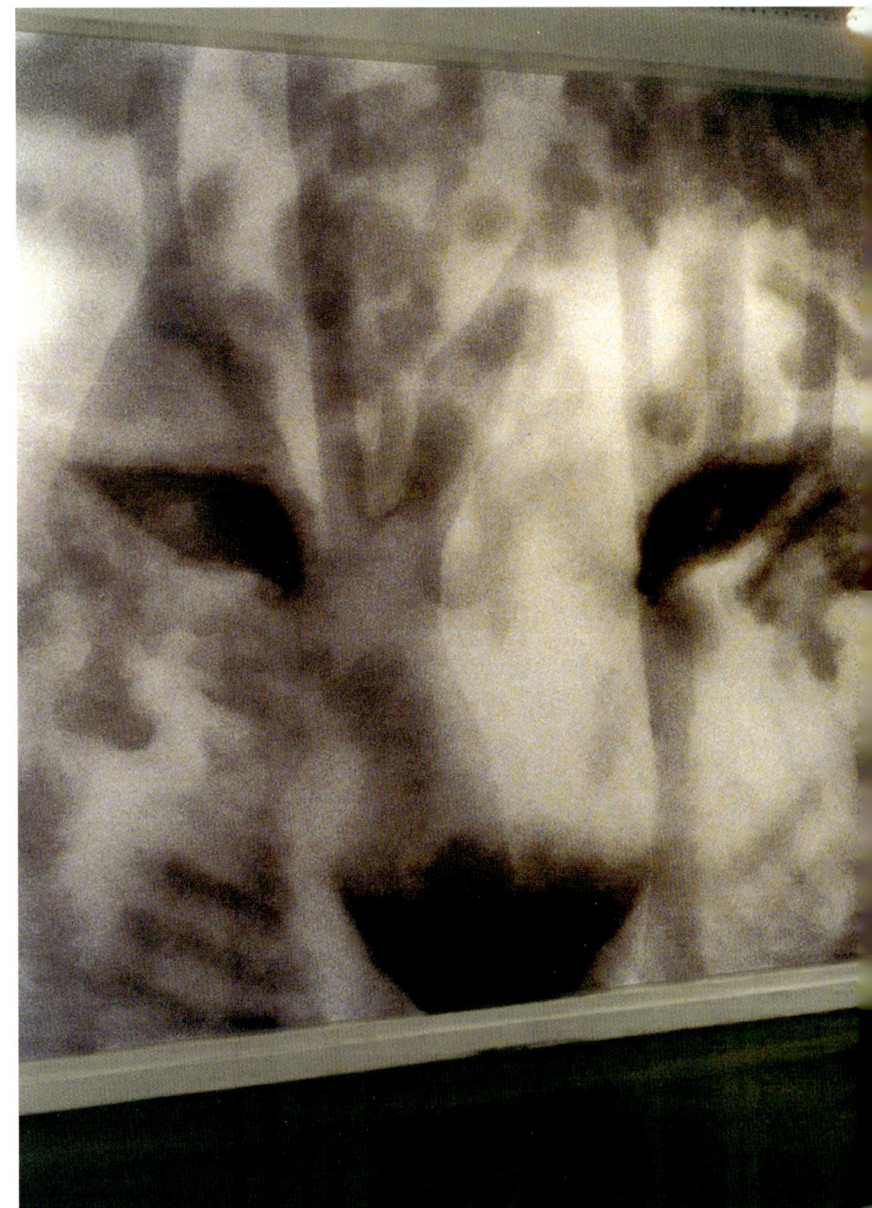

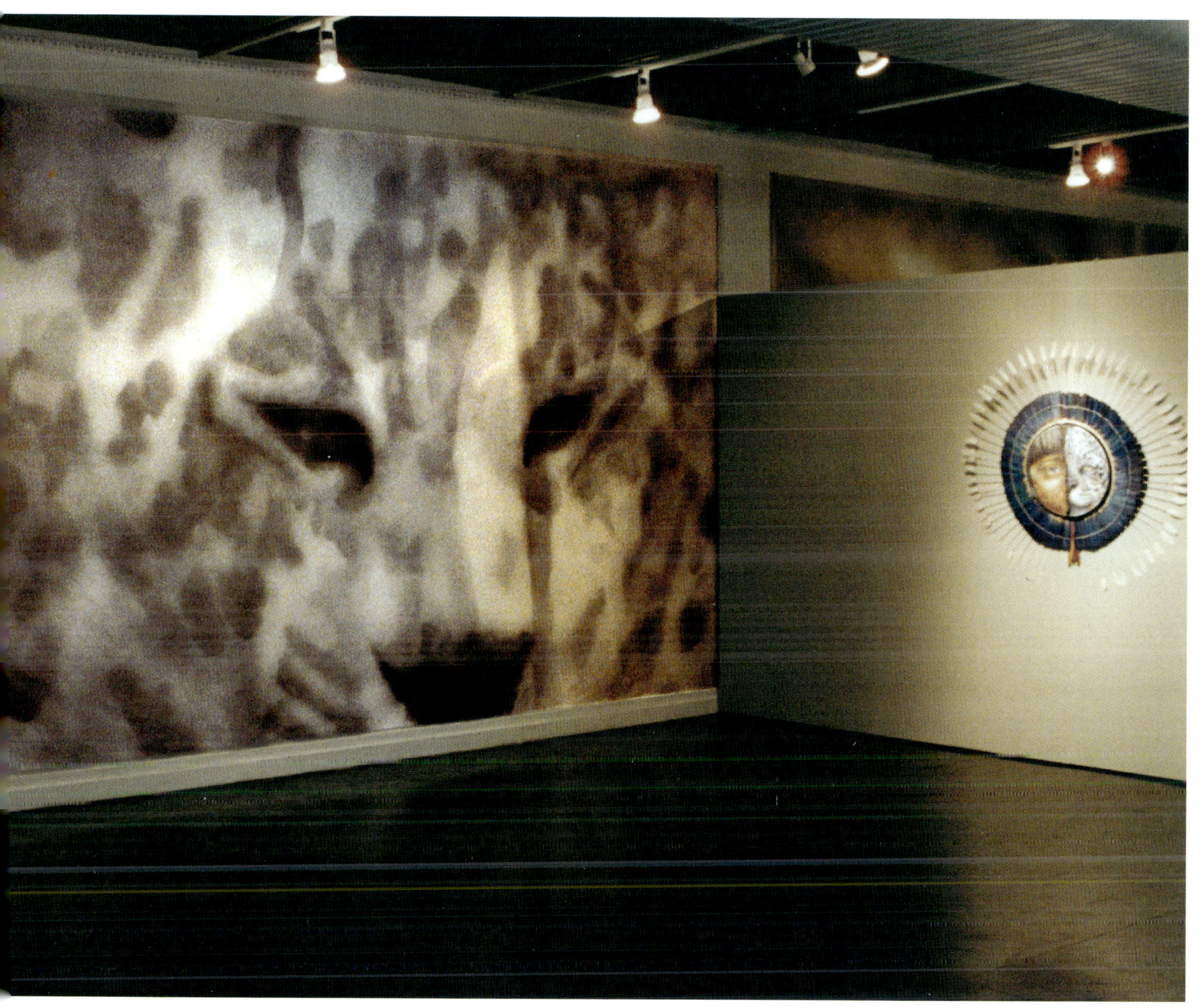

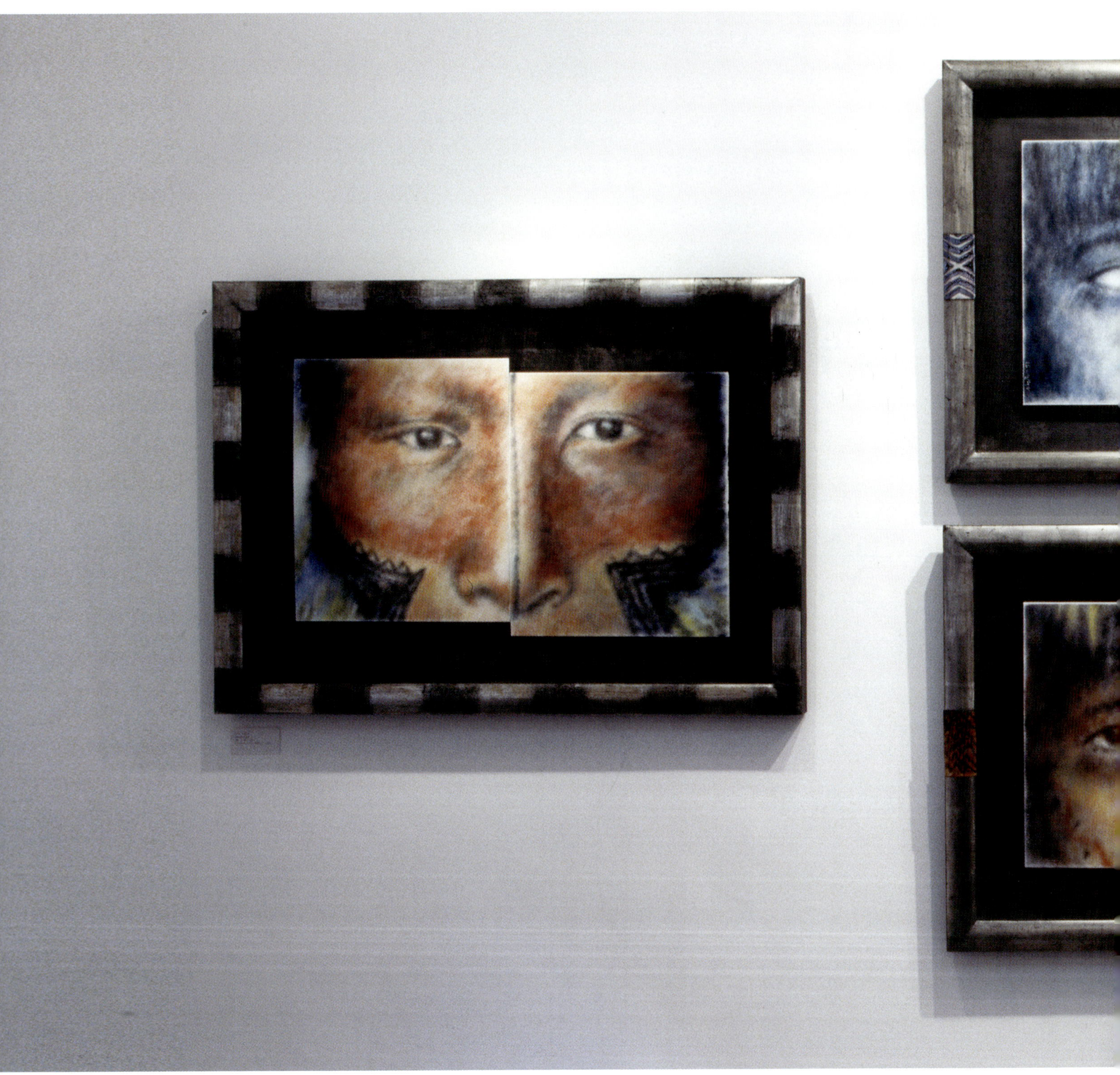

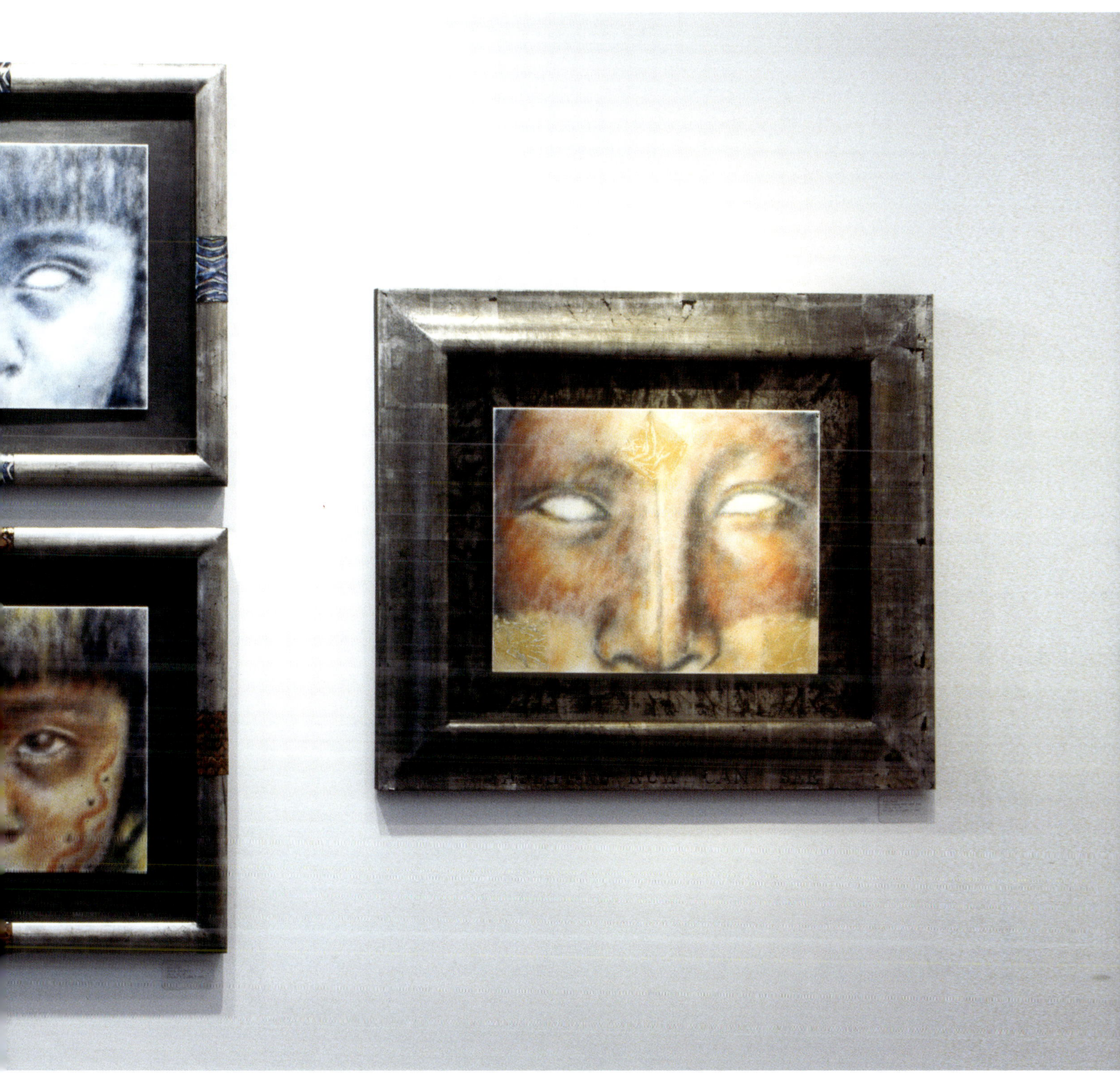

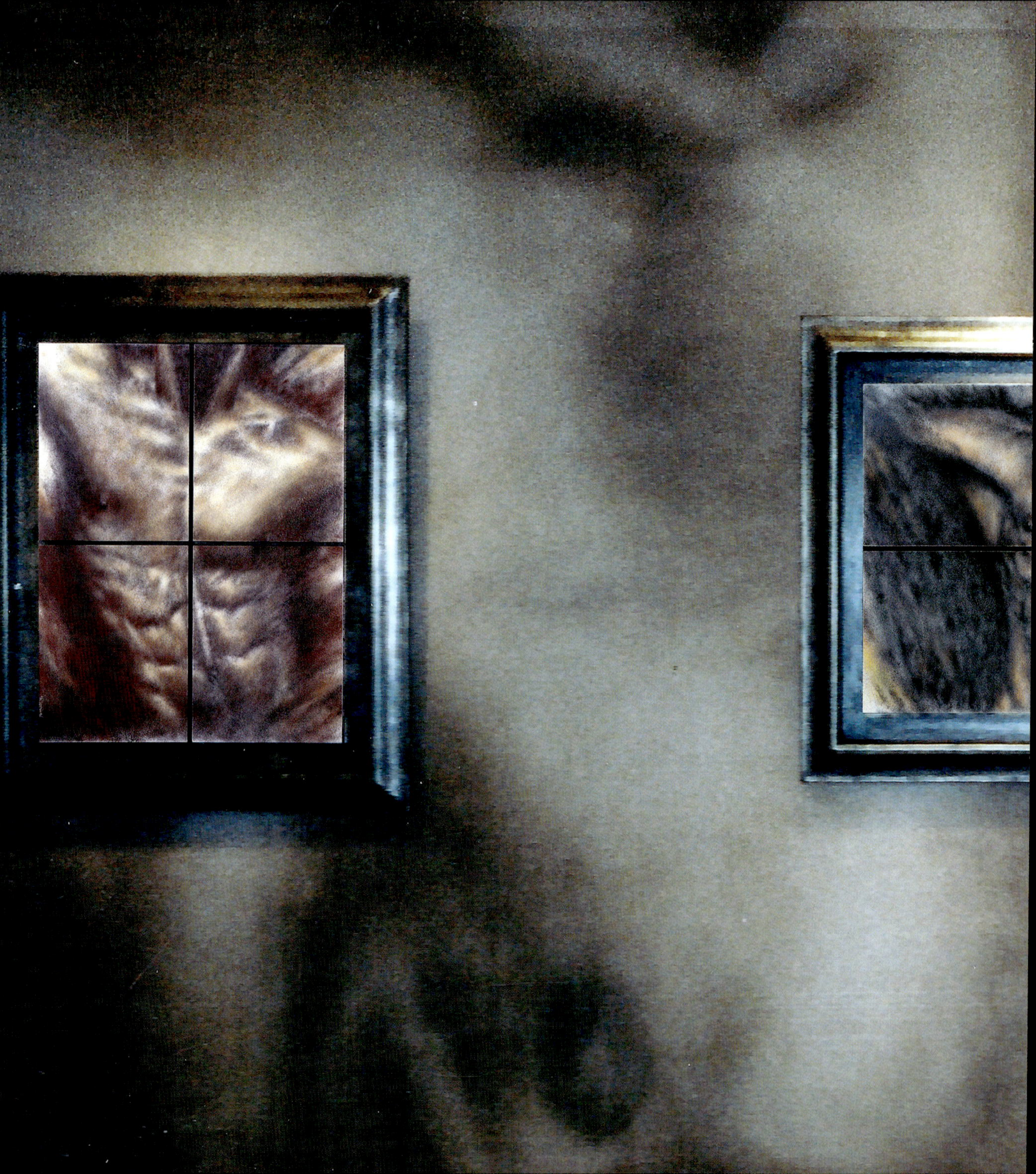

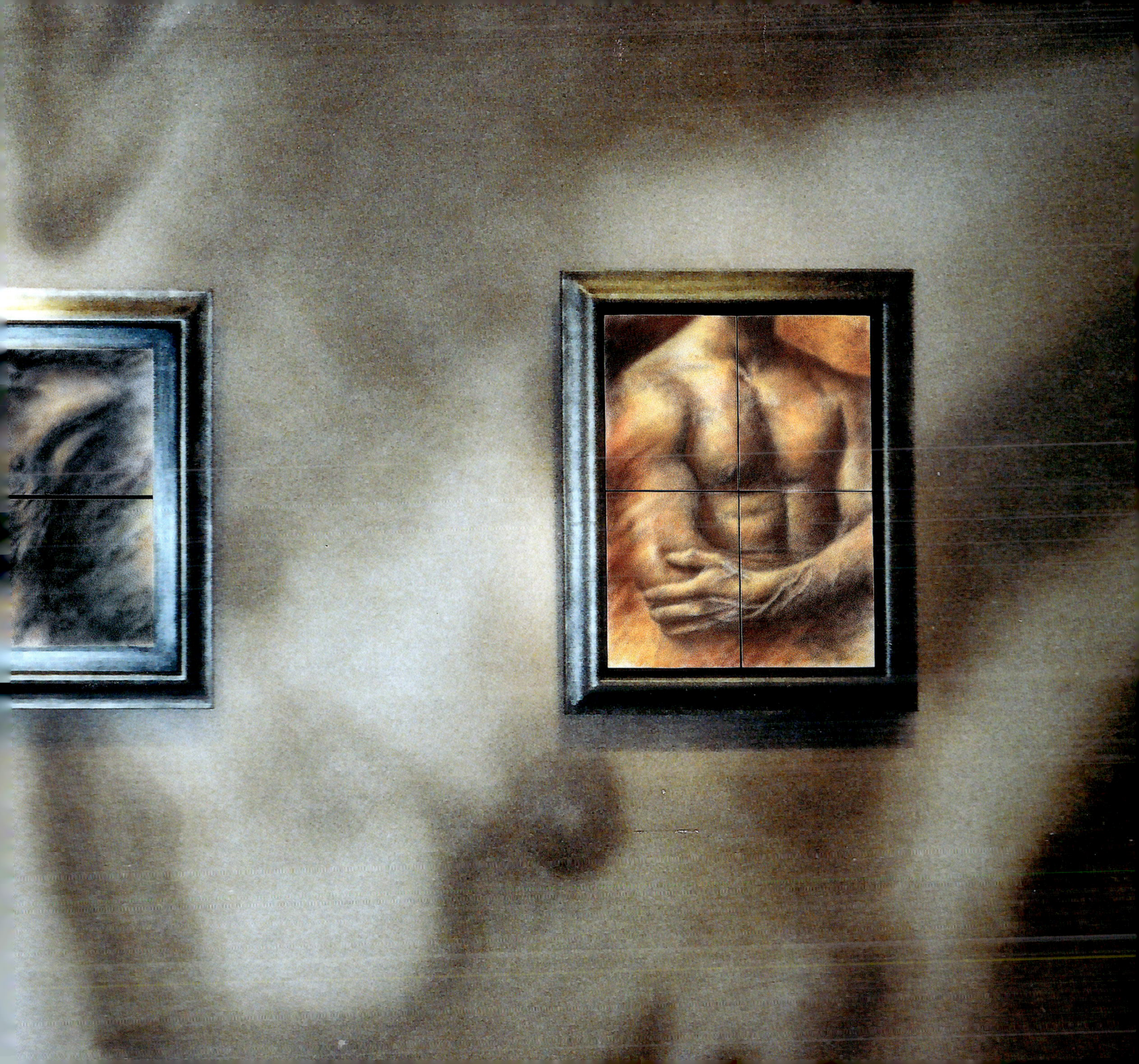

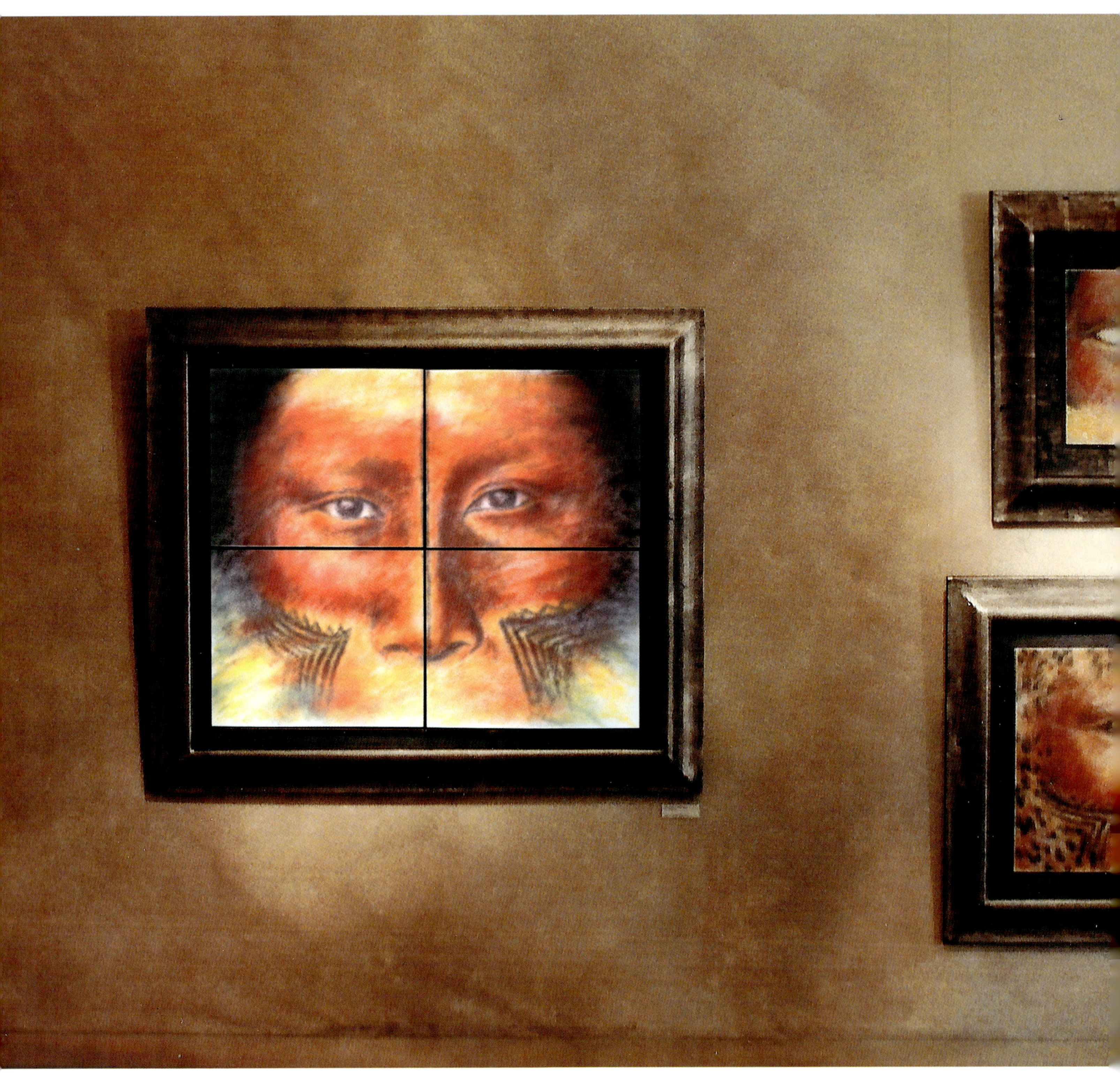

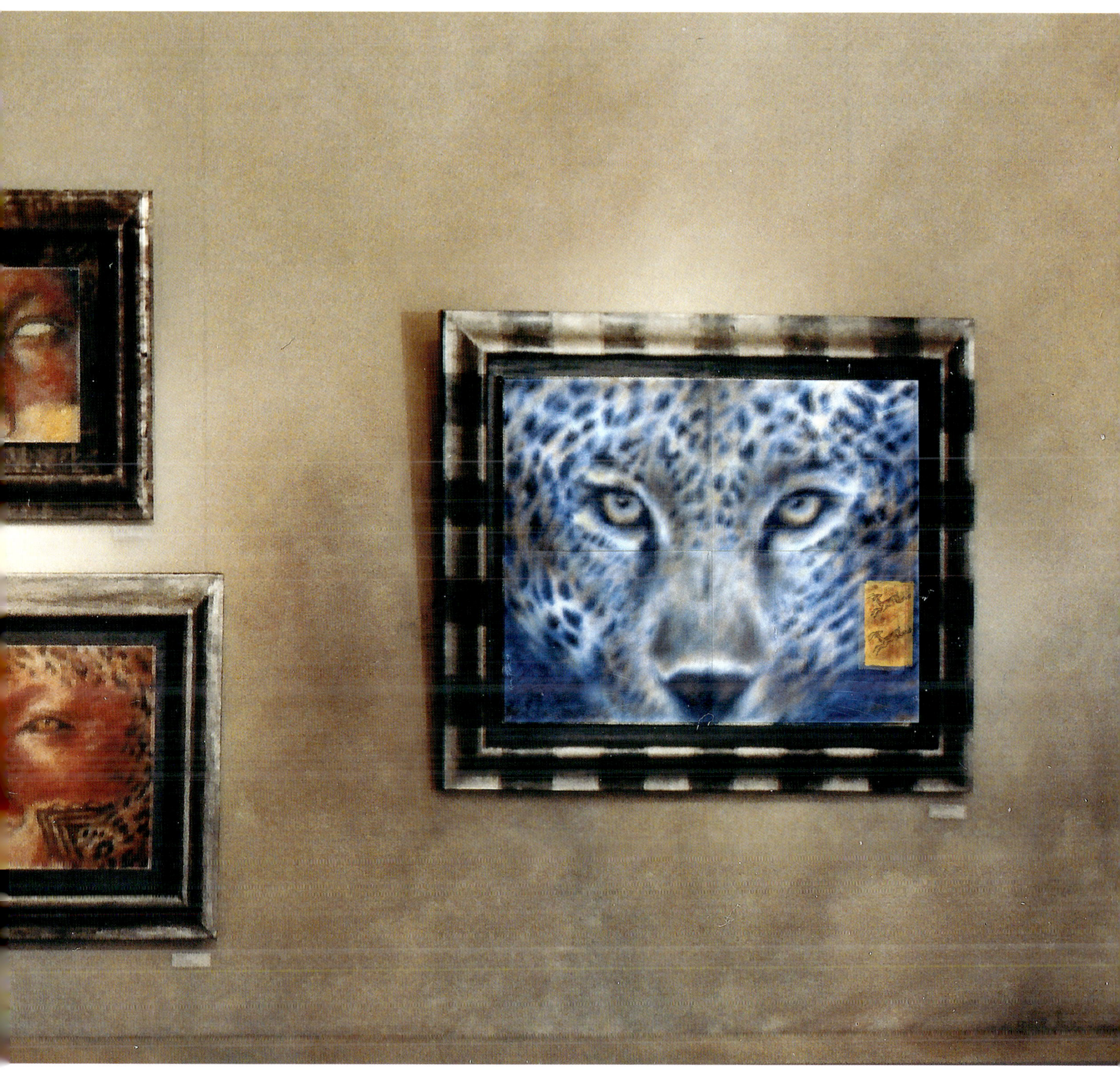

LEGENDS OF THE AMAZON

Exhibition at
Museu da Casa Brasileira
São Paulo

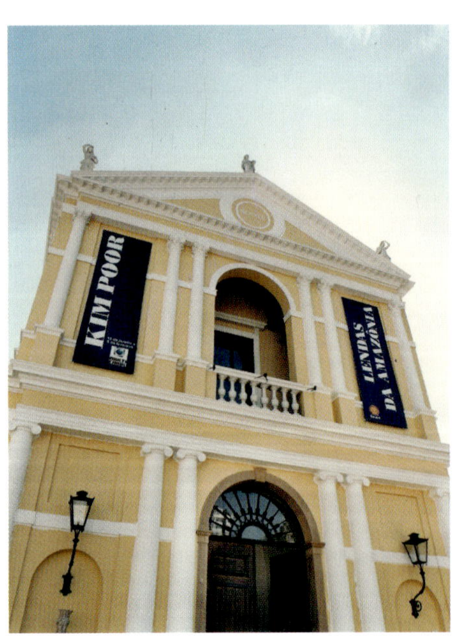

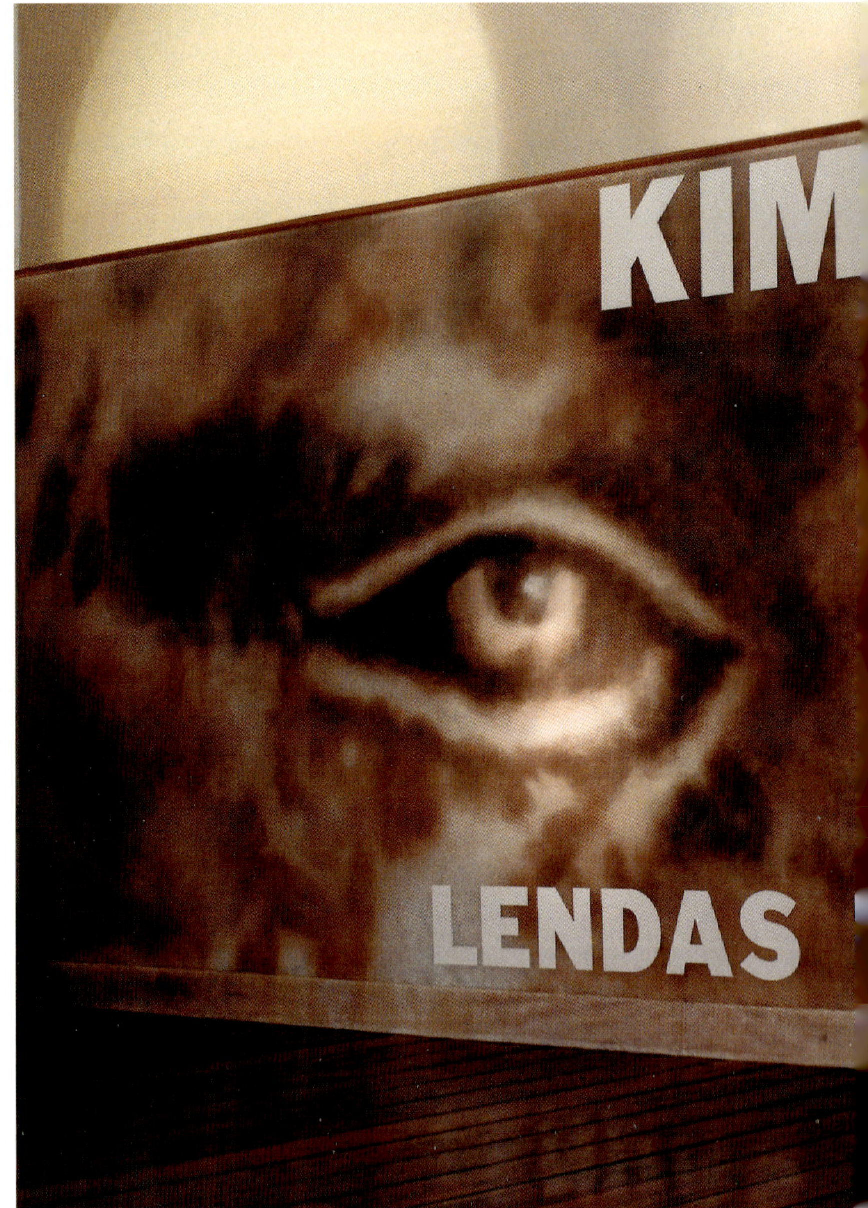

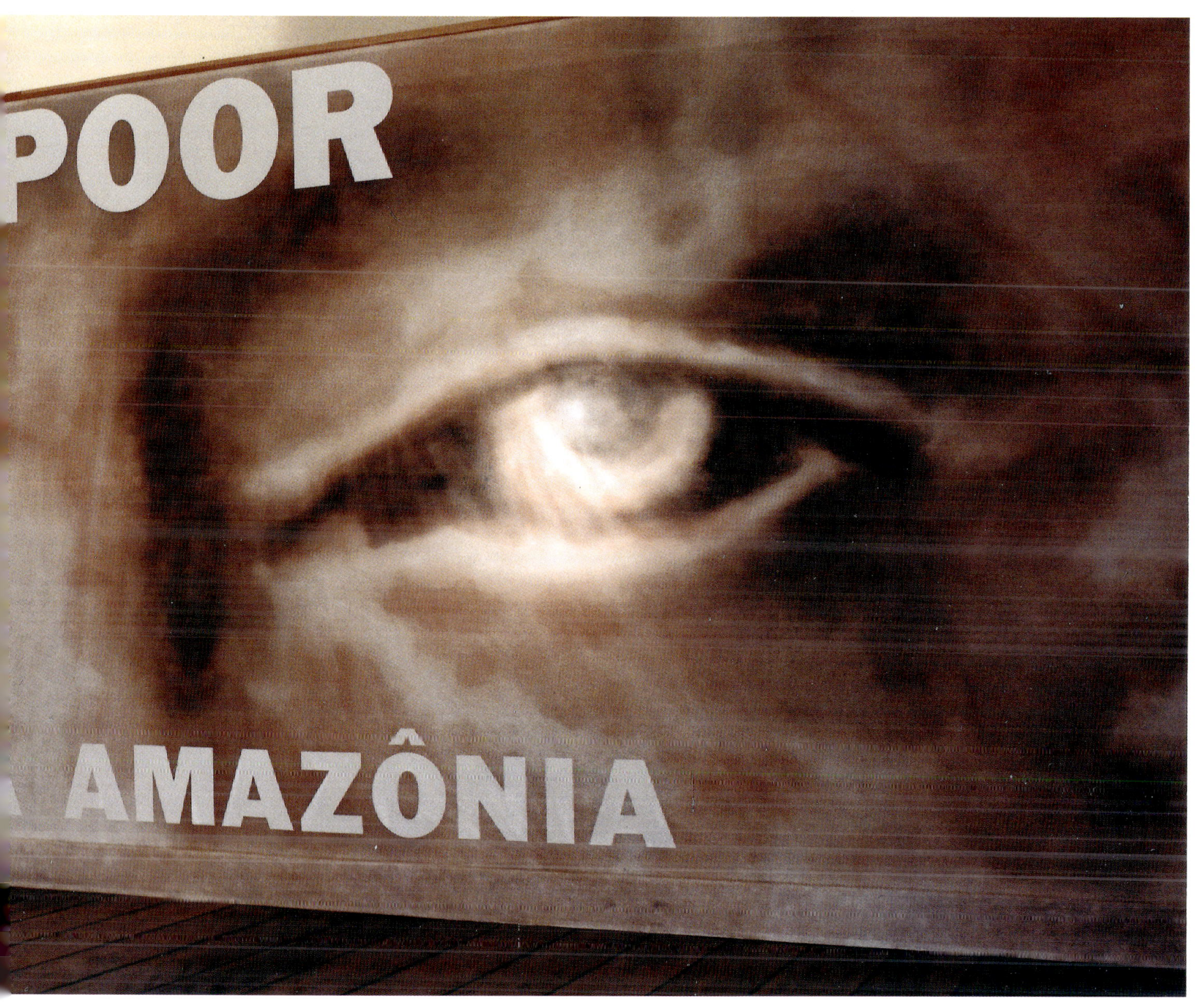
POOR
AMAZÔNIA

How The Stars Came To Be

In ancient times, the men in the tribes hunted, fished, and went into battle. But, in the village they did nothing. They just slept in their hammocks. Only the women worked.

One sunny afternoon, after they had filled the village baskets with grain, the women went into the forest, looking for corn. By the time it was dark, though, they had found nothing but a few withered ears.

The next day, they decided to take a young boy with them, because they believed that children always bring good luck.

The young boy - called Curumin in the Indian language - was able to guess where things could be found. He walked straight ahead, searching neither to one side nor the other. And he came right to a field of corn. The women were overjoyed.

They started to pick ear after ear of corn, and the boy filled his own basket. He sneaked away from them and ran back to the village with his corn, without even letting the women know that he was leaving.

'Grandmother', he said, when he was back in the village, 'make a cake for me with this corn.'

His grandmother ground up the corn meal, made it into a batter, and baked him a delicious cake.

'Come and have some of my cake', the boy yelled to his friends. The cake was hardly enough for so many hungry boys, and it disappeared in a moment.

'Now what are we going to do?' asked one of the boys. 'Our mothers are going to be angry that we used the corn and ate so much.'

'And your grandmother is going to tell them everything', said another.

'Let's hide her in that cave there in the forest', said one of the other boys.

'Well, we'd better hide the parrot with her', said the boy who had found the corn. 'That parrot talks too much!'

And that's what the boys did. 'I've got a good idea', said one of the boys. 'Let's climb that vine… and hide in the trees, so our mothers can't find us!'

When the women returned to the village, they were frightened to find the grandmother gone, the parrot gone and all of the boys disappeared. As they searched for them, they discovered that the boys had climbed the vine.

'Get down from there!' they screamed. But the boys would not come down.

'Well, we'll have to climb up after them. That's the only way we'll ever get them to come back', said one of the women. 'What stupid boys they are!'

So, one by one, the women climbed the vine, calling softly to the boys, and pleading with them to come back to the village and live with them.

When the boys saw what the women were doing, they called out to the colibri bird. 'Colibri, Colibri take this vine in your beak, and tie it to the sky!'

The bird, who knew what trouble the boys could make for him, did as they said. He anchored the vine up there in the sky.

The boy who had stolen the corn was lowest on the vine, and saw that the women were coming up to get them. In his fright, he cut the vine, and the women all fell to earth.

They weren't hurt by the fall, but all of them were changed into jaguars.

The boys were unable to return to earth, and, to this day, are up there in the sky. The punishment for the terrible things they did is to stay there forever, looking down to earth at what happened to their mothers. Their eyes are the stars, winking and blinking forever in the night sky.

IARA, Goddess of The River

Sunset is Iara's time of day. She lives at the bottom of the river, but late in the afternoon she comes to the surface. She collects the water flowers to decorate herself, and to play with the fish that live at the waters edge. Or she comes looking for a lover!

The Indians tell their sons: 'Stay away from the river when the sun is going down! Iara looks for little boys to keep.'

The boys listen to what they've been told, and they're frightened. They know that Iara is beautiful, and that she sings... and that she can cast a spell over them!

One day, a brave Tapuia boy was paddling along on the river, all alone. The sun was high in the sky, and the boy tried to catch some fish for his dinner. Time passed, and the first birds began flying back to their nests.

The first frogs began to croak in the distance, and night fell. As it did, the sun seemed slowly to sink into the waters of the river.

Suddenly, a flower rose to the surface of the river. But the flower was singing! And laughing, it shook its hair, as black as its luminous eyes. It wasn't a flower, it was Iara! The Indian boy turned his canoe and fled toward his village.

But Iara had already cast her spell over him. Her sweet voice never left his ears. A vision of her followed him everywhere.

And, at sunset, the Tapuia boy stared at his canoe, wanting to go back out on the river.

'Don't go', his mother pleaded with him. She knew that her son had met with the beautiful Iara.

And there in the distance, frolicking with the little fish and collecting her flowers, Iara sang... and waited. She also knew that the boy would have to return.

And, one afternoon, that's just what happened. The jasmine gave off its perfume. The birds flew back to their nests. And the Indian boy, forgetting all about his village and family, jumped into his canoe and paddled...

He paddled until he met with the beautiful Iara. And Iara, as she sang, took the brave Indian boy with her to the bottom of the river.

The Butterflies

A long time ago the butterflies resembled human beings and they always lived and played next to the beaches of salt water.

There were many villages and each one possessed a leader. Gamep was one of these leaders. He was the most powerful for being the smartest because he could pacify the civilised.

The Indians and the civilised became good friends and because of this they gave each other many presents of knives, machetes and jewellry.

There was however one chief who was very mean who was called Xanawai. He was always creating intrigue and fights including with the civilised.

Xanawai told the civilised that the great chief Gamep was no good because even though they exchanged presents he had killed their relatives.

This obviously was not true for the reality was that these relatives lived in Gamep's village and were all very well thank you.

The problem was that the civilised believed Xanawai's story and decided to attack Gamep. The fight occurred in a region where the waters were very salty and with very strong currents resembling large water falls. Gamep's men used very long canoes and one of them which was attacked by the civilised sunk and drowned many people.

The canoes that were saved managed to return to the beach and there they found many butterflies playing on the beach. They thought the butterflies resembled the civilised and started to shoot arrows at them, because the butterflies were so naive they did not realise that they were being attacked.

When they realised this many had already been killed in an attempt to run away they started to fly and transformed themselves back into real butterflies.

Gamep, realising what he had done and what had happened, became enraged towards Xanawai. He gathered all his men and attacked Xanawai's village. Gamep killed him himself and ordered that he be burned.

He ordered the remains to be put inside a basket and to be put outside the Maloca so that all could see the evil he had done.

It took many years before the butterflies would return and bless the beaches with their beauty and their colour.

The Eye Game

Because the crab's eyes have always stuck so far out from his head, people have always thought that he was able to throw his eyes to any place he wanted. And the Indians tell the story of how that whole idea got started.

One day, long, long ago, the crab threw his eyes all the way to Lake Palana. He said, 'Get over there, eyes. Go! Go! Go!' And his eyes flew away. There he was, without his eyes. The crab said, 'Oh, my eyes have flown away. I think I'd better call them back.' So, he said, 'Come back from Lake Palana, eyes Quick! Quick! Quick! Quick!' And his eyes came back to him.

His friend, the jaguar wanted to know how it was that the crab could make his eyes fly away. 'I want to see that again. Send your eyes away, cousin.'

The crab did it again:

'Fly to the shores of Lake Palana.
Go! Go! Go!'

The crab's eyes flew away again to the

shores of the lake. Then he asked the jaguar if he had seen how it worked. The jaguar asked the crab to call his eyes back again. So, the crab called:

'Eyes, come back to from the shores of Lake Palana. Quick! Quick! Quick!' And, his eyes came back in an instant.

The jaguar was really excited.

'Now, send my eyes, cousin. I want to see Lake Palana, too.'

The crab didn't want to send the jaguar's eyes. It was a big responsibility to take on, and what if it didn't work!

'It's not a good idea. The grandaddy of all the Traira fish lives there at the lake.'

The jaguar got angry.

'I want you to send my eyes over there… now!'

So his friend, the crab, told him to relax and close his eyes. Then the crab said:

'Fly to the shores of Lake Palana, eyes of my cousin! Go! Go! Go!'

The jaguar's eyes flew away to see the lake, and the jaguar couldn't see anything that was happening. So, he asked the crab to tell his eyes to come back to him.

'Come back from the shores of Lake Palana, eyes of my cousin! Quick! Quick! Quick!'

The jaguar's eyes came back, and the jaguar told the crab that what he had done was marvellous.

'That was terrific, cousin! Send my eyes over there again. I want to see the lake again.'

The crab didn't want to do it again. He said that the grandaddy of the Traira fish, who was swimming around in the lake, saw the jaguar's eyes and ate them up. Now, the jaguar couldn't see anything, and he began to shout:

'Call my eyes back, cousin! Right away!'

So, the crab called, 'Come back from the shores of Lake Palana, eyes of my cousin! Quick! Quick! Quick!'

But the eyes didn't come back. The crab called again. Nothing! He called again and again. No sign of the jaguar's eyes!

'The grandaddy of the Traira fish swallowed your eyes! I told you that would happen!' said the crab.

'You shouldn't have sent my eyes away! Now I can't see anything! I'm going to eat you up!'

The jaguar threw himself on the crab, but the crab jumped into the water and hid himself under a palm leaf. The crab clutched the stem to his back, with the leaf forming a breastplate, which, even today, all crabs have.

As he tried to escape from the anger of the jaguar, the crab ran, moving so that you couldn't tell if he was going forward or backward, like all crabs do.

The jaguar, stumbling through the forest, met up with the royal condor. The condor asked him:

'What are you doing here, cousin?'

'Nothing,' the jaguar said. 'The crab sent my eyes over to Lake Palana, and the grandaddy of the Traira fish swallowed them. Is there any way you can get me some eyes to replace the ones I lost?' The royal condor promised to help him.

'Let me see what I can do. Stay here, and don't move. I'm going to get some milk from the jatai tree.'

He flew away, looking for the milk from the jatai, but he didn't come back for a long time. Just as the jaguar was getting completely discouraged, the royal condor returned, saying that it had been very difficult to find any milk of the jatai. He heated the milk, and told the jaguar to lie down on the ground. He said:

'Be very still! If you want to have new eyes, you have to put up with the heat. Don't move, and don't say anything!'

The royal condor dropped the hot milk of the jatai into the place where the jaguar's left eye had been, and the jaguar didn't move or say anything. The eagle had dropped the rest of the milk into the place where the jaguar's right eye had been, and then using a twig, he extracted a bit of the milk from a bush that the Taulipangue Indians call kaikusezimpi. It was a different kind of milk, and the eagle used it to wash out the jaguar's eyes.

After he had washed the jaguar's eyes with the milk from the kaikusezimpi, the jaguar had eyes that were clear and beautiful. He turned his new eyes to one side and the other, and found that he could see things that were close and things that were far away.

He thanked the condor, but the condor said to him:

'Now, in exchange for your new eyes, I want you to hunt down a tapir for me.'

The jaguar went on the hunt, and came back with a big, fat tapir.

'Here is the tapir you ordered in exchange for my new eyes.'

'Good!. From now on, that's how it's going to be. I gave you your new eyes, cousin, and now you have to provide me with food to eat. One thing in exchange for the other. Every time you hunt down a deer, a tapir or any other prey, you have to give me a portion. Don't forget!'

Ever since then, the jaguar hunts to provide a portion of food for the royal eagle. He didn't know that the favour done for him would mean hard work for the rest of his life. But, on the other hand, it was worth it!

The jaguar's new eyes are clear and beautiful! He can see in the dark, and hunt even at night! And he is able to see things that are nearby and those that are far away!

Amazon - The River of Love

Everything in this story happened long before the God, Kanaxiwé, wandered the earth. The river that is called the Amazon was, in those days, a huge inland sea, surrounded by beautiful, endless land. There was no such thing, in those times, as a ceiling to the forest. The Sun provided that lost territory with light and warmth, and everything there grew well. The Moon gave dew to the land, and was the protective mother of its people, its animals and its plants.

These two stars that shone over that endless land fell in love, and agreed to marry. But, in order for them to be able to do so, they would have to abandon their celestial travels and live on the earth. Kanaxiwé warned them that their crazy idea about living on the earth would bring destruction to that steamy equatorial paradise. The Sun would burn the flowers, and the Moon would condemn all existing things to death. Fires would be extinguished by the Moon's dew; water would be evaporated by the heat of the sun, and it would be the end of the world.

Frustrated in their dream of marriage, the stars turned to meeting furtively in the West, where the sun was so beautiful at the end of its daily journey. One day, Kanaxiwé discovered his celestial pupils in their misbehaviour. He was furious, and decided to make changes in the forest. A cataclysm shook the world. Thunder sounded from one end of the forest to the other, and from the sky to the earth. Animals fled. People disappeared, or, running away fearfully, were swallowed in the storm. Mountains rose from the forest, reaching to the sky and belching fire. The huge inland sea was a confusion of giant waves, and then dried up.

Afterward, a luxuriant, flowery jungle covered the plains. The Sun was sent into the sky to follow a celestial orbit. The Moon, frantic with grief at having lost its companion, the Sun, searched at the top of the frigid mountain. But it never again saw the Sun - his friend that had been sent from the Earth by Kanaxiwé. In its desperation, the Moon fell to weeping. The tears fell to the ground, and as they evaporated, caused torrential rains to fall where once the inland sea had been.

A river of tears was formed, which the ancient Kiña people called 'aiaká-maé' which means 'The River of Love'. Today, that river is called The Amazon.

The Theft of The Fire

In ancient times, the earth belonged to everyone, but fire did not. Fire was owned by the Tucano. And the Tucano, wanting to stay warm, carried the fire hidden under his wings.

Baira was a brave and intelligent Parintintim Indian. His people were forced to dry their meals leaving them in the sun, so Baira decided that he would steal the fire. Then, his people could cook their food.

Baira was very smart. They say that it was Baira who taught the Parintintim to hunt birds using mistletoe for bait. And he taught them to fish using a sangab, an artificial fish or lure, to attract the larger fish. Baira taught his people many things.

One day he asked himself, 'Why should fire be owned by someone? It should belong to everyone! Does the water have an owner? No! Does the sun have an owner? No! Are the earth or the flowers owned by anybody? No! So, why does fire have an owner? It's not right; fire should belong to everyone.'

So, he made a plan to steal the fire from the Tucano. He went into the forest, and covered himself with leaves and termites. He lay motionless on the floor of the forest, appearing to be dead.

Soon, he heard a buzzing: buzz buzz buzz... it was the Blue Fly. He buzzed and buzzed, and flew off into the sky to tell the Tucano. In those times, the Tucano lived in the sky.

The Tucano wasted no time. He flew to the body, bringing the fire under his wings. His entire family came with him: his wife, his children, and some other urubus that were friends of his. The Indians say that, in those days, the urubus were like people. They had hands and everything. And, since they had hands, they were able to make a moquem, a kind of grill made with twigs that was used to cook meat or fish.

Tucano made himself a grill, and placed the fire beneath it. He blew and blew, and the fire became red-hot. Baira didn't move, but he opened one eye, and watched, learning how to make use of fire.

When the fire was ready, Tucano told his children to guard it.

Suddenly, without without meaning to, Baira twitched. The children saw that, and ran to tell Tucano.

'Daddy Daddy, the man moved!'

Tucano didn't believe them. But not wanting to make them feel bad, he sent them off to hunt blue flies, using small darts that he gave them. The youngsters enjoyed themselves hunting the flies, and forgot about the fire.

When he saw the flames reaching up through the grill, Baira jumped up stole the fire, and ran for home. When Tucano saw what had happened, he called his people together, and they all went hunting for the thief. Baira hid in a hollow tree, but the urubus found it, and tried to pull him out. Baira squeezed out the other side, and crawled in to some nearby underbush.

Tucano wanted to go in after him, but he couldn't because of his great wings. Baira was able to escape, and he reached the shore of a large river. There on the other side were his people - all of the Parintintim. But the river was too wide for him to cross.

He wanted to give the fire to his people, but there was the river between them and him. He called to a surradeira, one of the fastest snakes in the forest, and said:

'I have the fire here, and I have to take it to my people there on the other side. Take it to them quickly, before it goes out.'

Baira put the burning fire on the back of the snake, and told him to take it across the water. The snake, following Baira's orders, swam as fast as he could for the other side, but he couldn't make it.

Baira pulled the fire back to himself, using a branch as a hook, and called to the shrimp. He put the fire on the shrimp's back, and called to the shrimp, telling him to take it to his people there on the other side of the river. The shrimp reached the middle of the river, but, unable to stand the heat, turned into a fried shrimp. Baira pulled the fire back to himself again, and called for the crab. He put the fire on his back, and said to himself, 'It's the crab that's going to be able to bring the fire to my people.'

But the crab couldn't stand the heat, either, and when he reached the middle of the river, turned red, as he is today.

Baira wasn't discouraged. He pulled the fire back, and put it onto the back of a saracura, one of the birds of the river.

'I'll take the fire to your people', the bird promised Baira.

He flew off without even touching, but he couldn't make it. He felt the heat of the fire on his back and began to scream: 'I can't. Help! Help!'

Baira pulled the fire back, and called on the sapo-cururu, one of the frogs of the river. The frog grabbed the fire and jumped his way across the river, trying to reach the Parintintim people waiting on the opposite side. He got close, but he was so tired that he wasn't able to pull himself from the water. The Indians carried him to the shore, and took the fire from him.

Meanwhile, Baira had squeezed the river, and made it as narrow as a creek. He jumped and reached the other side easily. He went to his people, and they celebrated the feats of their hero for a week with feasts and dancing.

Ever since that day, thanks to Baira, the Parintintim have known how to use fire, cooking their fish and meat over a grill.

For having brought the fire across the river, Cururu, the frog, was made a witch- doctor. And, ever since, the Cururu has been called the 'fire-thief' and has been able to eat the blue fire of the fireflies without burning himself.

But, when it's cold, and there's no fire to warm him, he remembers the fire he carried across the river, and sings:

'Sapo-cururu on the bank of the river, when the sapo sings, the cururu is cold… '

The Turtle and The Deer

It seemed, out of all the animals in the forest, that the turtle and the deer could never get along. They were always arguing and bickering. They called each other names and, in general, were very disagreeable. While both were to blame, it must be said that the deer, being faster, larger, stronger and more prominent, was certainly the more boastful. Although this fact rankled the turtle, it was he who fancied himself as much keener, craftier and smarter than most of the animals in the jungle.

One day, the deer met the turtle on the main path through the jungle. "Hey! My friend! Why is it that you're always in the same spot? I am able to go swiftly to all sorts of places and, when I return, you haven't moved but ten yards. Why, last week you were by the river. I came back this morning and what did I find? My friend, the turtle, still by the river!"

"Well, my friend, the truth is that I have been far and now I am back."

"You've been where?"

"I've been to the other side of the world and back - all in a week! What do you say to that?"

"If you were able to go to the other side of the world and back in a week, then I could surely do the same thing in two days."

"Two days isn't very long, my friend. I'm pretty fast and I only just made it in one whole week."

"Ha!" exclaimed the deer, "I'm the one who's fast. Do you see that large stone over there in the elbow of the river? Watch how fast I am able to get there and back." The deer had hardly finished speaking when he shot away. He was back in two seconds. "Did you see that?"

The turtle, however, hadn't even finished turning his head. But he replied with a glimmer in his small beady eyes, "It's not just enough to have fast legs. You must also be able to think fast!"

"What do you mean? What does thinking fast have to do with it?" asked the deer, mockingly.

The turtle explained, "There are some distances that you travel with your legs. There are others that you must travel with your thoughts."

"Not I, my friend! No one, and no thing, runs faster than I do."

"Are you sure of that?"

"Well," replied the deer, "If you want to make a small bet, then, let's have a race and see who finishes first."

"Are you really sure?" continued the turtle.

"Never been surer."

"Then, I accept your challenge."

The deer responded eagerly, "Let's pick a day for the race." And he was certain he would win.

The sloth, who had been listening and observing from behind a large termite hill while occasionally licking up a tasty cluster of termites, cautioned the turtle, "Don't bet, turtle. You'll lose. Take it from me, another slow, surefooted creature, you cannot outrun the deer."

"It is not only a matter of how fast you run," said the turtle, "You must also learn to think fast!"

Lose or not, they agreed that the race would be run ten days later. The starting line would be on the left-hand side of the river and the finish line on the right.

All of the deer, rabbits and sloths in the forest decided they would watch the race and laugh at the poor turtle's fiasco. While they talked amongst themselves, laughing and making fun of the turtle, the turtle was busy making plans. He passed the word among some of his other turtle friends to instruct all the turtles in the jungle to station themselves at an equal distance from each other all along the route of the race. Lastly, he sent a message to one of his brothers, who lived on the right-hand side of the river. And then he pulled his head back into his shell and went to sleep.

On race day the deer and the turtle lined up at the river. By now a rather sizable group of spectators had come to watch. The deer jumped back and forth, doing exercises and showing off his strength and speed in little bursts and leaps.

The turtle said nothing, but he was thinking, "I'm not so sure that this is such a good idea after all," he thought, in a moment of doubt. "The deer is much larger and faster, but, then, what right does he have to make fun of me all the time."

As the turtle ruminated, the rabbit got ready to give the starting signal. "Are you ready?" he called out.

"Of course!" shouted the deer.

"I am," said the turtle, quietly.

So, the rabbit yanked the bellbird's tail and it gave out a metallic shriek.

The deer was so sure of himself that he offered to give the turtle a head start of one hundred yards.

"I don't need it," replied the turtle.

The deer turned and shot away from the starting line and was soon out of sight. All the other animals sniggered and turned around to wait for the arrival of the deer on the right-hand side of the river. They didn't see the turtle slip into a hole under a rock.

Two hundred meters ahead, the deer yelled out, "Are you back there, brother turtle?"

The voice of the turtle answered from just ahead, "Here I am!"

The deer couldn't understand how on earth the turtle had passed him so quickly and quietly. He began to run faster and passed the turtle. Two hundred yards further down the path he called out again, "Brother turtle, are you far behind now?"

"Here I am, up in front of you!" answered the turtle.

The deer was even more astonished than before. He began to run faster still and passed the turtle in a blur of speed.

And so it went on. Every two hundred yards the deer called out to the turtle, expecting him to be far behind. The turtle would always reply, "Here I am. Up in front!"

The deer ran faster and faster; harder and harder. His front and back legs seemed never to touch the ground. Finally, to the applause of all his friends, the deer reached the finish line on the right-hand side of the river, which was under a Jatoba tree. The bellbird squawked loudly to signal his arrival. The deer fell to the ground, exhausted. "I won!" he chanted in victory, while panting for breath.

"Who says?" said the turtle, as he came out from behind an anthill. "Why, I've been here for quite a while. In fact, I was here so early I decided to take a rest." And the turtle gave a dry little laugh, "Che, he, he..."

The rabbit, who was officiating, heard what the turtle said and was truly amazed, "Well, friend deer, a bet is a bet. And you lost!"

The deer was thoroughly embarrassed to have lost the race to such an insignificant little creature. Of course, he wasn't aware that it was not the same turtle all along the way. He really believed that the turtle had beaten him and won the race with speed of leg. To his credit, the deer was honourable and admitted defeat.

"You see." said the turtle, with a twinkle in his black beady eyes, "It is not always how fast you run, but how fast you think." And with that, he pulled his head into his shell and went to sleep.

Since then, the deer has never made fun of the turtle and they live peacefully and respectfully in the jungle together.

The Two Parrots

Sun was out hunting. Walking through the woods, he met a small boy who had two small parrots to sell. These were very young parrots. They had not yet learned to fly.

Sun decided to buy the parrots and take them home to raise. He would keep the one with the beautiful gold and blue feathers, and he would give the lovely green one to his companion, Moon.

In those days, Moon was still a young man.

The two friends fed the parrots, played with them every day. They taught the parrots to sit on their fingers, and while they were sitting there, they taught them how to speak.

Time passed. The parrots learned to speak as well as most people do, and better than some.

One day, one parrot said to the other, 'I feel sad for Sun. When he comes home from hunting, he is so tired. But he does not have time to rest, because he must prepare dinner. Let us help him.'

In no time the parrots had transformed themselves into two beautiful women. One began preparing dinner, the other watched at the door of the oca where they lived. She would warn her sister if anyone happened to come by, so they could both become parrots again and not give their secret away.

Sun and Moon returned from their hunting late in the afternoon. When they were still a distance from their oca, they heard a sound like this: Pum! Pum! Pum!

Sun put his ear to the ground. 'It sounds as if there is an animal nearby, larger than either of us have ever seen', he said to his companion, the Moon. 'The animal is coming through the woods. Let's walk faster.'

As they got closer to their oca, the pum-pum sounds grew louder.

'That's no animal sound!' said Moon. 'It is the sound of a mortar pounding a pestle. Someone is grinding corn with great force. It sounds as if they were in a great hurry, too.'

'You're right', said Sun. 'And it's funny, but the sound seems to be coming from our house. How can that be? We must find out.'

Sun and Moon were only a few steps from the door. The sound of mortar beating stopped.

They went into their house. No one was there, of course. But their food had been deliciously cooked and was laid out on the hearth.

They searched every corner. They turned over all the baskets. They even turned over the coals in their oven, determined to find whoever had fixed their dinner. But they found no one. Just their two parrots, of course, sitting on the roof beams, as they usually did. The parrots looked at them curiously, as they always did, blinking their eyes and stretching their necks, talking parrot-talk: 'Cra cra cra'.

There was no other person there.

'It must have been the parrots', said Moon laughingly. Our parrots can do anything.'

'No, no' said Sun. 'Even if they wanted to, they could not have made dinner. They have no hands! But look over here. People have been in our house.'

Sun showed Moon the prints of bare feet on the dirt floor. But the footprints stayed in the house; there was not a trace of them outside the front door! It was mysterious!

The next day, the same thing happened. As Sun and Moon returned from their day of hunting, they heard the same sound of a pestle pounding corn in a mortar. Pum! Pum! Pum!

Dinner was again prepared, footprints were again all over the dirt floor, but there was no one around! Sun and Moon searched even more carefully this time, but found no one. Just the parrots, watching curiously from the roof beam.

Every day it was the same. Sun, becoming more and more puzzled, finally said to Moon, 'Someone must be listening to us so they know when we leave on our hunts. I think we should say in loud voices that we are going out to hunt, and we will take our bows and arrows with us, but then we will hide in the jungle. I'll hide on one side of the house. You hide on the other. When we hear the sound of the mortar pounding corn, I will rush in the front door and you will rush in the back door.'

Sun and Moon followed this plan the next day. It wasn't long before they heard women's voices and women's laughter coming from inside their house. They heard the Pum! Pum! Pum! of mortar on pestle, and immediately Sun ran through the front door, and Moon came rushing in the back door.

At the same moment they saw two young maidens who, upon being discovered, bowed their heads and sat down without saying a word.

Sun and Moon had never seen two such beautiful women before. Their skin was golden brown and their long black hair was smooth and shining.

Moon wanted to talk first. He spoke to the prettier of the two women.

'So. You have been preparing our meals every day. Where do you come from?'

The maiden confessed, with her head still bowed.

'We transformed ourselves from parrots so that we could prepare your evening meal. We felt sad for you both. You work so hard, all day long, and then have to come home to make your own dinner. We wanted to help you. But now… '

'Now you will stay this way, forever!' exclaimed Sun, shining with satisfaction.

The maiden spoke again, still without raising her head. 'Then you will have to decide which of us each of you will marry.

'I will marry you,' said Sun.

The woman chosen by Sun had been the blue and gold parrot, Sun's parrot.

'Then you have chosen me twice', said the woman, laughing happily.

And Moon quickly told the other woman he wanted to marry her.

And so they married their chosen maidens. To this very day, Sun and Moon live happily together in that same house. The house is small for the four of them, though, so they decided to take turns. Sun and his wife sleep in the house at night. Moon and his wife stay in the house during the day.

And that's why Moon doesn't sleep at night, and instead roams about, waiting for his turn to go home in the morning. That's when Sun, taking his bow and arrow, goes out to hunt…

Turtle and The Jaguar

Turtle was cleaning his flute one day, near his den, while Jaguar was on the hunt.

Jaguar went slowly, carefully putting one

paw down here, another paw there.
But there wasn't a monkey to be seen!

Suddenly, Jaguar heard the sound of strong blows on a tree trunk: tam-tam-tam!

'Ah it's a woodpecker,' thought Jaguar.

Just then, the wind brought the scent of a capibara to the Jaguar. He raised his nose to the wind. 'Huuummm, huuummm,' Jaguar sniffed deeply. But the wind kept going, right past Jaguar, taking the delicious smell with it.

And then Jaguar heard someone singing this song:

'I made a flute from the bone of the Jaguar, fim... fin fin fim.'

Jaguar's eyes widened. Who would dare sing a song like that? He would certainly have to find out!

Jaguar did not have to stalk many metres ahead before he came upon Turtle, playing his flute. And indeed, it was a flute made of bone.

Jaguar did not want to startle the turtle, so he walked up very, very quietly, as only Jaguars can do.

When Jaguar was very close to the turtle, he said in a soft voice, 'How well you play the flute, Turtle. How does that song go again?'

Turtle was not fooled by Jaguar's soft voice. He knew Jaguar just wanted him to sing his song again so Jaguar could start a fight. So Turtle answered, 'I sang this song:

'I made my flute from the bone of a deer...'

Jaguar wasn't convinced. 'Now, Turtle, I think I am hearing a different song this time, he said in a menacing voice.

'Oh, no sir!' denied Turtle. 'That's just what I was singing. You were so far away you probably could not hear me clearly. Now that you are so close, the music probably won't sound as pretty, but stay here. I will move away a bit, and then the music will sound good again, you will hear it much better.'

Turtle moved just to the very entrance of his den. He started to sing his song:

'Fim... fin fin fim... I made a flute from the bone of a Jaguar!

Fim... fin fin fim... '

No sooner did Jaguar hear the words than he sprang at Turtle. But Turtle slipped easily into his den.

Snarling, Jaguar tried to dig his way in. He thrust his paw into the hole and grabbed Turtle's leg with his claws.

Feeling himself in Jaguar's grip, Turtle began to laugh out loud.

'Ha, ha! Look at this dumb Jaguar! He has grabbed a tree root, thinking it was my leg. What a dumb Jaguar!' said Turtle, as if he were speaking to someone else in his den.

Jaguar did not like the idea that Turtle and whoever else was in his den were laughing at him. He was furious, but if he were really clawing a tree root, what terrible humiliation! So he let go and pulled his paw out.

Jaguar heard Turtle laughing and laughing. Actually, Turtle could not stop laughing. He had fooled the Jaguar, the one animal who frightened all the animals in the jungle. What a grand joke this was! And he could not stop himself from sharing it with Jaguar.

'Hey, dummy!' Turtle hooted. 'You know, you really were clawing my leg. It wasn't a tree root at all. It was my leg!' And Turtle started laughing all over again.

Outside, Jaguar roared and snarled and snapped and paced in anger. He bared his fangs and settled down in front of Turtle's den, every muscle tensed.

'I will get that turtle,' said Jaguar in a murderous rage.

He lay in wait for Turtle, but Turtle very, very quietly pulled into his shell and went peacefully to sleep.

Jaguar did not sleep. He waited and waited for Turtle to come out. He was not going to let a turtle get the best of him!

Jaguar grew hungry, but he would not give up. 'I will eat turtle for my next meal!' he vowed silently.

But Jaguar grew thinner and thinner, weaker and weaker, until he knew he must eat something -- anything -- even if it wasn't Turtle.

But Jaguar had lost all his strength, waiting for Turtle to come out. He was too weak now to hunt. When he tried to walk, he fell over, right where he had been crouching all this time. And then he died!

In a while, Turtle peeked out of his den and saw that the Jaguar was dead. He took a bone from the leg of Jaguar, and made it into a flute.

For many years, because turtles live a very long time, Turtle could be heard, late at night, playing his flute, and singing this song, 'Fim... fin fin fim... '

KIM POOR

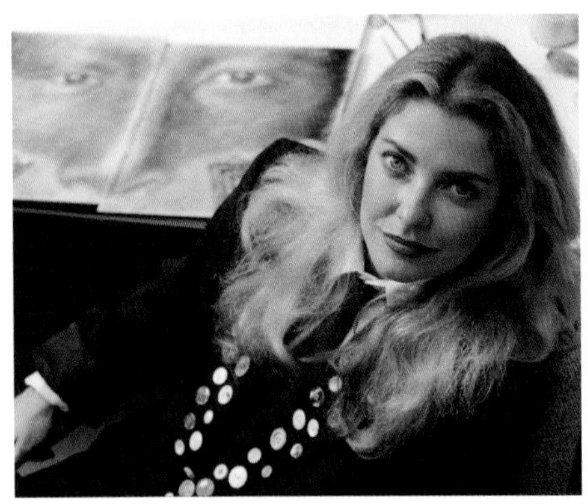

Biography
Kim Poor studied art at Skidmore College, at Parsons School in New York and at the Central School of Art in London. In the seventies Salvador Dali, on visiting a group show at the Soho Gallery, appeared perplexed by her idiosyncratic painting technique which used powdered glass on a steel plate and which he christened 'Diaphanism', a term subsequently incorporated in the Oxford English Dictionary to describe her technique. Her work has been exhibited in the galleries and museums of various cities worldwide, such as Rio, São Paulo, New York, London, Belgium and Athens and form part of important private collections such as Paul McCartney's, Baroness Thyssen's and Peter Gabriel's. Kim Poor is one of only four Brazilians cited in noted critic Edward Lucie-Smith's 'Art Today' from Phaidon – regarded as a bible amongst art collectors. Her CV also includes more than 30 record sleeves, not to mention a book of her illustrations of the work of the English group, Genesis. She has also found renown internationally with her jewellery designs, creating one-off sculptural pieces.

Selected One-Woman Shows:
1974 Portuguese Consulate, New York
1975 Ibeu Gallery, Rio
1979 Thumb Gallery, London
1992 Durini Gallery, London
1993 Durini Gallery, London
1997 Museum of Modern Art, Rio de Janeiro
1998 Museu da Casa Brasileira, São Paulo
2001 Gallery 32, London
2002 Claridge's Jewellery Design show
2004 Savoy Group show, Rio de Janeiro
2017 The Shadow of Angels at St. Stephen Walbrook, City of London

Selected Group Shows:
1966-72 OLM Gallery, Rio
1972 Chelsea Gallery, São Paulo
1973-76 Skidmore College Gallery, New York State
1974 Parsons Gallery, New York
1978-79 Soho Gallery, New York
1976-80 Beaux Arts Institute, Rio
1981-82 Graded School, São Paolo
1989-90 'No Boundaries On The Planet Of Tupis-Toris' (travelling exhibition)
London, Ecology CenterPraesent Tempor
Moscow, Global Forum On Environment & Development for Survival
New York, United Nations Foyer
1993 Contemporary Arts Museum, Hong Kong
Fine Arts Museum, Macau
Modern Art Museum, Bangkok
Atrium, London
Canning House, London (Latin American Women Artists)
'Masks - Real & Imagined' - Soho Gallery, London
1994 'War Child' - Flowers East, London
1995 'The Discerning Eye' - The Mall Gallery, London
1997 'Kiss Five' - Gallery K, London
2001 'Between Earth and Heaven' Museum of Modern Art, Ostend
2004 'Gods Becoming Men' Frissiras Museum, Athens
2005 'What Is Realism?' Albemarle Gallery, London
2006 Grosvenor Jewellery Show
2007 Coutts London Jewellery
2008 Coutts London Jewellery

Prizes:
1976/77/78 Gold Medal, Beaux Arts Institute of Brazil, Rio
1976 Album Cover of the Year - Voyage of the Acolyte
1976 Honors – Bachelor of Arts – Skidmore College

Private Collections:
Rothschild
Chagas Freitas
Paulo Geyer
Peter Gabriel
Ambassador João Quintela
Paul McCartney
Baroness Thyssen
Spiros Polemis
Museum of Contemporary Art, Buenos Aires

Commissions:
Albany State College
Princess Yamani
American School, Rio
Skidmore College, New York
Sidgwick and Jackson

Books:
1979 'Genesis Lyrics' Illustrated by Kim Poor
2012 'Artwear' (the stones of Burle Marx)
2017 'Amazonia Imagined'

Bibliography:
1995 'Art Today' by Edward Lucie-Smith
1998 'Adam' by Edward Lucie-Smith
'Zoo, Animals In Art' by Edward Lucie-Smith
2009 'The Glory of Angels' by Edward-Lucie-Smith

Forthcoming Projects:
Illustrated anthology of Brazilian legends - 'Legends of The Amazon - The Myths and Fables of the Amazon Indians'.
e-Book - 'Legends of the Amazon'